Beyond God the Father

D0037476

Beyond God the Father

Toward a Philosophy
of Women's Liberation

by Mary Daly

Beacon Press   Boston

Beacon Press books are published under the auspices
of the Unitarian Universalist Association of
Congregations in North America,
25 Beacon Street, Boston, Massachusetts 02108
Published simultaneously in Canada by
Fitzhenry and Whiteside Limited, Toronto

Printed in the United States of America

(hardcover) 9 8 7 6 5 4 3 2 1
(paperback) 9 8 7 6 5 4 3 2 1

Library of Congress Cataloging In Publication Data

Daly, Mary.
  Beyond God the Father.

  Bibliography: p.
  Includes index.
  1. Feminism.   2. Women in Christianity.   I. Title.
HQ1154.D3   1984   305.4'2   84–45067
ISBN 0–8070–1502–4 (hard)
ISBN 0–8070–1503–2 (pbk.)

Emily Oddwoman

I

In memory of Anna and Frank,
who gave me their hope

II

Tyger! Tyger! burning bright
In the forests of the night
What immortal hand or eye
Dare frame thy fearful symmetry?

William Blake

Contents

Original Reintroduction

This book, first published in 1973, was written in an atmosphere of exhilaration and great hope. As Linda Barufaldi describes her memory of that time/space, it was one of "communal inspiration."[1] To Name the process implied in that communal inspiration, I have invented the word *Be-Friending,* which means "the creation of a context/atmosphere in which leaps of Metamorphosis can take place."[2] *Be-Friending* is Realizing the Lust to share happiness, and it is possible when women begin to re-member our Elemental potency and therefore experience Be-Longing, the Lust for happiness. Happiness, understood in this context, is not a mere passing emotion. It is a life of activity, of Unfolding spiritual, intellectual, sensory, physical, e-motional potency.

It was deep experiential knowledge of Elemental potency/potential in women that made possible the writing of *Beyond God the Father,* and this knowledge has sustained my own journey. Certainly, women pursuing the task and journey of radical feminism through the late seventies and on through the eighties have lived through disheartening as well as exhilarating times. The horrors of the 1980s—experienced concretely in the day-by-day struggle to survive with our bodies/minds intact—have been Lived through and surmounted to the degree that we have been able to Realize our own potency.

As this Reintroduction is being written, seemingly contradictory events are occurring rapidly. On the foreground level—the level of the state of patriarchal possession—there is more and more cause for despair; the dis-ease of phallocracy is extending its organs everywhere. Yet there are Other dimensions—the Realm of the Wild reality of women's Selves—which Denise Connors first Named the *Background.*[3] Here, in these dimensions, there is a resurgence of communal inspiration arising from a more complex appreciation of sisterhood, and some feminists sense that we are once again entering a Time of hope. This hope is volcanic, breaking through the foreground dimensions of experience in explosions of Ecstasy, desperation, and Rage. Many women have been jolted out of complacency. Radical feminists who have been Traveling since the late sixties and early seventies—sometimes feeling cast into the role of Cassandra, the unheard prophetess—are now joined by newly arriving sisters/friends who experience surprising eruptions of buried Natural/Elemental powers.

As Soothsayers, deviant/defiant women see through the society of godfather, son, and company. Beyond this, Crones sense astonishing yet perfectly sensible synchronicities—or Syn-Crone-icities. Spinning Crones who have Lived through earthquakes, tornadoes, tidal waves, parching sojourns in deserts of the spirit, are stronger than before; Norns know our Hour is arriving.

The droners' doomsday clock ticks on.* Weaving our own Time/Space on the boundaries of clockocracy, Websters Doom these doomers. Denouncing the destroyers, Nags announce the resurgence of female powers. Wild women will to shift the shapes of words, of worlds. Naming Elemental sources/forces, Sirens call women to a metapatriarchal journey of exorcism and ecstasy. Responding to this call, which corresponds to the promptings of our inner voices, women are strengthened for the struggle on the boundaries of fatherland, while moving more deeply into our own reality, our be-ing.

Mythic Paradigms Revisited, or Breaking Out of Man-Made Amnesia

If this book had not been written, my later books, *Gyn/Ecology* and *Pure Lust* could not have happened.** The actual writing was

---

* The "doomsday clock" is a popular symbol which appears regularly in the *Bulletin of the Atomic Scientists.* In 1984 the hands were reset to "three minutes before midnight," indicating "extreme and immediate danger" of nuclear holocaust.

** My first feminist book, *The Church and the Second Sex* (Harper and Row, 1968), was also a milestone in my journey. The situation with that completed in 1972, thirteen years before the publication of this *Original Reintroduction.* Since Crones understand thirteen to be an auspicious number, the timing would seem to be Crone-logical. *Thirteen* can be taken as a metaphor of metamorphosis, signifying Tidal Time, outside tidy measurements of the clocks, watches, and calendars of father time.[4] Insofar as this book participates in Tidal Time, it continues to be the expression of a process that Unfolds unendingly. *Beyond God the Father* opens doors of perception and maps the beginnings of a route. Since, however, this is not a flat, linear route but rather a spiraling journey, the beginnings cannot simply be left behind. Rather, they are taken up again and again, understood and heard more and more deeply, in an ever-evolving context.

The direction of the journey is foretold in this book, for example in the discussion of three "myths of transcendence."[5] The first mythic paradigm—separation and return—represents pseudo-transcendence in the form of dead circles of repetition, going nowhere. The second—conflict and vindication—reduces the meaning of transcendence to fighting an oppressor, thereby making perpetual oppression necessary. The third paradigm—integrity and transformation—implies spiraling movement, liberating the elements of truth embedded in the other myths by locating these in a biophilic context.

---

book is different, however. As I explained in the *Feminist Postchristian Introduction* to the 1975 edition of that work, during the years following its initial publication I moved from "reformist" feminism to identifying as a postchristian radical feminist. Therefore, my reevaluation of *The Church and the Second Sex* expresses my view of the earlier Daly as a foresister whose work is an essential source and to whom I am indebted but with whom I largely disagree. The *Feminist Postchristian Introduction* to that book is a milestone in my *radical* feminist journey, and its publication together with the original text forms an important bridge—a place of dual perspective that can be helpful to women who are making that essential crossing *now.*

Reintroducing *Beyond God the Father,* however, is a profoundly different experience, for I basically still agree with its major theses, understanding many of them more deeply than I did when I wrote the book. Although I have changed my vocabulary to a great extent, and although my ideas have evolved, I recognize this work as prophetic in many ways, as explained in this *Original Reintroduction.*

Within this Metaphoric, Metamorphic atmosphere, then, the patterns of separation and return are transformed, their momentum channeled into directions which Emily Culpepper has described as "spiraling paths."[6] The past is repeatedly encountered, but it is also transmuted, since the context in which it is remembered is moving. The paradigm of conflict and vindication also is taken up and transformed, for the necessity of fighting oppression is Realized as but one aspect of the journey of exorcism and ecstasy.

In recent years, Furious women have experienced in agonizing detail the mazes constructed by the patriarchal backlashers whose intent is to obstruct this movement of integrity and transformation, tracking women into repetitive circles and pointless death marches. We have witnessed an escalation of rape, woman battering, incestuous abuse of female children, pornographic degradation, impoverishment of every kind. All of these gynocidal atrocities function to re-turn women to their masters, physically and psychically. These manifestations of physical violence, combined with such inventions as man-made plastic feminism,[7] have reinforced the ruts, already violently embedded into women's psyches, which track women into dying out their lives in patterns of pointless circling and re-acting.

An insidious consequence of this tracking of women's thoughts, words, passions, and behavior has been the *fixing* of original feminist insights. Terrified, women become frozen/stuck at elementary stages of analysis. Typically, a woman in this state of paralysis mistakenly identifies mere labeling with creative thinking/speaking/acting—which is Naming. Illogically, she may assume that having used the term *patriarchy* or having called herself a feminist with sufficient frequency relieves her of responsibility for action and for further analysis of the meanings and practical implications of these words. Although this description may seem exaggerated, it was in fact predictable and is "normal" in a society characterized by devaluation of words. Bombarded by the constant babble of the media and of ordinary conversation in a verbicidal, gynocidal, biocidal environment, women *forget* the deep Background of words and of our own Selves.

One passage from Nietzsche cited in this book is especially relevant here:

Whenever man has thought it necessary to create a memory for himself, his effort has been attended with torture, blood, sacrifice.[8]

Re-membering/Musing women know that man continues to manufacture memories for himself and that to this end he is escalating the use of torture, blood, sacrifice—physical and psychic. The man-made memories embedded in women—particularly through the master-minded media—torture, batter, and bury Deep Memory, afflicting women with amnesia.

Despite the many and solid gains of recent years, the battering of women's psyches in this period of backlash has dis-couraged many from the process of understanding phallocracy and imagining ways of breaking out. Indeed, women are terrorized into amnesia and made afraid to know the full implications of patriarchal power. For many know enough to know that real knowledge implies participation in the Craft/Wisdom of Witches (Witchcraft) and that this knowing is a crime punishable by death.

Tracked by the terrorists, a woman may feel convinced that she need not "take time" to pursue her analysis of and activism against the gynocidal society as such, that she should "move on" to other subjects. Indeed, the term *gynocide* may seem "extreme" to her. Having mistakenly—and conveniently—overlooked the essential point that violence against women is the source and paradigm of all other manifestations of violence, she "moves" to the conclusion that feminism is a stage, to be replaced by concern with other causes.

Caught on the wheels of such fixed thinking, some women have turned back to male-led movements and allegiance to patriarchal institutions. Re-turning to the hope of influencing men rather than trusting Elemental powers and choosing to *be* the Powerful Outsiders' Society,[9] women are sentenced to confinement in senescent circles of pseudorebellion.

Beyond God the Father issues warnings against the temptations to re-turn, pointing to the reality of woman-identified hope.

It dis-covers rapism as the paradigm of all oppression, as the root and model of the nuclear arms buildup, racism, man-made poverty, chemical contamination. Clearly:

The logical extension of the mentality of rape is the objectification of all who can be cast into the role of victims of violence.[10]

The struggle to break out of the circles of rapism has in some ways become more difficult, since the sovereigns of sado-society have augmented their assaults, using their religion, their politics, their professions, their media as rituals for erasure of female powers, imprisoning women in the state of the grateful dead. Lulled/dulled into the sleeping death which is the condition designed for patriarchally possessed women, "forgetting" the reality of gynocide, women react to each other as if they were the primary sources of their oppression. The old embedded mechanisms of self-hatred and horizontal violence are tapped by the tricksters, and women are trapped/sapped.

As foretold in this book, television has been a major instrument of this ritual reinforcement of self-destructive mechanisms, so that

the majority, drugged by the perpetual presence of the politics of rape on the TV screen, sees it all but sees nothing. The horrors of a phallocentric world have simultaneously become more visible and more invisible.[11]

Not surprisingly, then, the women's movement in recent years has appeared partially paralyzed. Burnout is an experience not unfamiliar to long-term feminists.

Yet it is also true that the biophilic process of *anamnesia*— of unforgetting one's own deep experience—can be intensified amid the blatant horrors of godfather reagan, pentagon, and company. These horrors have indeed simultaneously become more visible as well as more invisible. *Choice,* therefore, is of ultimate significance. It is possible to allow knowledge of Be-ing to become ever more subliminal, to let it fade hopelessly. But it is also possible to choose to see the patterns of patriarchally perpetrated atrocities, to render the terrifying knowledge more and more explicit, Naming the agents and their strategies for destruction of life. Summoning the courage to See and to Name and to Act is a process of exorcism, clearing away the smog of deception so that ways of escape can be imagined and Realized.

Realizing the way out of stag-nation, the state of bondage, *is* living the spiraling journey of integrity and transformation, of re-membering ourSelves as verbs, as participators in the Verb, Be-ing.*

From God the Father to God the Verb, and Beyond

This book takes on the task of de-reifying "God," that is, of changing the conception/perception of god from "the supreme being" to Be-ing. The Naming of Be-ing as Verb—as intransitive Verb that does not require an "object"—expresses an Other way of understanding ultimate/intimate reality. The experiences of many feminists continue to confirm the original intuition that Naming Be-ing as Verb is an essential leap in the cognitive/affective journey beyond patriarchal fixations.

Since the original publication of *Beyond God the Father,* major developments have taken place under the aegis of "women's spirituality."[12] The variety of approaches and the resurgence of gynergy attending these developments have in large measure been inspiring and encouraging. Without breakthroughs in woman-identified spirituality, the "women's movement" would be a non-movement—hopelessly dead and deadening. Yet, of course, there are problems.

Serious and unacknowledged difficulties can arise when those who speak and/or write of *The Goddess* or *goddesses* avoid the giant step/leap of Realizing ultimate/intimate reality as movement, as Verb. One result, though unintended, is complicity in Verbicide—killing of the living, transformative energy of words,

---

* I am not saying that every woman has to use these words to Name herSelf as verb. Women may use very different language. I do think that the basic intuition of potential for movement and the Realizing of this potential in a large, biophilic context must *be* there.

muting of the metamorphic, shapeshifting powers inherent in words. Thus *The Goddess* can be reduced to a static symbol, a mere replacement for the noun *God.*

Such replacement can amount to a "change" as minimal as a transsexual operation on the patriarchal god. Since, as Jan Raymond has shown , a "transsexed" male is still male (a "she-male" or a male-to-constructed female),[13] it is clear that such an operation—whether men perform it on each other or their god—cannot be expected to bring about profound psychic or social change. A transsexed patriarchal god is still patriarchal and will function (at least in subliminal or subterranean ways) to serve the interests of the fathers, for such a symbol is external to the experienced reality of women and nature.

If we want to dis-cover how *The Goddess* (singular or plural) is functioning for women, it will be useful to observe how this affects our be-ing in the world. Insofar as the image inspires passivity, self-absorption, the plastic passion of full-fullment,[14] and in general the therapeutic syndrome of rage-less re-turning,[15] there is ample indication that it is functioning as a noun. The noun-goddess, tokenized derivative of the christian god, serves the cockocratic establishment, perpetuating the status quo.

The noun-goddess, then, is a simple off-shoot of the noun-god, who is a reified reversal of the ancient Verb-Goddess, the Triple Goddess of many Names.[16] As derivative of this reified reversal, she-he is indeed a baffling and bamboozling phenom-enon.* She-he can be found lurking in many circles, including christian circles, and she-he legitimates the endless senescent circling of such circles.

In contrast to all of this, Goddess-images—insofar as these inspire creative activity, Self-Realizing bonding with Other women

---

* The ordination of female christian priests also is an imitative, deriv-ative phenomenon. Since christian priests function as reversers of the biophilic work of Pagan priestesses, reducing religion to a static state, female christian priests would seem to be in the unfortunate condition of imitation reversers, serving dead symbols and serving these up to starving congregations of bamboozled believers who are doubly tricked by this incorporation of females into the processions of priestly predators.

in the work of Weaving, and Dragon-identified passions such as Rage and Lust for Nemesis—can function as Metaphors of Metamorphosis, as verbs fostering participation in the Verb, Be-ing.

In these instances, *Goddess* Names active participation in Powers of Be-ing.[17] As Metaphor of Metabeing, she calls for action, for movement. As Nelle Morton has explained, she evokes a shock, a clash with the "going logic," introducing a new logic.[18] Metaphors are not mere "figures of speech." Derived from the Greek *meta* (meaning after, behind, transformative of, beyond) and *pherein* (meaning to bear, carry), *metaphor* in the deepest sense suggests the power of words to carry us into a Time/Space that is after, behind, transformative of, and beyond static being —the stasis maintained by phallocracy. Insofar as they function as Metaphors of Metabeing, Goddess-words transport us into this Time/Space.

Susanne Langer recognized that "our literal language is a very repository of 'faded metaphors,' " and I have suggested that there is a sexual politics of the fading of metaphors, which is a logical corollary of the withering of women's auras in the state of servitude which is patriarchy.[19] Powerful old words whose Metaphoric force has been faded under the phallocratic rule include *Spinster, Webster, Weird, Hag, Witch, Sibyl, Muse*, and many Others, as well as *Goddess.* The waning of such words' powers is part of the program of elimination of female powers.

Yet these words as Metaphors of Metabeing are accessible to women as Muses, as Wonderlusters who choose to break out of man-made mind-molds. *Goddess,* then, can become our broom, our flying Nightmare, carrying Wild wanderers beyond the dulling daydreams programmed by the perpetual soap operas of the sado-state. This happens when women dare to Realize our Elemental, woman-bonding powers.

Such Realizing is no simple matter, however. Traveling beyond the godfather and his transsexed substitutes continues to be a difficult task. A major pitfall for some women in recent years has been the delusion that they have accomplished this task by a mere semantic shift in their own vocabulary, unaccompanied by profound alteration of consciousness and behavior—that is, of the *context* in which words are spoken. When a woman is caught in this delusion she does not see that all the propaganda of patriarchy—fairy tales, popular songs and films, psychology, advertising, political speeches—is replication of the godfather, son, and holy ghost theology *and that she is susceptible to its influence.* Continually caught off guard and full-filled with false confidence, she is a prime target of the paternal public relations experts.

Really moving beyond god the father and his surrogates means Living the process of participation in Powers of Be-ing. Elementally Metaphoric words and the actions they encourage and reflect are signals of these Powers. They are Metamorphic, shifting the shapes of space and time, rearranging energy patterns, breaking through and relocating boundaries.

Living "On the Boundary": Then and Now

This book announces the moral imperative to live "on the boundary" of patriarchal institutions. "The boundary"—the location of new space/new time—is understood primarily in a psychic sense of woman-identified integrity, but this is closely associated with the claiming of physical space/time by and for women. Such space/time is "on the boundary of all that has been considered central."[20]

It is hardly surprising that patriarchal attitudes toward women's space/time have remained unchanged since the writing of this book. What has been shocking to many feminists is the extent to which bore-ocrats have managed to repossess spaces/ times that women had succeeded in claiming for ourSelves.

Although on one level this is discouraging, there are dimensions of understanding that can be expanded in the light of such recent history. At the very minimum, these sobering experiences can help to dispel from our psyches any remnants of the delusion that phallocracy can be reformed or improved. One logical consequence of such total and positive dis-illusionment is a shifting of the focus of hope away from unredeemable structures to the Selves of women and other biophilic creatures, engendering intensified concentration upon our own powers of creation, our own Final Cause. The shedding of false hopes can and should be invigorating, making possible the dis-covering of new energy patterns, the release of more gynergy. Wonderlusting Journeyers are learning to rid ourSelves of excess baggage such as misguided expectations that weigh us down and divert us from our course.

The sources of authentic hope are to be found within Wild women—Self-proclaimed Witches/Hags who choose the creation of our own space/time as a primal expression of intellectual/e-motional vitality, knowing that without this we will suffocate in the ranks of the living dead. Having learned from recent experience to understand more deeply than before that assimilation is deadly, deviant women can focus with renewed ferocity upon understanding the possibilities of our territory—the boundary—where/when we can Live the metapatriarchal journey of exorcism and ecstasy.

Such dis-covering of deeper dimensions of boundary be-ing is Metamorphic Musing. Living "on the boundary," then, implies continual unfolding of Elemental potential. This in turn implies that the boundaries themselves change. Such transformation of boundaries does not imply abandonment of the struggle to *be* in this world. Quite the opposite is true: It is the practice of Prudent/Prudish[21] worldliness itself that enables women to move to Other boundaries.

The metapatriarchal adventure of boundary living implies the awakening of Other senses—senses that have been muted in the state of depression/repression that is patriarchy. A woman who experiences/Lives this awakening may drastically change her occupation. Or again, a boundary-living woman may appear to be working at the "same kind" of job that she held previously. However, the intensification and expansion of her Elemental powers of perception affect all of her activities. While looking and listening steadily with her "ordinary" eyes and ears, she sees and hears with her Third Eye and Third (Inner) Ear. The boundaries on which she lives and works, then, continue to be transmuted.

Thirteen or so years ago some women—radical feminists—knew quite clearly what boundary living meant for us. Some of that clarity became obscured as a result of escalating assaults. Clearly it is Time for the emergence of qualitatively Other clarity and hope, which can be fierce enough to take into account the heightened malignancy of the man's world and Lusty enough to leap more boldly beyond its gruesome grasp.

Such Leaping is possible because there are Elemental bio-philic Forces that *are* ineffably stronger than the framers' fabrications. These Forces are knowable by women Living "on the boundary" precisely because the Elemental location of *the Boundary* which underlies all the shifts and variations of boundaries is *between the worlds*.[22] These worlds are the fixers' stage-set of fictions/falsifications (the foreground) and the deep Background of Elemental Life.

Qualitative Leaping continues to happen because some women not only refuse to forget the Background but go on Weaving into this Realm, whirling beneath, above, through, and beyond the butchers'/botchers' state of boredom, exploding the backlashers' bags of dirty tricks, wandering/wondering outside the cruel rules of rakes and rippers who preach and promote "the end of the world." Prudent Pro-Lifers* pronounce an end to the mashers' mirror world of lies, the reversal realms of knifers/"pro-lifers" whose not-be-ing/not-seeing rapes and kills the core of conscience/consciousness.

As Raging women Race into the Background, the energy of that Other World—the This World that is hidden by the hucksters'/hackers' heaps of pseudoinformation—is Elementally encouraging. We Rage with the rhythms of Tidal Time.

Countering the clocks of father time, Raging/Racing women become Counterclock-Wise, asking Counterclock-Whys. Boundary-shifting Sibyls become Other-Wise, uttering Other Whys. Our very be-ing vibrates with earth, air, fire, water and with the moon, sun, and farthest stars. Participating in communications/vibrations that range through spirit-space and time, boundary-breaking, Boundary-Living Prudes and Websters experience Presence in new and ancient ways. Therefore we are ready to re-examine the meaning of power of the present, power of Presence, now.

---

* By the word *Pro-Lifers* here I mean biophilic, that is, Life-loving women who are committed to *quality* of life and to freedom of choice to ensure that quality in all dimensions. I also mean to snatch back that word, which rightfully is a Lusty women's word, and which has been ripped off by self-righteous "right to lifers" whose indifference to women's lives is manifested in this characteristic use of the strategy of reversal.

Power of Presence, Now

Furious women have struggled to survive the manifold androcratic attempts to undermine our power of Presence—the power of the woman-identified Self that radiates outward, attracting other Others. The undermining basically takes the form of covering over all evidence of our own reality, so that women come to disbelieve in our own powers. The assaults against our ability to Realize our own Presence come from the media, education, all of the professions. Degraded caricatures of women—from hard-core porn images to mindlessly adoring wives of politicians—instill self-loathing, woman-hatred, and terror.

As the foreground fabrications become ever more vile and violent, women coming into Touch with the Background weave and re-weave faith and hope in our power of Presence. This continuing Webster-Work incorporates learning from experiences, including sometimes plodding through seemingly boundless wasteland. It is a process of Self-strengthening and of reinforcing the bonds among Survivors/Thrivers[23] who have consciously weathered the backlash, developing keener senses, more precise modes of understanding, re-membering the capacity for radical Aloneness as essential for biophilic bonding.

Self-presentiating Websters are learning about physical ultimacy, finding that the cumulative effects of qualitative leaps into metapatriarchal be-ing *now* resonate across the limits set by the tidy timekeepers and territorial terrorists of fatherland.[24]

Surviving women Realize Presence. Conjuring the Courage to See, Viragos/Gorgons expel the phallic presence of absence—that glut of non-sense which expands meaninglessly, suffocating meaning. As Sibyls, we are becoming prescient, presentient. As Soothsayers, Survivors are learning to presentiate Other reality, causing this to be Realized as present.

Beyond Beyond God the Father:
Continuing the Journey[25]

Continuing the Journey requires discarding some old semantic baggage so that travelers will be unencumbered by malfunctioning (male-functioning) equipment. I have already dealt with *God*—from

which it is impossible to remove male/masculine imagery. Two
other eminently discardable terms are *androgyny* and *homosexuality*. These were dismissed in the preface to *Gyn/Ecology:*

The second semantic abomination, androgyny, *is a confusing term
which I sometimes used in attempting to describe integrity of
be-ing. The word is misbegotten—conveying something like "John
Travolta and Farrah Fawcett-Majors scotch-taped together"—as
I have reiterated in public recantations. The third treacherous
term,* homosexuality, *reductionistically "includes," that is, excludes,
gynocentric be-ing/Lesbianism.*[26]

The fact that such terms are discarded in the Journey beyond
Beyond God the Father does not mean that the *process* of Naming
was faulty or that the impetus behind the choice of such words
was misguided. They can be seen now as transitional words and,
in fact, as self-liquidating words. From hindsight, they can be
recognized as having a built-in, though not consciously planned,
obsolescence. Be-ing continues. The process of Naming proceeds.

Be-ing at home on the road means continuing the metapatriarchal Metamorphosis. As I have explained in *Pure Lust,* it involves breaking taboos (especially the Terrible Taboo against
Women-Touching women),* breaking sound barriers, Racing in
Tidal Time, becoming Pyrogenetic, learning Volcanic Virtue, moving with Elemental E-motion, Realizing Elemental Potency. It means
Wanderlusting and Wonderlusting with the elements. It means
Be-Longing, Be-Friending, Be-Witching.

---

* Terribly Taboo Women-Touching is not simply a matter of sexual
contact. I am referring also to contact with women's Spiritual Touching
Powers, which is just as much prohibited under patriarchy as direct physical and even sexual contact with another Female Self. The fetishizing of
that part of the Total Taboo that concerns sexual contact is a ruse of the
patriarchs. Fixing women with fears of physical contact, they distract
from the Gyn/Ecological context that gives full meaning to such contact.
Nonfeminist women who are simply "gay" can remain bound libidinally
on other levels to the institutional fathers. But if violation of the Taboo
against woman-bonding both encompasses and transcends the sexual
sphere and leads to refusal and rebellion that is holistic and Elemental,
the Powers of women are freed to change our lives.

Be-ing at home on the road means summoning the Courage to Be, the Courage to See, the Courage to Sin.* It means be-ing Wicked. Wicked women are Wiccen women, speaking Be-Witching words. As Websters, Wicked Wiccen women unwind the bindings of mummified/numbified words. This involves hearing/speaking through Other time/space, unwinding the clocks of tidy time.

Wicked Websters declare that women and words have served the fathers' sentences long enough. We ride the rhythms of Racing Rage, freeing words. Like birds uncaged, these soundings rush and soar, seeking sister-vibrations. Wicked women, when heard, sound the signal that Tidal Time has come.

Women moving beyond god the father find that the mysticism of words is twined with the mysticism of creation. Wording is one fundamental way of Be-Witching—Sparking women to the insights and actions that change our lives. Wording is expression of shape-shifting powers, weaving meanings and rhythms, unleashing Original forces/sources. Arranging words to convey their Archaic meanings, Websters release them from cells of conventional senses.

Releasing words to race together, Websters become Muses. We do not use words; we Muse words. Metapatterning women and words have magical powers, opening doorways of memories, transforming spaces and times. Rhymes, alliterations, alteration of senses—all aid in the breaking of fatherland's fences. Thus liberation is the work of Wicked Grammar, which is a basic instrument, our Witches' Hammer.

Wicked women strive to overcome the amnesia, aphasia, and apraxia inflicted by phallocracy.[27] We actively pronounce certain ideologies, institutions, practices to be blameworthy and evil. This pronouncing/denouncing portends the end of such evil, auguring an Other reality.

---

* Self-presentiating women—be-ing WRONG according to the prevailing assumptions—may be said to Sin. The word *sin* is probably etymologically akin to the Latin *est*, meaning (s)he *is*, and is derived from the Indo-European root *es-*, meaning *to be* (*American Heritage Dictionary*). Clearly, the ontological courage of feminists, our courage to be, implies the courage to be WRONG. Elemental be-ing outside the fathers' rule(s) is Sinning; it requires the Courage to Sin.

The ideologies, institutions, practices thus denounced have as their common method *usage*. Websters denounce the patriarchal usage of women and nature and of words. We denounce both good usage and bad usage, proclaiming the termination of usage. Journeying Websters are enabled to declare words free from usage insofar as we Speak our lives in an Other context.

The Muses/Daimons attending all Wicked wanderers/wonderers are Guides on the Journey beyond *Beyond God the Father*. Guided by Muses, we tour the Realms of Words, unleash these Sisters, ungag these Holy Crones. We see/hear that words fly together, sounding each other to freedom. Wise women, who know that the Race of Wild women is akin to the Race of Weird Words, find here clues to our own liberation. Words and women reclaim our own nations, our tribes and formations. In this process, words and women guide each other. Our guiding is reciprocal, requited. United, our movements are directed by sagacious Sin-Tactics. Together we work to expel the bore-ocratic chairmen of the bored. We strive to make the world Weirder.

One task of Wandering/Wondering women is Be-Fooling. This involves denouncing snoolish stupidity as evil. Such denouncing is not mere "fooling around." It punctures the pomposity of want-wits and windbags, whose malignant mindlessness would destroy the world. Be-Fooling is Elemental humor. It is ontological Fooling.

Be-Fooling is threefold. First there is Nixing. As Nixes, Websters weaving beyond god the father veto, ban, and forbid the droolings of fools, the dronings of clones, the mindless devastations wrought by stag-nations. Next, there is Hexing. As Witches, Websters hex, cast spells, pronouncing the Doom of doomdom. Third, there is X-ing. X is the symbol for the unknown or variable quantity/quality. For Be-Fooling Websters it signals the quantum leaps, the Weirdward Intergalactic Galloping of Nag-Gnostic Voyagers. X-ing means foretelling the arrival of the X-factor. It means announcing the convergence of conditions for concordance, for encountering the Fates.

Regaining the Sense of Direction

Sibyls/Soothsayers developing a Sense of Direction map the dimensions of metapatriarchal Space/Time. We practice Space-

Craft. Crafty Crones walk/talk the Wrong Way. (For example, we practice moving widdershins, that is, counterclockwise.) Moving in Wicked directions, we open doors to Other dimensions, Other Spatial perceptions. By thus reversing the reversals of the righteous space controllers, we enter a different context. Here Spinsters Spin on our heels, facing the "four directions" from different angles.

A Sibyl sees that the "four directions" are laden with Elemental and mythic associations, that they are connected with winds, seasons, Goddesses, Angels. This knowledge of her Elemental tradition gives grounding and legitimation to her Sylph-identified Sense of Direction, her Archaic/Original orientation, her Fate-directed destination—her Final Cause.

Stopping the Doomsday Clock

The Moon-Goddesses—Gorgons—look toward men and turn them to stone—the doomsday men with their doomsday clocks whose tick-tocks mimic the rhythms of Lunar Time. Gorgons look outward, refusing to serve the masters' commands to peer into mirrors. They tear off the blindfold from captive Justice, crying that the Time has come to activize, to See with Active Eyes. They say that Eye/I-beams can stop the doomsday clock, that moonward-turning Eyes can stop the spells of twelves, Spelling Thirteen.

Twelve is the measure of master-minded monotony. Crones need only recall the twelve apostles, the twelve days of christmas, twelve men on a jury, et cetera, ad nauseam. In general, Brewsters prefer a baxter's dozen,[28] a coded reminder of the Elemental number thirteen. In tune with the moon, Lusty women sense the primal potency of the Elemental, thirteen-month lunar year.

Thirteen represents the Other Hour, beyond the direction of disaster. It suggests the Time/Space of Spelling Doom to the would-be doomers. It Spells awakening of Memory, of Metamemory, unveiling of Mystery, whose Eye-Bite snaps the chains of fettered Time. *Thirteen* signals the hitherto and always Unknown, the Elemental Forces/Sources that can save even planets doomed to destruction. It signals Realms not neatly measurable, the Call of the Wild, the ever-recurring dawn of new creation, the Spin-

ning of spiral galaxies whose majestic arms ponderously rotate
in magnificent celestial ballets.

This context Spells hope—the hope of the Thirteenth Hour—
the hope of jumping off the clock, off the parameters of the predators' predictability. The context suggested by Metaphoric *Thirteen*
is the context of Leaping, of carrying Threads of Life through
galaxies of gynergetic/gynergenetic creation. The Tapestries thus
woven are records of re-membering and foretelling of future Memories. They are recordings of celestial sound waves and light
waves, chorusing morphogenetic resonances with stars.

Metaphoric *Thirteen* suggests Possibilities of Metamorphosis.
Available to all who will to shift the shapes of words, of worlds,
it points to spaces/times of new beginnings, of whirring whirls.
It conjures whirlpools, whirlwinds, whose force unwinds the
doomers' clocks, unlocks pent-up Elemental flocks of Weaving
spirits.

In this Other Hour, wonders never cease. Now released, in-
numerable flying Websters fleck the spheres with particulate parti-
colored designs. Party lines are disconnected. In their stead,
threads of cosmic communication are re-spun—all in fun. Crissing
and crossing, soaring and tossing, tumbling to earth while touching the sun, the Weavers carry filaments of hope to the women
of this world and others.

If this description of journeying beyond *Beyond God the
Father* seems farfetched to some, let these doubters rest assured:
It *is*. Elemental faith is farfetched. The words of the Fates are
fetched from remote times and places as well as from the innermost depths of Here and Now. Faces that can stop the doomsday
clock are faces of Crones who have come from afar and continue
to travel. The numbers of such cosmic messengers are increasing very rapidly, faster than the speed of flight.

So, too, the tribes of women who are jumping off the face/
foreground of the impoverished doomsday world are growing.
Since patriarchy is the perpetual poorhouse in which women are
stored/restored, afflicted with poverty of spirit, imagination, intellect, passion, physical vigor, as well as economic poverty, it is
clear—and clearer than ever—that we have basically Nothing to
lose.

In fact, each Time a woman makes the quantum leap into Tidal Time, the death knell of phallocracy sounds more loudly and our hopes soar more Spritefully. The Race of women is enriched by each individual movement of fey faith, hopping hope, and biophilic bonding. As this book announces:

The power of sisterhood is not warpower. There have been and will be conflicts, but the Final Cause causes not by conflict but by attraction. Not by the attraction of a Magnet that is All There, but by the creative drawing power of the Good Who is self-communicating Be-ing, Who is the Verb from whom, in whom, and with whom all true movements move.[29]

The magnetizing powers of Be-Witching women are creative drawing powers of presentiating Presence, dis-closing participation in Self-communicating Be-ing. The Journey can and does continue because the Verb continues—from whom, in whom, and with whom all true movements move.[30]

Notes

1. Telephone communication, August 1984.
2. Mary Daly, *Pure Lust: Elemental Feminist Philosophy* (Boston: Beacon Press, 1984), p. 373.
3. Conversation, Boston, October 1976.
4. See Daly, *Pure Lust,* pp. 289–314.
5. Chapter 1, pp. 24–26.
6. Emily Culpepper, "Philosophia in a Feminist Key: Revolt of the Symbols," unpublished Th.D. dissertation, Harvard University, 1983, p. 379. In this work, which will be published in revised form as a book, Culpepper explains: "With the model of the spiral in mind, we can value even one small step toward change as being that slight shift of degree which can transform the confining path of the circle, channeling its momentum into a spiral path that can really move us onward."
7. See Daly, *Pure Lust,* pp. 67–72, 112, 144–46, 166–69, 202–06.
8. Chapter 5, p. 142.
9. Virginia Woolf first Named the Outsiders' Society in *Three Guineas* (New York: Harcourt, Brace & World, Harbinger Books, 1938), pp. 106–44.
10. The context of this statement is chapter 4, p. 118. The basic thesis is sustained throughout the book.
11. Chapter 4, p. 120.
12. An excellent anthology, which can lead the reader to further investigations, is *The Politics of Women's Spirituality: Essays on the Rise of Spiritual Power Within the Feminist Movement,* ed. by Charlene Spretnak (Garden City, N.Y.: Doubleday and Company, Inc., 1982). See also Starhawk, *The Spiral Dance* (San Francisco: Harper and Row, 1979).
13. See Janice G. Raymond, *The Transsexual Empire: The Making of the She-Male* (Boston: Beacon Press, 1979).
14. See Daly, *Pure Lust,* pp. 200–06.
15. See Daly, *Gyn/Ecology: The Metaethics of Radical Feminism* (Boston: Beacon Press, 1978), pp. 223–92.
16. See Merlin Stone, *When God Was a Woman* (New York: Harcourt Brace Jovanovich, Harvest Books, 1976); *Ancient Mirrors of Woman-*

hood (Boston: Beacon Press, 1984). See also Patricia Monaghan, *The Book of Goddesses and Heroines* (New York: E. P. Dutton, Dutton Paperbacks, 1981); Barbara G. Walker, *The Woman's Encyclopedia of Myths and Secrets* (San Francisco: Harper and Row, 1983); Marta Weigle, *Spiders & Spinsters: Women and Mythology* (Albuquerque: University of New Mexico Press, 1982). Never to be forgotten is Elizabeth Gould Davis, *The First Sex* (New York: G. P. Putnam's Sons, 1971).

17. See Daly, *Pure Lust,* pp. 27, 423.

18. Nelle Morton develops her theory of metaphor and of *goddess* in her many articles and in her book *The Journey Is Home* (Boston: Beacon Press, 1985).

19. See Susanne K. Langer, *Philosophy in a New Key* (New York: New American Library, Mentor Books, 1942). Also see Daly, *Pure Lust,* p. 28.

20. Chapter 1, pp. 40–41.

21. See Daly, *Pure Lust,* pp. 263–74.

22. The idea of the Boundary as "between the worlds" was Named by Suzanne Melendy. Conversation, Boston, September 1984. As Emily Culpepper suggested, *Beyond God the Father* is "like a window between the worlds." Telephone communication, August 1984.

23. I defined *Surviving* as Thriving in *Gyn/Ecology,* p. 9: "Surviving (from the Latin *super* plus *vivere*) I take to mean living above, through, around the obstacles thrown in our paths. This is hardly the dead 'living on' of possessed tokens. The process of Survivors is meta-living, be-ing."

24. See Daly, *Pure Lust,* pp. 147–52.

25. Many of the ideas suggested in this and the following sections will be developed in the forthcoming book, *Websters' First New Intergalactic Wickedary of the English Language,* Conjured by Mary Daly, in Cahoots with Jane Caputi.

26. Daly, *Gyn/Ecology,* p. xi. Farrah Fawcett herself discarded her bubbleheaded feminine role since this passage was written, particularly in the 1984 television drama "The Burning Bed."

27. These words were first used by feminist novelist and theoretician Louky Bersianik to describe patriarchally imposed forgetfulness, inability to make verbal connections, and incapacity to take appropriate action. See *Les agénésies du vieux monde* (Outremont, Quebec: L'Intégrale, éditrice, 1982).

28. *Baxter* originally meant female baker. "Baxter's dozen," therefore, is an Original way of expressing the proverbial "baker's dozen," meaning thirteen. As Elizabeth Gould Davis pointed out in *The First Sex* (p. 111), the number thirteen became "unlucky" under patriarchy because of its association with gynocracies.

29. Chapter 7, p. 198.

30. A connecting Leap in the Journey between this book and *Gyn/Ecology* is my article "The Qualitative Leap Beyond Patriarchal Religion," *Quest: A Feminist Quarterly,* vol. 1, no. 4 (Spring 1975), pp. 20–40. The *Feminist Postchristian Introduction* to the 1975 edition of *The Church and the Second Sex* is also an essential and by no means missing link to *Gyn/Ecology* and beyond.

Preface

This book is in a real sense a sequel to *The Church and the Second Sex*, published in the late sixties, just before the contemporary tide of women's liberation writings burst forth. The earlier book manifested some of the anger and ebullient hope that characterized the period immediately following the Second Vatican Council.

The perceptive reader will notice that essentially the same anger and the same hope are the wellsprings of this book, but that the focus has shifted and the perspective has been greatly radicalized. The transition to a wider and deeper perspective within the author's own consciousness has been dramatic—as have been the five years between publication dates. For women involved in liberation, these have been years of intense living "on the boundary"—a veritable full generation of change measured by the accelerated time flow of this age.

If the transition has been dramatic, it has also had its funny side. It has been a source of amusement to friends and to myself that some of the critique of language made in this book could be applied to the earlier one. Hopefully, neither they nor I will now regress to a position of standing still or even of running more slowly—which in these times would be equivalent to running backwards.

Some of the footnote references in this book are to other books and articles. Others are references to conversations with women, the best discussions I have ever had. The free-floating creativity in these discussions has outranked in the quality of its intellectuality most of the scholarly material I have read. I suspect that a great deal of this material had its source in the intuitions and reasoning of women who, of course, did not receive credit and were consigned to the customary role of having ideas stolen from them. Having been denied equal access to the realm of the printed word, women still have primarily an oral tradition.[1] My references to conversations are meant to be a reminder of that tradition, as well as an effort to set precedent for giving women some of the credit due to them, finally.

I thank Jan Raymond, Linda Barufaldi, Emily Culpepper, and Jean MacRae, whose friendship, ideas, and process of becoming are woven into the fabric of this book. For their support I thank also my friends, especially Pauli Murray, Kaye Ashe, Nelle Morton, Pat and Joe Green, Mary Lowry, Ann and Irvin Cobb, Clare Hall, Helen and John Gray, Mary Lou Thompson, Betty Farians, Frances McGillicuddy, Bill Wilson, Jim Burke, Cele and Eli Leavitt. I thank Yolanda Gringeri for helping me with the preparation of the manuscript.

INTRODUCTION

The Problem, the Purpose, and the Method

I want a women's revolution like a lover.
I lust for it, I want so much this freedom,
this end to struggle and fear and lies
we all exhale, that I could die just
with the passionate uttering of that desire.
  —ROBIN MORGAN

When you are criticizing the philosophy of an epoch, do not chiefly direct your attention to those intellectual positions which its exponents feel it necessary explicitly to defend. There will be some fundamental assumptions which adherents of all the various systems within the epoch unconsciously presuppose. Such assumptions appear so obvious that people do not know what they are assuming because no other way of putting things has ever occurred to them.

  —ALFRED NORTH WHITEHEAD

The basic presuppositions of this book have been proposed in detail elsewhere.[1] I shall briefly highlight some of these ideas before proceeding to a discussion of purpose and method.

Recent years have witnessed a series of crescendos in the women's movement. Women of all "types," having made the psychic breakthrough to recognition of the basic sameness of our situation as women, have been initiated into the struggle for liberation of our sex from its ancient bondage. The bonding together of women into a sisterhood for liberation

is becoming a widespread feature of American culture, and the movement is rapidly taking on worldwide dimensions.

The bonding is born out of shared recognition that there exists a
worldwide phenomenon of sexual caste, basically the same whether one
lives in Saudi Arabia or in Sweden. This planetary sexual caste system
involves birth-ascribed hierarchically ordered groups whose members
have unequal access to goods, services, and prestige and to physical
and mental well-being. Clearly I am not using the term "caste" in its
most rigid sense, which would apply only to Brahmanic Indian society.
I am using it in accordance with Berreman's broad description, since
our language at present lacks other terms to describe systems of rigid
social stratification analogous to the Indian system.[2]

It may be that the psychological root of selective nit-picking about
the use of the term "caste" to describe women's situation is a desire
not to be open to the insights made available by the comparison.[3] Such
rigidity overlooks the fact that language develops and changes in the
course of history. The term is the most accurate available. Precisely
because it is strong and revealing, many feminists have chosen to
employ it. As Jo Freema˙ points out, caste systems are extremely difficult although not impossible to change. Moreover, since they are composed of interdependent units, to alter one unit is to alter all.[4]

The exploitative sexual caste system could not be perpetuated without the consent of the victims as well as of the dominant sex, and such
consent is obtained through sex role socialization—a conditioning process which begins to operate from the moment we are born, and which
is enforced by most institutions. Parents, friends, teachers, textbook
authors and illustrators, advertisers, those who control the mass media,
toy and clothes manufacturers, professionals such as doctors and
psychologists—all contribute to the socialization process. This happens
through dynamics that are largely uncalculated and unconscious, yet
which reinforce the assumptions, attitudes, stereotypes, customs, and
arrangements of sexually hierarchical society.

The fact of women's low caste status has been—and is—disguised. It is masked, first of all, by *sex role segregation*. This is more
subtle than spatial segregation, as in a ghetto, for it makes possible
the delusion that women should be "equal but different." Sexual caste
is hidden also by the fact that women have various forms of *derivative
status* as a consequence of relationships with men. That is, women

have duality of status, and the derivative aspect of this status—for example, as daughters and wives—divides us against each other and encourages identification with patriarchal institutions which serve the interests of men at the expense of women. Finally, sexual caste is hidden by *ideologies* that bestow false identities upon women and men. Patriarchal religion has served to perpetuate all of these dynamics of delusion, naming them "natural" and bestowing its supernatural blessings upon them. The system has been advertised as "according to the divine plan."

The history of antifeminism in the Judeo-Christian heritage already has been exposed.[5] The infamous passages of the Old and New Testaments are well known. I need not allude to the misogynism of the church Fathers—for example, Tertullian, who informed women in general: "You are the devil's gateway," or Augustine, who opined that women are not made to the image of God. I can omit reference to Thomas Aquinas and his numerous commentators and disciples who defined women as misbegotten males. I can overlook Martin Luther's remark that God created Adam lord over all living creatures but Eve spoiled it all. I can pass over the fact that John Knox composed a "First Blast of the Trumpet against the Monstrous Regiment of Women." All of this, after all, is past history.

Perhaps, however, we should take just a cursory glance at more recent history. Pope Pius XII more or less summarized official Catholic views on women when he wrote that "the mother who complains because a new child presses against her bosom seeking nourishment at her breast is foolish, ignorant of herself, and unhappy." In the early 1970s the Roman church launched all-out warfare against the international movement to repeal anti-abortion laws. In 1972, Pope Paul VI assumed his place as champion of "true women's liberation," asserting that this does not lie in "formalistic or materialistic equality with the other sex, but in the recognition of that specific thing in the feminine personality—the vocation of a woman to become a mother."[6]

Meanwhile in other Christian churches things have not really been that different. Theologian Karl Barth proclaimed that woman is ontologically subordinate to man as her "head." Dietrich Bonhoeffer in his famous *Letters and Papers from Prison*, in which he had proclaimed the attack of Christianity upon the adulthood of the world to be pointless, ignoble, and unchristian—in this very same volume—insists that women should be subject to their husbands. In 1972, Episcopal Bishop C. Kilmer Myers asserted that since Jesus was male, women cannot be ordained. Some Protestant churches pride themselves upon the fact that they do ordain women, yet the percentages are revealing. The United Presbyterian Church, for example, has women ministers, but they constitute less than 1 percent of fully ordained ministers in that church.

Theology and ethics which are overtly and explicitly oppressive to women are by no means confined to the past. Exclusively masculine symbolism for God, for the notion of divine "incarnation" in human nature, and for the human relationship to God reinforce sexual hierarchy. Tremendous damage is done, particularly in ethics, when ethicists construct one-dimensional arguments that fail to take women's experience into account. This is evident, for example, in biased arguments concerning abortion. To summarize briefly the situation: the entire conceptual systems of theology and ethics, developed under the conditions of patriarchy, have been the products of males and tend to serve the interests of sexist society.

To a large extent in recent times the role of religion in supporting the sexual caste system has been transferred to the professions of psychiatry and psychology. Feminists have pointed out that it is by no accident that Freudian theory emerged as the first wave of feminism was cresting. This was part of the counterrevolution, the male backlash. Psychiatry and psychology have their own creeds, priesthood, spiritual counseling, rules, anathemas, and jargon. Their power of psychological intimidation is enormous. Millions who might smile at being labeled "heretic" or "sinful" for refusing to conform to the norms of sexist society can be cowed and kept in line by the labels "sick," "neurotic," or "unfeminine." Together these professions function as "Mother" Church of contemporary secular patriarchal religion, and they send missionaries everywhere.

It isn't "prudent" for women to see all of this. Seeing means that everything changes: the old identifications and the old securities are gone. Therefore the ethic emerging in the women's movement is not an ethic of prudence but one whose dominant theme is existential courage. This is the courage to *see* and to *be* in the face of the nameless anxieties that surface when a woman begins to see through the masks of sexist society and to confront the horrifying fact of her own alienation from her authentic self.

There are many devices available both to women and to men for refusing to see the problem of sexual caste. One way is *trivialization*. One is asked: "Are you on that subject of women again when there are so many important problems—like war, racism, pollution of the environment?" One would think, to hear this, that there is no connection between sexism and the rape of the Third World, the rape of the blacks, or the rape of land and water. Another way of refusing to see the oppression of women is *particularization*. For instance, one hears: "Oh, that's a Catholic problem. The Catholic Church is so medieval." One would imagine, to listen to this, that there is no patriarchy anywhere else. Particularization is not uncommon among scholars, who frequently miss the point of the movement's critique of patriarchy itself as a system of social arrangements, and become fixated upon one element or pseudo-element of feminist theory as a target for rebuttal. That is, they spend energy answering questions that women are not really asking. An example of this is the labored defense of Paul by Scripture scholars who would have us know that "the real Paul" was not the author of the objectionable passages against women and was *not* the all time male chauvinist.[7] From the point of view of scriptural scholarship the distinction between the deutero-Pauline authors and "the real Paul" is important, no doubt. However, the discussion is hardly central to women's concern with the oppressiveness of patriarchal religion. The point is that for nearly two thousand years the passages have been used to enforce sexual hierarchy. They represent an established point of view. It is rather obscene to be more concerned with justifying an author long dead and with berating women for an alleged lack of scholarship than with the deep injustice itself that is being perpetrated by religion. The women's critique is not of a few passages but of a universe of sexist suppositions.

Another related method of refusing to see is *spiritualization*, that is, refusal to look at concrete oppressive facts. For example, would-be pacifiers of women seem to be fond of quoting the Pauline text which proclaims that "in Christ there is neither male nor female." This invites the response that *even if* this were true, the fact is that everywhere else there certainly is. Moreover, given the concrete facts of social reality and given the fact that the Christ-image is male, one has to ask what meaning-content the passage possibly can have.

Finally, some people, especially academics, attempt to make the problem disappear by *universalization*. One frequently hears: "But isn't the real problem *human* liberation?" The difficulty with this approach is that the words used may be "true," but when used to avoid confronting the specific problems of sexism they are radically untruthful.

The Purpose of This Book

It is easy, then, simply not to see. So overwhelming and insidious are the dynamics that function to support the sexist world view that women are constantly tempted to wear blinders—even in the very process of confronting sexism. Then the result is cooptable reformism that nourishes the oppressive system. In the process of writing this book, I have tried to be constantly aware of this dynamic. Asked if this work is intended to be a "new theology," I must point out that the expression is misleading. To describe one's work as "theology" or even as "new theology" usually means that the basic assumptions of patriarchal religion will be unchallenged and that they constitute a hidden agenda of the work. I am concerned precisely with questioning this hidden agenda that is operative even in so-called radical theology. I do *not* intend to apply "doctrine" to women's liberation. Rather, my task is to study the potential of the women's revolution to transform human consciousness and its externalizations, that is, to generate human becoming. If one must use traditional labels, my work can at least as accurately be called philosophy. Paul Tillich described himself as working "on the boundary" between philosophy and theology. The work of this book is not merely on the boundary *between* these (male-created) disciplines, but on the boundary *of* both, because it speaks out of the experience of that half of the human species which has been represented in neither discipline.

But if the word "theology" can be torn free from its usual limited and limiting context, if it can be torn free from its function of legitimating patriarchy, then my book can be called an effort to create theology as well as philosophy. For my purpose is to show that the women's revolution, insofar as it is true to its own essential dynamics, is an ontological, spiritual revolution, pointing beyond the idolatries of sexist society and sparking creative action in and toward transcendence. The becoming of women implies universal human becoming. It has everything to do with the search for ultimate meaning and reality, which some would call God.

Women have been extra-environmentals in human society. We have been foreigners not only to the fortresses of political power but also to those citadels in which thought processes have been spun out, creating a net of meaning to capture reality. In a sexist world, symbol systems and conceptual apparatuses have been male creations. These do not reflect the experience of women, but rather function to falsify our own self-image and experiences. Women have often resolved the problems this situation raises by simply not seeing the situation. That is, we have screened out experience and responded only to the questions considered meaningful and licit within the boundaries of prevailing thought structures, which reflect sexist social structures.

As Simone de Beauvoir sadly notes, women who have perceived the reality of sexual oppression usually have exhausted themselves in breaking through to discovery of their own humanity, with little energy left for constructing their own interpretation of the universe. Therefore, the various ideological constructs cannot be imagined to reflect a balanced or adequate vision. Instead, they distort reality and destroy human potential, female and male. What is required of women at this point in history is a firm and deep refusal to limit our perspectives, questioning, and creativity to any of the preconceived patterns of male-dominated culture. When the positive products of our emerging awareness and creativity express dimensions of the search for ultimate meaning, they can indeed be called both philosophical and theological, but in the sense of pointing beyond the God of patriarchal philosophy and religion.

The Problem of "Method"

The question arises, therefore, of the method I propose to use in this book in dealing with questions of religious symbols and concepts, and with ethical problems. I will begin my description with some indications of what my method is *not*. First of all it obviously is not that of a "kerygmatic theology," which supposes some unique and changeless revelation peculiar to Christianity or to *any* religion.[8] Neither is my approach that of a disinterested observer who claims to have an "objective knowledge about" reality.[9] Nor is it an attempt to correlate with the existing cultural situation certain "eternal truths" which are presumed to have been captured as adequately as possible in a fixed and limited set of symbols.[10] None of these approaches can express the revolutionary potential of women's liberation for challenging the forms in which consciousness incarnates itself and for changing consciousness.

The method that is required is not one of correlation but of *liberation*. Even the term "method" must be reinterpreted and in fact wrenched out of its usual semantic field, for the emerging creativity in women is by no means a merely cerebral process. In order to understand the implications of this process it is necessary to grasp the fundamental fact that women have had the power of *naming* stolen from us. We have not been free to use our own power to name ourselves, the world, or God. The old naming was not the product of dialogue—a fact inadvertently admitted in the Genesis story of Adam's naming the animals and the woman. Women are now realizing that the universal imposing of names by men has been false because partial. That is, inadequate words have been taken as adequate. In this respect—though with a different slant—the new woman-consciousness is in accord with the view of Josiah Royce that it is impossible to consider any term apart from its relations to the whole.[11]

To exist humanly is to name the self, the world, and God.[12] The "method" of the evolving spiritual consciousness of women is nothing less than this beginning to speak humanly—a reclaiming of the right to name. The liberation of language is rooted in the liberation of ourselves.

It would be a mistake to imagine that the new speech of women can be equated simply with women speaking men's words. What is happening is that women are really *hearing* ourselves and each other, and out of this supportive hearing emerge *new words*.[13] This is not to say necessarily that an entirely different set of words is coming into being full blown in a *material* sense—that is, different sounds or combinations of letters on paper. Rather, words which, materially speaking, are identical with the old become new in a semantic context that arises from qualitatively new experience. The word *exodus* as applied to the community of women that is now emerging exemplifies this phenomenon.[14] The word's meaning is stripped of its patriarchal, biblical context, while at the same time speaking *to* and *beyond* that context. So also the word *sisterhood* no longer means a subordinate mini-brotherhood, but an authentic bonding of women on a wide scale for our own liberation.

Moreover, this liberation of language from its old context implies a breakthrough to new semantic fields. The new context has its source and its verification in the rising consciousness women have of ourselves and of our situation. Since this consciousness contradicts the established sense of reality which is reflected in the prevailing social and linguistic structures, its verbal expressions sometimes involve apparent contradictions. The words of women's becoming function in such a way that they raise questions and problems and at the same time give clues to the resolution of those problems. A number of examples of this naming process can be found in this book.

Occasionally such expressions may be deliberately transitional. When, for example, I have spoken of "the sisterhood of man" the result has been a sense of contradiction and a jarring of images. "Intellectually" everyone "knows" that "man" is a generic term. However, in view of the fact that we live in a world in which full humanity is attributed only to males, and in view of the significant fact that "man" also means male, the term does not come through as truly generic. For this reason many feminists would like to erase the specious generic term "man" from the language, and rightly so. What "sisterhood of man" does is to give a generic weight to "sisterhood" which the term has never before been called upon to bear. At the same time it emasculates the pseudo-generic "man." The expression, then, raises the problem of a sexually oppressive world and it signals other possibilities. I would not use the pseudo-generic "man" in any other kind of context than in this contradictory and problematic setting. The point is not to legitimate the use of "man" for the human species, but to point to the necessity of the death of this false word, its elimination from our language.

The method of liberation, then, involves a *castrating* of language and images that reflect and perpetuate the structures of a sexist world. It castrates precisely in the sense of cutting away the phallocentric value system imposed by patriarchy, in its subtle as well as in its more manifest expressions. As aliens in a man's world who are now rising up to name—that is, to create—our own world, women are beginning to recognize that the value system that has been thrust upon us by the various cultural institutions of patriarchy has amounted to a kind of gang rape of minds as well as of bodies.

Feminists are accustomed to enduring such labels as "castrating females." Some have rightly retorted that if "to castrate" essentially means to deprive of power, potency, creativity, ability to communicate, then indeed it is women who have been castrated by a sexist society. However, I would push the analysis a bit further. It is also true that men are castrated by such a social system in which destructive competitiveness treats men who are low on the totem pole (e.g., black males, poor males, noncompetitive males, Third World males, etc.) *like women*. Yet all of these can still look down upon the primordially castrated beings—women. Now these primordial eunuchs are rising up to castrate not people but *the system* that castrates—that great "God-Father" of us all which indulges senselessly and universally in the politics of rape.

The cutting away of this phallocentric value system in its various incarnations amounts also to a kind of *exorcism* that essentially must be done by women, who are in a position to experience the demonic destructiveness of the super-phallic society in our own being. The *machismo* ethos that has the human psyche in its grip creates a web of projections, introjections, and self-fulfilling prophecies. It fosters a basic alienation within the psyche—a failure to lay claim to that part of the psyche that is then projected onto "the Other." It is essentially demonic in that it cuts off the power of human becoming.

The method of *liberation-castration-exorcism*, then, is a becoming process of "the Other"—women—in which we hear and speak our own words. The development of this hearing faculty and power of speech involves the dislodging of images that reflect and reinforce the prevailing social arrangements. This happens in one way when women assume active, creative roles. I am not referring to women as "role models" in the commonly accepted sense of patriarchy's "models." Rather, I mean to call attention to the emergence of free persons whose lives communicate a kind of contagious freedom.

This dislodging process requires a refusal of the false identity of tokenism. This refusal sometimes is expressed by dramatic action, which is multidimensional in meaning. There is no single prescription for such symbolic acts. They grow organically out of particular situations. They are revelatory, since they not only unmask the fact of sexism but also give signals and clues of transcendence. Generally they involve rejection of tokenism, breaking with the past, dramatic action, the living out of something really new—which gives the impetus for further action.[15]

Women may judge that in some cases the names imposed upon reality by male-dominated society and sanctified by religion are basically oppressive and must be rejected. In other instances, it may be that partial truth has been taken for the whole in the past, and that the symbols and conceptualizations that are biased have to be liberated from their partiality. Women will free traditions, thought, and customs only by hearing each other and thus making it possible to speak our word. This involves interaction between insight and praxis, not in the sense of "reflection" upon "social action" (a false dualism), but rather in the sense of a continual growth, flexibility, and emergence of new perceptions of reality—perceptions that come from being where one is.[16]

The becoming of women in sisterhood is the countercultural phenomenon *par excellence* which can indicate the future course of human spiritual evolution. As I have pointed out, none of the methods acceptable to male philosophers and theologians can begin to speak to this task. Women are not merely "re-thinking" philosophy and theology but are participating in new creation. The process implies beautiful, self-actualizing anger, love, and hope.

Overcoming Methodolatry

One of the false gods of theologians, philosophers, and other academics is called Method. It commonly happens that the choice of a problem is determined by method, instead of method being determined by the problem. This means that thought is subjected to an invisible tyranny. Suzanne Langer wrote:

The limits of thought are not so much set from outside, by the fullness or poverty of experiences that meet the mind, as from within, by the power of conception, the wealth of formulative notions with which the mind meets experiences. Most new discoveries are suddenly-seen things that were always there.[17]

The tyranny of methodolatry hinders new discoveries. It prevents us from raising questions never asked before and from being illumined by ideas that do not fit into pre-established boxes and forms. The worshippers of Method have an effective way of handling data that does not fit into the Respectable Categories of Questions and Answers. They simply classify it as nondata, thereby rendering it invisible.

It should be noted that the god Method is in fact a subordinate deity, serving Higher Powers. These are social and cultural institutions whose survival depends upon the classification of disruptive and disturbing information as nondata. Under patriarchy, Method has wiped out women's questions so totally that even women have not been able to hear and formulate our own questions to meet our own experiences. Women have been unable even to experience our own experience.

This book is an effort to begin asking nonquestions and to start discovering, reporting, and analyzing nondata. It is therefore an exercise in Methodicide, a form of deicide. The servants of Method must therefore unacknowledge its nonexistence (a technique in which they are highly skilled). By the grace of this double negative may they bless its existence in the best way they know. High treason merits a double cross.

The order of nonquestions to be treated in this book is as follows: I have begun by bringing into focus the phenomenon of the death of God the Father in the rising woman-consciousness and the consequent breakthrough to conscious, communal participation in God the Verb. This is followed by an exercise in exorcising evil from Eve, which involves a Fall into freedom. Since this Fall is redemptive and healing, it signals the arrival of New Being. Therefore, the next problem to be confronted is Christolatry, which hinders this arrival. Next comes an effort to look beyond phallocentric morality. The last three chapters focus upon the community of sisterhood under three aspects: as Antichurch, as Cosmic Covenant, and as Final Cause.

This writing has been done in hope. Hopefully it represents not merely a continuation but a new beginning. Certainly it is not The Last Word. But insofar as it brings forth the right word it will be heard, for the right word will have the power of reality in it.

CHAPTER ONE

After the Death of God the Father

The first step in the elevation of women under all systems of religion is to convince them that the great Spirit of the Universe is in no way responsible for any of these absurdities.

—ELIZABETH CADY STANTON

The biblical and popular image of God as a great patriarch in heaven, rewarding and punishing according to his mysterious and seemingly arbitrary will, has dominated the imagination of millions over thousands of years. The symbol of the Father God, spawned in the human imagination and sustained as plausible by patriarchy, has in turn rendered service to this type of society by making its mechanisms for the oppression of women appear right and fitting. If God in "his" heaven is a father ruling "his" people, then it is in the "nature" of things and according to divine plan and the order of the universe that society be male-dominated.

Within this context a mystification of roles takes place: the husband dominating his wife represents God "himself." The images and values of a given society have been projected into the realm of dogmas and "Articles of Faith," and these in turn justify the social structures which have given rise to them and which sustain their plausibility. The belief system becomes hardened and objectified, seeming to have an unchangeable independent existence and validity of its own. It resists social change that would rob it of its plausibility. Despite the vicious circle, however, change can occur in society, and ideologies can die, though they die hard.

As the women's movement begins to have its effect upon the fabric of society, transforming it from patriarchy into something that never existed before—into a diarchal situation that is radically new—it can

Ɪecomҽ the greatest single challenge to the major religions of the world, Western and Eastern. Beliefs and values that have held sway for thousands of years will be questioned as never before. This revolution may well be also the greatest single hope for survival of spiritual consciousness on this planet.

The Challenge: Emergence of Whole Human Beings

There are some who persist in claiming that the liberation of women will only mean that new characters will assume the same old roles, and that nothing will change essentially in structures, ideologies, and values. This supposition is often based on the observation that the very few women in "masculine" occupations often behave much as men do. This kind of reasoning is not at all to the point, for it fails to take into account the fact that tokenism does not change stereotypes or social systems but works to preserve them, since it dulls the revolutionary impulse. The minute proportion of women in the United States who occupy such roles (such as senators, judges, business executives, doctors, etc.) have been trained by men in institutions defined and designed by men, and they have been pressured subtly to operate according to male rules. There are no alternate models. As sociologist Alice Rossi has suggested, this is not what the women's movement in its most revolutionary potential is all about.[1]

What *is* to the point is an emergence of woman-consciousness such as has never before taken place. It is unimaginative and out of touch with what is happening in the women's movement to assume that the becoming of women will simply mean uncritical acceptance of structures, beliefs, symbols, norms, and patterns of behavior that have been given priority by society under male domination. Rather, this becoming will act as catalyst for radical change in our culture. It has been argued cogently by Piaget that structure is maintained by an interplay of transformation laws that never yield results beyond the system and never tend to employ elements external to the system.[2] This is indicative of what *can* effect basic alteration in the system, that is, a potent influence *from without*. Women who reject patriarchy have this power and indeed *are* this power of transformation that is ultimately threatening to things as they are.

The roles and structures of patriarchy have been developed and sustained in accordance with an artificial polarization of human qualities into the traditional sexual stereotypes. The image of the person in authority and the accepted understanding of "his" role has corresponded to the eternal masculine stereotype, which implies hyper-rationality (in reality, frequently reducible to pseudo-rationality), "objectivity," aggressivity, the possession of dominating and manipulative attitudes toward persons and the environment, and the tendency to construct boundaries between the self (and those identified with the self) and "the Other." The caricature of human being which is represented by this stereotype depends for its existence upon the opposite caricature—the eternal feminine. This implies hyper-emotionalism, passivity, self-abnegation, etc. By becoming whole persons women can generate a counterforce to the stereotype of the leader, challenging the artificial polarization of human characteristics into sex-role identification. There is no reason to assume that women who have the support of each other to criticize not only the feminine stereotype but the masculine stereotype as well will simply adopt the latter as a model for ourselves. On the contrary, what is happening is that women are developing a wider range of qualities and skills. This is beginning to encourage and in fact demand a comparably liberating process in men—a phenomenon which has begun in men's liberation groups and which is taking place every day within the context of personal relationships. The becoming of androgynous human persons implies a radical change in the fabric of human consciousness and in styles of human behavior.

This change is already threatening the credibility of the religious symbols of our culture. Since many of these have been used to justify oppression, such a challenge should be seen as redemptive. Religious symbols fade and die when the cultural situation that gave rise to them and supported them ceases to give them plausibility. Such an event generates anxiety, but it is part of the risk involved in a faith which accepts the relativity of all symbols and recognizes that clinging to these as fixed and ultimate is self-destructive and idolatrous.

The becoming of new symbols is not a matter that can be decided arbitrarily around a conference table. Rather, symbols grow out of a changing communal situation and experience. This does not mean that we are confined to the role of passive spectators. The experience of the becoming of women cannot be understood merely conceptually and abstractly but through active participation in the overcoming of servitude. Both activism and creative thought flow from and feed into the the evolving woman-consciousness. The cumulative effect is a surge of awareness beyond the symbols and doctrines of patriarchal religion.

The Inadequate God of Popular Preaching

The image of the divine Father in heaven has not always been conducive to humane behavior, as any perceptive reader of history knows. The often cruel behavior of Christians toward unbelievers and toward dissenters among themselves suggests a great deal not only about the values of the society dominated by that image, but also about how that image itself functions in relation to behavior. There has been a basic ambivalence in the image of the heavenly patriarch—a split between the God of love and the jealous God who represents the collective power of "his" chosen people. As historian Arnold Toynbee has indicated, this has reflected and perpetuated a double standard of behavior.[3] Without debating the details of his historical analysis, the insight is available on an experiential level. The character of Vito Corleone in *The Godfather* is a vivid illustration of the marriage of tenderness and violence so intricately blended in the patriarchal ideal. The worshippers of the loving Father may in a sense love their neighbors, but in fact the term applies only to those within a restricted and unstable circumference, and these worshippers can "justifiably" be intolerant and fanatic persecutors of those outside the sacred circle.

How this God operates is illustrated in contemporary American civil religion.[4] In one of the White House sermons given during the first term of Richard Nixon, Rabbi Louis Finkelstein expressed the hope that a future historian may say "that in the period of great trials and great tribulations, the finger of God pointed to Richard Milhous Nixon, giving the vision and the wisdom to save the world and civilization; and also to open the way for our country to realize the good that the twentieth century offers mankind."[5] Within this context, as Charles Henderson has shown, God is an American and Nixon is "his" annointed one.[6] The preachers carefully selected for the White House sermons stress that this nation is "under God." The logical conclusion is that its policies are right. Under God, the President becomes a Christ figure. In 1969, the day the astronauts would set foot on the moon, and when the President was preparing to cross the Pacific "in search of peace," one of these preachers proclaimed:

And my hope for mankind is strengthened in the knowledge that our intrepid President himself will soon go into orbit, reaching boldly for the moon of peace. God grant that he, too, may return in glory and that countless millions of prayers that follow him shall not have been in vain.[7]

A fundamental dynamic of this "theology" was suggested by one of Nixon's speech writers, Ray Price, who wrote:

Selection of a President has to be an act of faith. . . . This faith isn't achieved by reason: it's achieved by charisma, by a feeling of trust. . . .[8]

Price also argued that the campaign would be effective only "if we can get people to make the *emotional* leap, or what theologians call 'leap of faith.' "[9] This is, of course, precisely the inauthentic leap that Camus labeled as philosophical suicide. It is the suicide demanded by a civil religion in which "God," the Savior-President, and "our nation" more or less merge. When the "leap" is made, it is possible simply not to see what the great God-Father and his annointed one are actually doing. Among the chosen ones are scientists and professors who design perverse methods of torture and death such as flechette pellets that shred the internal organs of "the enemy" and other comparable inhumane "anti-personnel" weapons. Also among the elect are politicians and priests who justify and bestow their blessing upon the system that perpetrates such atrocities. "Under God" are included the powerful industrialists who are making the planet uninhabitable.

Sophisticated thinkers, of course, have never intellectually identified God with a Superfather in heaven. Nevertheless it is important to recognize that even when very abstract conceptualizations of God are formulated in the mind, images survive in the imagination in such a way that a person can function on two different and even apparently contradictory levels at the same time. Thus one can speak of God as spirit and at the same time imagine "him" as belonging to the male sex.[10] Such primitive images can profoundly affect conceptualizations which appear to be very refined and abstract. So too the Yahweh of the future, so cherished by the theology of hope, comes through on an imaginative level as exclusively a He-God, and it is consistent with this that theologians of hope have attempted to develop a political theology which takes no explicit cognizance of the devastation wrought by sexual politics.

The widespread conception of the "Supreme Being" as an entity distinct from this world but controlling it according to plan and keeping human beings in a state of infantile subjection has been a not too subtle mask of the divine patriarch. The Supreme Being's plausibility and that of the static worldview which accompanies this projection has of course declined, at least among the more sophisticated, as Nietzsche prophesied. This was a projection grounded in specifically patriarchal societal structures and sustained as subjectively real by the usual processes of producing plausibility such as preaching, religious indoctrination, and cult. The sustaining power of the social structure has been eroded by a number of developments in recent history, including the general trend toward democratization of society and the emergence of technology. However, it is the women's movement which appears destined to play the key role in the overthrow of such oppressive elements in traditional theism, precisely because it strikes at the source of the societal dualism that is reflected in traditional beliefs. It presents a growing threat to the plausibility of the inadequate popular "God" not so much by attacking "him" as by leaving "him" behind. Few major feminists display great interest in institutional religion. Yet this disinterest can hardly be equated with lack of spiritual consciousness. Rather, in our present experience the woman-consciousness is being wrenched free to find its own religious expression.

It can legitimately be pointed out that the Judeo-Christian tradition is not entirely bereft of elements that can foster intimations of transcendence. Yet the liberating potential of these elements is choked off in the surrounding atmosphere of the images, ideas, values, and structures of patriarchy. The social change coming from radical feminism has the potential to bring about a more acute and widespread perception of qualitative differences between the conceptualizations of "God" and of the human relationship to God which have been oppressive in their connotations, and the kind of language that is spoken from and to the rising woman-consciousness.

Castrating "God"

I have already suggested that if God is male, then the male is God. The divine patriarch castrates women as long as he is allowed to live on in the human imagination. The process of cutting away the Supreme Phallus can hardly be a merely "rational" affair. The problem is one of transforming the collective imagination so that this distortion of the human aspiration to transcendence loses its credibility.

Some religious leaders, notably Mary Baker Eddy and Ann Lee, showed insight into the problem to some extent and tried to stress the "maternal" aspect of what they called "God."[11] A number of feminists have referred to "God" as "she." While all of this has a point, the analysis has to reach a deeper level. The most basic change has to take place in women—in our being and self-image. Otherwise there is danger of settling for mere reform, reflected in the phenomenon of "crossing," that is, of attempting to use the oppressor's weapons against him. Black theology's image of the Black God illustrates this. It can legitimately be argued that a transsexual operation upon "God," changing "him" to "her," would be a far more profound alteration than a mere pigmentation change. However, to stop at this level of discourse would be a trivialization of the deep problem of human becoming in women.

Beyond the Inadequate God

The various theologies that hypostatize transcendence, that is, those which in one way or another objectify "God" as *a being*, thereby attempt in a self-contradictory way to envisage transcendent reality as finite. "God" then functions to legitimate the existing social, economic, and political status quo, in which women and other victimized groups are subordinate.

"God" can be used oppressively against women in a number of ways. First, it occurs in an overt manner when theologians proclaim women's subordination to be God's will. This of course has been done throughout the centuries, and residues remain in varying degrees of subtlety and explicitness in the writings of twentieth century thinkers such as Barth, Bonhoeffer, Reinhold Niebuhr, and Teilhard de Chardin.[12]

Second, even in the absence of such explicitly oppressive justification, the phenomenon is present when one-sex symbolism for God and for the human relationship to God is used. The following passage illustrates the point:

To believe that God is Father is to become aware of oneself not as a stranger, not as an outsider or an alienated person, but as a son who belongs or a person appointed to a marvelous destiny, which he shares with the whole community. To believe that God is Father means to be able to say "we" in regard to all men.[13]

A woman whose consciousness has been aroused can say that such language makes her aware of herself as a stranger, as an outsider, as an alienated person, not as a daughter who belongs or who is appointed to a marvelous destiny. She cannot belong to *this* without assenting to her own lobotomy.

Third, even when the basic assumptions of God-language appear to be nonsexist, and when language is somewhat purified of fixation upon maleness, it is damaging and implicitly compatible with sexism if it encourages detachment from the reality of the human struggle against oppression in its concrete manifestations. That is, the lack of explicit relevance of intellection to the fact of oppression in its precise forms, such as sexual hierarchy, is itself oppressive. This is the case when theologians write long treatises on creative hope, political theology, or revolution without any specific acknowledgment of or application to the problem of sexism or other specific forms of injustice. Such irrelevance is conspicuous in the major works of "theologians of hope" such as Moltmann, Pannenberg, and Metz. This is not to say that the vision of creative eschatology is completely irrelevant, but that it lacks specific grounding in the concrete experiences of the oppressed. The theorizing then has a quality of unreality. Perhaps an obvious reason for this is that the theologians themselves have not shared in the experience of oppression and therefore write from the privileged distance of those who have at best a "knowledge about" the subject.

Tillich's ontological theology, too, even though it is potentially liberating in a very radical sense, fails to be adequate in this regard. It is true that Tillich *tries* to avoid hypostatization of "God" (though the effort is not completely successful) and that his manner of speaking about the ground and power of being would be difficult to use for the legitimation of any sort of oppression.[14] However, the specific relevance of "power of being" to the fact of sexual oppression is not indicated. Moreover, just as his discussion of God is "detached," so is the rest of his theology—a point that I will pursue later on. This detachment from the problem of relevance of God-language to the struggle against demonic power structures characterizes not only Tillich but also other male theoreticians who have developed a relatively nonsexist language for transcendence. Thinkers such as Whitehead, James, and Jaspers employ God-language that soars beyond sexual hierarchy as a specific problem to be confronted in the process of human becoming.

The new insight of women is bringing us to a point beyond such direct and indirect theological oppressiveness that traditionally has centered around discussions of "God." It is becoming clear that if God-language is even implicitly compatible with oppressiveness, failing to make clear the relation between intellection and liberation, then it will either have to be developed in such a way that it becomes explicitly relevant to the problem of sexism or else dismissed. In asserting this I am employing a pragmatic yardstick or verification process to God-language in a manner not totally dissimilar to that of William James. In my thinking, the specific criterion which implies a mandate to reject certain forms of God-talk is expressed in the question: Does this language hinder human becoming by reinforcing sex-role socialization? Expressed positively—a point to be developed later on—the question is: Does it *encourage* human becoming toward psychological and social fulfillment, toward an androgynous mode of living, toward transcendence?

It is probable that the movement will eventually generate a new language of transcendence. There is no reason to assume that the term "God" will always be necessary, as if the three-letter word, materially speaking, could capture and encapsulate transcendent being. At this point in history, however, it is probable that the new God-word's essential newness will be conveyed more genuinely by its being placed in a different semantic field than by a mere material alteration in sound or appearance of the word. Since the women's revolution implies the liberation of all human beings, it is impossible to believe that during the course of its realization the religious imagination and intelligence will simply lie dormant. Part of the challenge is to recognize the poverty of all words and symbols and the fact of our past idolatry regarding them, and then to turn to our own resources for bringing about the radically new in our own lives. It is this living that is generating the new meaning context for God, some elements of which can now be examined.

Women's Liberation and Revelatory Courage

I have already indicated that it would be unrealistic to dismiss the fact that the symbolic and linguistic instruments for communication—which include essentially the whole theological tradition in world religions—have been formulated by males under the conditions of patriarchy. It is therefore inherent in these symbolic and linguistic structures that they serve the purposes of patriarchal social arrangements. Even the usual and accepted means of theological dissent have been restricted in such a way that only some questions have been allowed to arise. Many questions that are of burning importance to women now simply have not occurred in the past (and to a large extent in the present) to those with "credentials" to do theology. Others may have been voiced timidly but quickly squelched as stupid, irrelevant, or naïve. Therefore, attempts by women theologians now merely to "up-date" or to reform theology within acceptable patterns of question-asking are not likely to get very far.

Moreover, within the context of the prevailing social climate it has been possible for scholars to be aware of the most crudely dehumanizing texts concerning women in the writings of religious "authorities" and theologians—from Augustine to Aquinas, to Luther, to Knox, to Barth—and at the same time to treat their unverified opinions on far more imponderable matters with utmost reverence and respect. That is, the blatant misogynism of these men has not been the occasion of a serious credibility gap even for those who have disagreed on this "point." It has simply been ignored or dismissed as trivial. By contrast, in the emerging consciousness of women this context is beginning to be perceived in its full significance and as deeply relevant to the worldview in which such "authorities" have seen other seemingly unrelated subjects, such as the problem of God. Hence the present awakening of the hitherto powerless sex demands an explosion of creative imagination that can withstand the disapproval of orthodoxy and overreach the boundaries cherished by conventional minds.

The driving revelatory force that is making it possible for women to speak—and to *hear* each other speak—more authentically about God is courage in the face of the risks that attend the liberation process. Since the projections of patriarchal religion have been blocking the dynamics of existential courage by offering the false security of alienation, that is, of self-reduction in sex roles, there is reason to hope for the emergence of a new religious consciousness in the confrontation with sexism that is now in its initial stages. The becoming of women may be not only the doorway to deliverance which secular humanism has passionately fought for—but also a doorway *to* something, that is, a new phase in the human spirit's quest for God.

This becoming who we really are requires existential courage to confront the experience of nothingness. All human beings are threatened by nonbeing. In Tillich's analysis, the resultant anxiety surfaces in relation to the threat of fate and death, guilt and condemnation, and meaninglessness.[15] While Tillich analyzes courage in universalist, humanist categories, he does not betray any awareness of the relevance of this to women's confrontation with the structured evil of patriarchy. I am suggesting that at this point in history women are in a unique sense called to be the bearers of existential courage in society.

People attempt to overcome the threat of nonbeing by denying the self. The outcome of this is ironic: that which is dreaded triumphs, for we are caught in the self-contradictory bind of shrinking our being to avoid nonbeing. The only alternative is self-actualization in spite of the ever-present nothingness. Part of the problem is that people, women in particular, who are seemingly incapable of a high degree of self-actualization have been made such by societal structures that are products of human attempts to create security. Those who are alienated from their own deepest identity do receive a kind of security in return for accepting very limited and undifferentiated identities. The woman who single-mindedly accepts the role of "housewife," for example, may to some extent avoid the experience of nothingness but she also avoids a fuller participation in being, which would be her only real security and source of community. Submerged in such a role, she cannot achieve a breakthrough to creativity. Many strong women are worn out in the struggle to break out of these limits before reaching the higher levels of intellectual discovery or of creativity.

The beginning of a breakthrough means a realization that there is an existential conflict between the self and structures that have given such crippling security. This requires confronting the shock of nonbeing with the courage to be. It means facing the nameless anxieties of fate, which become concretized in loss of jobs, friends, social approval, health, and even life itself. Also involved is anxiety of guilt over refusing to do what society demands, a guilt which can hold one in its grip long after it has been recognized as false. Finally, there is the anxiety of meaninglessness, which can be overwhelming at times when the old simple meanings, role definitions, and life expectations have been rooted out and rejected openly and one emerges into a world without models.

This confrontation with the anxiety of nonbeing is revelatory, making possible the relativization of structures that are seen as human products, and therefore not absolute and ultimate. It drives consciousness beyond fixation upon "things as they are." Courage to be is the key to the revelatory power of the feminist revolution.

The Struggle Toward Self-Transcendence

The drive toward transcendence can be envisaged mythically in different but interrelated ways. This point has been made in an original way by Herbert Richardson, whose typology I am relating to sex role socialization in the following analysis.[16] The myth of separation and return (going away and coming home again—like Ulysses) is obviously a cyclic vision and it is often bound up with parental images. Birth means separation from the mother, but the child immediately returns to its parents in its dependency for the necessities of life. Popular Christianity envisages human life in these terms, looking forward to a return to the Father in heaven. The theme of *exitus-reditus* (exit and return) was commonly used in medieval theology to describe the human relationship to God. Although this theme was developed in a subtle and intricate way and although the journey did involve transformation through grace, the imagery of "return" that was attached to it lent itself easily to an attitude of detachment from social injustice. Taken on the imaginative level the myth of separation and return reflects quite well the limited sort of transcendence that has been the only possibility for most women in the course of history—separation from the home of parents only to return to paternalistic domination in the home of a husband. The eternal circle of separation from and return to infantile dependence has been the story of the feminine mode of existence.

Another kind of transcendence myth has been dramatization of human life in terms of conflict and vindication. This focuses upon the situation of oppression and the struggle for liberation. It is a short-circuited transcendence when the struggle against oppression becomes an end in itself, the focal point of all meaning. There is an inherent contradiction in the idea that those devoted to a cause have found their whole meaning in the struggle, so that the desired victory becomes implicitly an undesirable meaninglessness. Such a truncated vision is one of the pitfalls of theologies of the oppressed. Sometimes black theology, for example that of James Cone, resounds with a cry for vengeance and is fiercely biblical and patriarchal. It transcends religion as a crutch (the separation and return of much old-fashioned Negro spirituality) but tends to settle for being religion as a gun. Tailored to fit only the situation of racial oppression, it inspires a will to vindication but leaves unexplored other dimensions of liberation. It does not get beyond the sexist models internalized by the self and controlling society—models that are at the root of racism and that perpetuate it. The Black God and Black Messiah apparently are merely the same patriarchs after a pigmentation operation—their behavior unaltered.[17]

Fortunately, the danger that the new spiritual consciousness of women will be truncated in a similar way is greatly reduced by the fact that the stereotypically male symbols of Christianity do not lend themselves to this kind of easy adaptation by feminism. There is less "opportunity" for us to fall into facile repetition of the same mistakes. With the rise of feminism, women have indeed come to see the necessity of conflict, of letting rage surface and of calling forth a will to liberation. Yet—partially because there is such an essential contrast between feminism and patriarchal religion's destructive symbols and values, and partially because women's lives are intricately bound up with those of men—biologically, emotionally, socially, and professionally—it is quite clear that women's liberation is essentially linked with full human liberation. Women generally can see very well that the movement will self-destruct if we settle for vengeance. The more imminent danger, then, is that some women will seek premature reconciliation, not allowing themselves to see the depth and implications of feminism's essential opposition to sexist society. It can be easy to leap on the bandwagon of "human liberation" without paying the price in terms of polarization, tensions, risk, and pain that the ultimate objective of real human liberation demands.

A third myth of transcendence (still using Richardson's typology) is integrity and transformation. Within this perspective, the individual seeks self-transformation and spiritual rebirth. This involves the becoming of psychic unity, which means that one does not have to depend upon another for "complementarity" but can love independently. Richardson's analysis in this essay hints at but does not quite convey explicit recognition that such independence means the becoming of psychologically androgynous human beings, since the basic crippling "complementarity" has been the false masculine/feminine polarity. Androgynous integrity and transformation will require that women cease to play the role of "complement" and struggle to stand alone as free human beings.

Nonbeing, Power of Being, and Hope

The striving toward psychic wholeness, or androgyny, incorporates the insights and clues in the less adequate modes of envisaging transcendence. The separation and return motif, at its best, pointed to the dimension of depth in human existence. Its basis lay in intimations of the holiness of what *is*. The vision that it entailed, however, often tended to be nonsocial and abstracted from history, or—to borrow (somewhat out of context) a phrase from Moltmann—the nonhistorical mysticism of the solitary soul. At its best, this ontological-sacramental faith gave a kind of interior freedom. A high point of cyclic theological expression was the Thomistic synthesis. The conflict and vindication motif rests more upon a kind of moral faith, an intimation of the holiness of what *ought to be*. It too has tended to be individualistic and, with the help of Kant, has bred a kind of split-level consciousness in which personal struggles for transcendence can exist side by side with social conformity. In the recently developed theology of hope, the conflict and vindication motif is brought to a level of social concern that transcends some of the limitations of the Protestant ethic. Yet the ontological dimension of the holiness of what *is* is generally rejected as Hellenic and unbiblical. I am suggesting that the vision of human becoming as a process of integration and trans-formation, *as this vision is emerging in the women's revolution*, poten-tially includes *both* the individualistic ontological dimension of depth and revolutionary participation in history. It does this precisely because it strikes at the externalized structures and internalized images of pa-triarchy that have cut us off from realizing psychic wholeness in our-selves and consequently have cut down our capacity for genuine par-ticipation in history.

The seeds of such a synthesis were present to some extent in Til-lich's vision, especially as expressed in *The Courage to Be*, even though this was not developed as a political theology. As he explains, existential courage is dynamic and it has two sides: the courage to be as a self and the courage to be as a part. I suggest that such courage makes creative, communal, revolutionary hope possible to the extent that the courage is expressed in confrontation with earthly powers and principalities that embody nonbeing in our patriarchal culture. It is this di-mension of confrontation that makes courage give rise to creative hope.

This synthesis of hope and courage, potentially in the dynamics of the feminist revolution, includes separation and return since by break-ing from the past and consciously creating our own history we change the past, that is, change and expand our understanding of it. This separa-tion and return happens, for example, when we establish the significance of events that historians have disregarded, such as the achievements of great women and major landmarks in the history of the oppression of women. The synthesis also includes conflict and vindication, not in the sense of attempting to reduce those in power to objects, but in the sense of breaking down the masculine/feminine models thrust upon us by the powers and principalities that shrink the human potential of women and men.

If one were to judge by theological writings of the past several years, from Gogarten to Harvey Cox to Leslie Dewart to Pannenberg, it would appear that the sense of being is disappearing from the contemporary consciousness. Before jumping to such conclusions, however, it would be well to consider at least two points. In the first place, existential ques-tions have never been expressed explicitly in ontological terms most of the time by most people, who indeed seem to have spent most of their energy evading such questions. The question of being and nonbeing (to be or not to be) in all of its poignancy, arises in times of great distress, that is, in "marginal situations" (Berger) such as proximity to death, and occasionally in times of extremely positive "peak experiences."[18] In the second place, it is becoming increasingly evident that among disaffected members of the younger generation—younger in years and/or in spirit—there is a resurgence of ontological awareness which theologians recently have tended to overlook.[19] It appears that there has been a loss of the sense of being in our culture, and that this is essentially what the alienated are experiencing and communicating—an awareness of depth of reality that liberates from false consciousness. As I have indicated, the liberation of women involves susceptibility to the experience of nonbeing in a most dramatic way, for women have been the most radically alienated of all segments of society.

I am proposing that all authentic human hope is ontological, that is, that it requires facing nothingness. This experience gives a sense of distance and relativity in relation to the symbols prevailing in one's culture. Without it, the mind tends to perceive these as literally "true" or at least as permanently adequate for all cultural situations, which means that the human mind becomes paralyzed by its own products. This is, I think, the essential inadequacy of non-ontological "theology of hope," which obstinately stays within the terrain of biblical language.[20] When women reach the point of recognizing that we are aliens in this terrain, the sense of transcendence and the surge of hope can be seen as rooted in the power of being, which, perhaps for lack of a better word, some would still call "God."

Why Speak about "God"?

It might seem that the women's revolution should just go about its business of generating a new consciousness, without worrying about God. I suggest that the fallacy involved in this would be an overlooking of a basic question that is implied in human existence and that the pitfall in such an oversight is cutting off the radical potential of the movement itself.

It is reasonable to take the position that sustained effort toward self-transcendence requires keeping alive in one's consciousness the question of ultimate transcendence, that is, of God. It implies recognition of the fact that we have no power *over* the ultimately real, and that whatever authentic power we have is derived from *participation in* ultimate reality. This awareness, always hard to sustain, makes it possible to be free of idolatry even in regard to one's own cause, since it tells us that all presently envisaged goals, lifestyles, symbols, and societal structures may be transitory. This is the meaning that the question of God should have for liberation, sustaining a concern that is really open to the future, in other words, that is really ultimate. Such a concern will not become fixated upon limited objectives. Feminists in the past have in a way been idolatrous about such objectives as the right to vote. Indeed, this right is due to women in justice and it is entirely understandable that feminists' energies were drained by the efforts needed to achieve even such a modicum of justice. But from the experience of such struggles we are in a position now to distrust token victories within a societal and structural framework that renders them almost meaningless. The new wave of feminism desperately needs to be not only many-faceted but cosmic and ultimately religious in its vision. This means reaching outward and inward toward the God beyond and beneath the gods who have stolen our identity.

The idea that human beings are "to the image of God" is an intuition whose implications could hardly be worked through under patriarchal conditions. If it is true that human beings have projected "God" in their own image, it is also true that we can evolve beyond the projections of earlier stages of consciousness. It is the creative potential itself in human beings that is the image of God.[21] As the essential victims of the archaic God-projections, women can bring this process of creativity into a new phase. This involves iconoclasm—the breaking of idols. Even—and perhaps especially—through the activity of its most militantly atheistic and a-religious members, the movement is smashing images that obstruct the becoming of the image of God. The basic idol-breaking will be done on the level of internalized images of male superiority, on the plane of exorcising them from consciousness and from the cultural institutions that breed them.

One aspect of this expurgation is dethronement of false Gods—ideas and symbols of God that religion has foisted upon the human spirit (granted that the human spirit has created the religions that do this). I have already discussed this to some extent, but it might be well to focus specifically upon three false deities who still haunt the prayers, hymns, sermons, and religious education of Christianity. The three usurpers I have in mind have already been detected and made the targets of attack by liberal male theologians, but the point in mentioning them here is to indicate the specific relevance of feminism to their demise.

One of the false deities to be dethroned is the God of explanation, or "God as a stop-gap for the incompleteness of our knowledge," as Bonhoeffer called him.[22] This serves sometimes as the legitimation of anomic occurrences such as the suffering of a child, a legitimation process which Peter Berger lucidly analyzes in discussing the problem of theodicy.[23] Such phenomena are "explained" as being God's will. So also are socially prevailing inequalities of power and privilege, by a justifying process which easily encourages masochistic attitudes. Clearly, this deity does not encourage commitment to the task of analyzing and eradicating the social, economic, and psychological roots of suffering. As marginal beings who are coming into awareness, women are in a situation to see that "God's plan" is often a front for men's plans and a cover for inadequacy, ignorance, and evil. Our vantage point offers opportunities for dislodging this deity from its revered position on the scale of human delusions.

Another idol is the God of otherworldliness. The most obvious face of this deity in the past has been that of the Judge whose chief activity consists in rewarding and punishing after death. As de Beauvoir indicated, women have been the major consumers of this religious product. Since there has been so little self-realization possible by the female sex "in this life," it was natural to focus attention on the next. As mass consumers of this image, women have the power to remove it from the market, mainly by living full lives here and now. I do not mean to advocate a mere re-utterance of the "secularization" theology that was so popular in the sixties. This obvious shape of the God of otherworldliness has after all been the target of male theologians for some time, and the result has often been a kind of translation of religion into humanism to such an extent that there is a kind of "self-liquidation of theology."[24] What I see beginning to happen with women coming into their own goes beyond this secularization. The rejection of the simplistic God of otherworldliness does not mean necessarily reduction to banal secularism. If women can sustain the courage essential to liberation this can give rise to a deeper "otherworldliness"—an awareness that the process of creating a counterworld to the counterfeit "this world" presented to consciousness by the societal structures that oppress us is participation in eternal life.

It should be noted that the God lurking behind some forms of Protestant piety has functioned similarly to the otherworldly God of popular Roman Catholic piety. In his analysis of the effects of Luther's doctrine of salvation by faith alone, Max Weber uncovers serious problems of ethical motivation, involving a complicated series of phenomena: "Every rational and planned procedure for achieving salvation, every reliance on good works, and above all every effort to surpass normal ethical behavior by ascetic achievement is regarded by religion based on faith as a wicked preoccupation with purely human powers."[25] Transworldly asceticism and monasticism tend to be rejected when salvation by faith is stressed, and as a result there may be an increased emphasis upon vocational activity within the world. However, as Weber explains, emphasis upon personal religious relationship to God tends to be accompanied by an attitude of individualism in pursuit of such worldly vocational activity. One consequence is an attitude of patient resignation regarding institutional structures, both worldly and churchly.[26] It is precisely this schizophrenic attitude that combines personal vocational ambition within the prevailing set of social arrangements and passive acceptance of the system that radical feminism recognizes as destructive.

A third idol, intimately related to those described above, is the God who is the Judge of "sin," who confirms the rightness of the rules and roles of the reigning system, maintaining false consciences and self-destructive guilt feelings. Women have suffered both mentally and physically from this deity, in whose name they have been informed that birth control and abortion are unequivocally wrong, that they should be subordinate to their husbands, that they must be present at rituals and services in which men have all the leadership roles and in which they are degraded not only by enforced passivity but also verbally and symbolically. Although this is most blatant in the arch-conservative religions, the God who imposes false guilt is hardly absent from liberal Protestantism and Judaism, where his presence is more subtle. Women's growth in self-respect will deal the death blow to this as well as to the other demons dressed as Gods.

Women's Liberation as Spiritual Revolution

I have indicated that because the becoming of women involves a radical encounter with nothingness, it bears with it a new surge of ontological hope. This hope is essentially active. The passive hope that has been so prevalent in the history of religious attitudes corresponds to the objectified God from whom one may anticipate favors. Within that frame of reference human beings have tried to relate to ultimate reality as an object to be known, cajoled, manipulated. The tables are turned, however, for the objectified "God" has a way of reducing his producers to objects who lack capacity for autonomous action. In contrast to this, the God who is power of being acts as a moral power summoning women and men to act out of our deepest hope and to become who we can be. I am therefore in agreement with Johannes Metz that authentic hope will be active and creative.[27] The difference is that I see the specific experiential basis for this as an ontological experience. This experience in its first phase is one of nonbeing. In its second phase it is an intuition of being which, as Jacques Maritain described it, is a *dynamic* intuition.[28] Clearly, from what has preceded in this chapter, I see this ontological basis of hope to be particularly available to women at this point in history because of the marginal situation of females in an androcentric world.

This hope is communal rather than merely individualistic, because it is grounded in the two-edged courage to be. That is, it is hope coming from the experience of individuation *and* participation. It drives beyond the objectified God that is imagined as limited in benevolence, bestowing blessings upon "his" favorites. The power of being is that in which all finite beings participate, but not on a "one-to-one" basis, since this power is in all while transcending all. Communal hope involves in some manner a profound interrelationship with other finite beings, human and nonhuman. Ontological communal hope, then, is cosmic. Its essential dynamic is directed to the universal community.

Finally, ontological hope is revolutionary. Since the insight in which it is grounded is the double-edged intuition of nonbeing and of being, it extends beyond the superstitious fixations of technical reason. The latter, as Tillich has shown, when it is cut off from the intuitive knowledge of ontological reason, cannot get beyond superstition.[29] The rising consciousness that women are experiencing of our dehumanized situation has the power to turn attention around from the projections of our culture to the radically threatened human condition. Insofar as women are true to this consciousness, we have to be the most radical of revolutionaries, since the superstition revealed to us is omnipresent and plagues even the other major revolutionary movements of our time. Knowing that a Black or White, Marxist or Capitalist, countercultural or bourgeois male chauvinist deity (human or divine) will not differ essentially from his opposite, women will be forced in a dramatic way to confront the most haunting of human questions, the question of God. This confrontation may not find its major locus within the theological academy or the institutional churches and it may not always express itself in recognizable theological or philosophical language. However, there is a dynamism in the ontological affirmation of self that reaches out toward the nameless God.[30] In hearing and naming ourselves out of the depths, women are naming *toward* God, which is what theology always should have been about. Unfortunately it tended to stop at fixing names *upon* God, which deafened us to our own potential for self-naming.

The Unfolding of God

It has sometimes been argued that anthropomorphic symbols for "God" are important and even necessary because the fundamental powers of the cosmos otherwise are seen as impersonal. One of the insights characteristic of the rising woman consciousness is that this kind of dichotomizing between cosmic power and the personal need not be. That is, it is not necessary to anthropomorphize or to reify transcendence in order to relate to this personally. In fact, the process is demonic in some of its consequences.[31] The dichotomizing-reifying-projecting syndrome has been characteristic of patriarchal consciousness, making "the Other" the repository of the contents of the lost self. Since women are now beginning to recognize in ourselves the victims of such dichotomizing processes, the insight extends to other manifestations of the pathological splitting off of reality into falsely conceived opposites. Why indeed must "God" be a noun? Why not a verb—the most active and dynamic of all? Hasn't the naming of "God" as a noun been an act of murdering that dynamic Verb? And isn't the Verb infinitely more personal than a mere static noun? The anthropomorphic symbols for God may be intended to convey personality, but they fail to convey that God is Be-ing. Women now who are experiencing the shock of nonbeing and the surge of self-affirmation against this are inclined to perceive transcendence as the Verb in which we participate—live, move, and have our being.

This Verb—the Verb of Verbs—is intransitive.[32] It need not be conceived as having an object that limits its dynamism.[33] That which it is over against is nonbeing. Women in the process of liberation are enabled to perceive this because our liberation consists in refusing to be "the Other" and asserting instead "I am"—without making another "the Other." Unlike Sartre's "us versus a third" (the closest approximation to love possible in his world) the new sisterhood is saying "us versus nonbeing." When Sartre wrote that "man [sic] fundamentally *is* the desire to be God," he was saying that the most radical passion of human life is to be a God who does not and cannot exist. The ontological hope of which I am speaking is neither this self-deification nor the simplistic reified images often lurking behind such terms as "Creator," "Lord," "Judge," that Sartre rightly rejects.[34] It transcends these because its experiential basis is courageous *participation* in being. This ontological hope also has little in common with the self-enclosed "ontological arguments" of Anselm or Descartes. It enables us to break out of this prison of subjectivity because it implies commitment together.

The idea that breakthrough to awareness of transcendence comes through some sort of commitment is not new, of course. It has not been absent from existential philosophy. Karl Jaspers, for example, writing of the problem of getting beyond the subject-object split (which, of itself, without awareness of the Encompassing, yields nothing but dead husks of words), affirms that this happens when people live in commitment, but it is not too clear what sort of commitment he had in mind—a not uncommon unclarity among existentialist philosophers.[35] The commitment of which I am speaking has a locus. It is a "mysticism of sorority." I hasten to put this phrase in quotes even though it is my own, since it is a re-baptism of Metz's "mysticism of fraternity"—a correction I deem necessary since—as by now is obvious—a basic thesis of this book is that creative eschatology must come by way of the disenfranchised sex.[36]

What I am proposing is that the emergence of the communal vocational self-awareness of women is a *creative political ontophany*. It is a manifestation of the sacred (*hierophany*) precisely because it is an experience of participation in being, and therefore a manifestation of being (*ontophany*). A historian of religions such as Eliade insists that there was a sort of qualititive leap made by the biblical religions in the realm of hierophany.[37] Whether or not this is historically true is not my concern at this point. What I do suggest is that the potential for *ontological* hierophany that is already beginning to be realized in the participatory vocational self-consciousness of women does involve a leap, bridging the apparent gap between being and history. In other words, women conscious of the vocation to raise up this half of humanity to the stature of acting subjects in history constitute an ontological locus of history. In the very process of becoming actual persons, of confronting the non-being of our situation, women are bearers of history.

In his analysis of history-bearing groups, Tillich saw vocational con-sciousness as a decisive element.[38] He did not believe that humanity as a whole can become the bearer of history instead of particular groups. There is a particular *eros* or sense of belonging which provides the iden-tity of a group to the exclusion of others.[39] This much is true of the women's movement as existing essentially in polarity with the predomi-nantly androcentric society and its institutions. However, there is an essential way in which the women's movement does *not* meet Tillich's specifications for a history-bearing group. I am suggesting that this "non-qualification" arises precisely from the fact that our transformation is so deeply rooted in being. Tillich insists that a history-bearing group's ability to act in a centered way requires that the group have a "central, law-giving, administering, and enforcing authority."[40] In contrast to this, our movement is *not* centrally administered—although it includes or-ganizations such as NOW and WEAL[41]—and many (perhaps most) radicalized women resist attempts to bring this about because their out-look is nonhierarchical and multidimensional.

I am suggesting that the women's movement is *more than* a group governed by central authority in conflict with other such hierarchical groups. If it were only this it would be only one more subgroup within the all-embracing patriarchal "family." What we are about is the human becoming of that half of the human race that has been excluded from humanity by sexual definition. This phenomenon, which is mushrooming "up from under" (to use Nelle Morton's phrase) in women from various "classes," races, and geographical areas, can hardly be described as a group. What is at stake is a real leap in human evolution, initiated by women. The ground of its creative hope is an intuition of being which, as Janice Raymond has suggested, *is* an intuition of human integrity or of androgynous being.[42]

When this kind of sororal community-consciousness is present—this "us versus nonbeing"—there are clues and intimations of the God who is without an over-against—who is Be-ing. The unfolding of the woman-consciousness is an intimation of the endless unfolding of God. The route to be followed by theoreticians of the women's revolution, then, need not be contiguous with that followed by Marxist theoreticians such as Roger Garoudy and Ernst Bloch, even though we share their concern to maintain an absolutely open future, and even though in some sense we must share also in their insistence upon atheism. We agree with their atheism insofar as this means rejection of hypostatized God-projections and the use of these to justify exploitation and oppression.[43] However, there is a difference which I believe arises from the fact that Marxism does not fully confront patriarchy itself. Roger Garoudy wrote:

If we reject the very name of God, it is because the name implies a presence, a reality, whereas it is only an exigency which we live, a never-satisfied exigency of totality and absoluteness, of omnipotence as to nature and of perfect loving reciprocity of consciousness.[44]

In effect, Garoudy distinguishes his position from that of even the most progressive Christian theologians by asserting that the exigency of the Christian for the infinite is experienced and/or expressed as presence, whereas for him it is absence. What I am suggesting is that women who are confronting the nothingness which emerges when one turns one's back upon the pseudo-reality offered by patriarchy are by that very act saying "I am," that is, confronting our own depth of *being*. What we are experiencing, therefore, is not *only* the sense of absence of the old Gods—a sense which we fully share with Garoudy and Bloch. Our exclusion from identity within patriarchy has had a totality about it which, when faced, calls forth an ontological self-affirmation. Beyond the absence, therefore, women are in a situation to experience *presence*. This is not the presence of a super-reified Something, but of a power of being which both is, and is not yet.

One could hasten to point out that various theories of a developing God have been expounded in modern philosophy. Some women might find it helpful to relate their perception of the spiritual dynamics of feminism to ideas developed by such a thinker as William James, who offers the possibility of seeing the perfecting of God as achieved through our active belief, which can be understood as an enrichment of the divine being itself.[45] Others might find it helpful to correlate this experience with Alfred North Whitehead's functional approach to the problem of God, who is seen as a factor implicated in the world and philosophically relevant.[46] Other helpful insights on the problem of the developing God can be found in the work of such thinkers as Max Scheler, Samuel Alexander, E. S. Brightman, and Charles Hartshorne. In my opinion it would not be the most fruitful expenditure of energy at this point to attempt to fit our thoughts concerning the spiritual implications of radical feminism into theories that might appear tempting as prefabricated molds. Rather, it seems to me far more important to listen to women's experiences to discover the spiritual dynamics of this revolution and to speak these dynamics in our own lives and words.

I have already said that this does not mean that an entirely new language for God, materially speaking, will emerge, *ex nihilo*, but rather that a new meaning context is coming into being as we re-create our lives in a new experiential context. Because the feminist experience is radically a coming out of nothing into a vocational/communal participation in being, I have suggested that it can be perceived in terms of ontological hope. Paradoxical though it may seem, this being-consciousness may mean that our new self-understanding *toward God* may be in some ways more in affinity with medieval thought than with some modern theological and philosophical language about God. It is fascinating to observe that in beginning to come to grips with the problem of our own self-naming in a world in which women are nameless, feminism is implicitly working out a naming toward God that is comparable to, though different from, the famous three "ways" the medieval theologians employed in speaking of God.[47]

There was first of all the *negative way*, variously described, but meaning essentially that we can show "what God is not" by systematically denying of God the imperfections of creatures. A prominent scholar has suggested that current epistemology, influenced by recent developments in science, holds resources for a comparable "negative way," but with a different slant. That is, science itself, by constantly opening up more and more unpredicted aspects of reality, is making us aware that there *is* an unknown, aspects of which may be transcendent. This doesn't "prove" Transcendence, but makes room for it.[48] I am suggesting that a new *via negativa* is coming not just from science but from the experience of liberation. Women are living out this negative way by discovering more and more the androcentrism of God-language and being compelled to reject this, and, beyond this, by discovering the male-centeredness of the entire society which this legitimates. Since women are excluded from the in-group of the male intellectual community, and since in fact we begin actively to *choose* self-exclusion as we become more conscious of the limitations on thought and creativity that the in-breeding of the power-holding group involves (witness the deadness of meetings and journals of the "learned societies"), we may be less trapped in the old delusions — such as word games about God that pass for knowledge among those who play them. This discovery, followed by active choice of "not belonging" on the part of creative women, can lead to our finding previously untapped resources within ourselves, and the process yields clues to further possibilities of becoming. The realization of our exclusion from the world-building process is a *neo-negative way*, in that we are discovering our previously unknown being, which points our consciousness outward and inward toward as yet unknown Being, that some would call the hidden God.

Second, there was the traditional *affirmative way*, which presupposed that God prepossessses all the perfections of creatures and that therefore any perfection found in a creature which does not by definition include limitation can be predicated of God. Thus it was considered legitimate to say that God is good, wise, etc.[49] I am suggesting that feminism is giving rise also to the beginnings of a *neo-affirmative way*. This is a *living* "analogy of being" (*analogia entis*), and the particular aspect of our existence from which we are enabled to draw the analogy is the courage that is experienced in the liberation process. The *analogia entis* of Aquinas involved an extremely complex reasoning, based upon certain premises, including the notion that God is the first cause of all finite reality and the idea that there is some kind of resemblance between effects and their causes.[50] By contrast, what I am pointing to by the use of the expression "analogy of being" is an experience of the dynamic content of the intuition of being as experienced in existential courage. Women now have a special opportunity to create an *affirmative way* that is not simply in the arena of speculation, but especially in the realm of active self-affirmation. Since through the existential courage now demanded of us we can have consciousness of *being toward* the image of God, this process can give us intimations of the Be-ing in and toward which we are participating. That is, it can be in some sense a theophany, or manifestation of God.

A third way of naming God, the traditional *way of eminence*, was not totally distinct from the other two "ways" but rather included both. Medieval theologians, including the so-called Denis the Areopagite and Thomas Aquinas, believed that even names said affirmatively of God fall far short of saying *what* God is: "So when we say 'God is good,' the meaning is not, [merely] 'God is the cause of goodness,' or 'God is not evil,' but the meaning is, 'Whatever good we attribute to creatures pre-exists in God' and in a more excellent and higher way."[51]

I propose that the becoming of women is potentially a new and very different *way of eminence*. The positive and unique element in our speaking toward God has to do with what Buber called "the primary word I-Thou [which] establishes the world of relation."[52] By refusing to be objectified and by affirming being, the feminist revolution is creating new possibilities of I-Thou. Therefore, the new *way of eminence* can be understood as follows:

In modern society, technical controlling knowledge has reached the point of violating the privacy and rights of individuals and destroying the natural environment. In reaction against this, social critics sometimes call for the awakening of interpersonal consciousness, that is, of intersubjectivity. But this cannot happen without communal and creative refusal of victimization by sexual stereotypes. This creative refusal involves conscious and frequently painful efforts to develop new lifestyles in which I-Thou becomes the dominant motif, replacing insofar as possible the often blind and semi-conscious mechanisms of I-It, which use the Other as object. In the realm of knowledge, this means removing the impediments to that realm of knowing which is subjective, affective, intuitive, or what the Scholastics called "connatural." It means breaking down the barriers between technical knowledge and that deep realm of intuitive knowledge which some theologians call ontological reason.[53]

Objective or technical knowledge is necessary for human survival and progress. It is the capacity for "reasoning." Clarity of thinking and the construction of language require its use. So also does the ability to control nature and society. However, by itself, cut off from the intuitive knowledge of ontological reason, technical knowledge is directionless and ultimately meaningless. When it dominates, life is deprived of an experience of depth, and it tends toward despair.

Technical knowledge of itself is detached. It depends upon a subject-object split between the thinker and that which is perceived. It is calculative, stripping that which is perceived of subjectivity. Technical knowledge, cut off from ontological reason, degrades its object and dehumanizes the knowing subject. Because it reduces both to less than their true reality, at a certain point it even ceases to be knowledge in any authentic sense. When it is thus separated from ontological reason, the psychological and social sciences which it dominates become dogmatic, manipulative, and destructive. Under its dominion, philosophy, theology, and all of religion deteriorate.

Widening of experience so pathologically reduced can come through encounter with another subject, an I who refuses to be an It. If, however, the encounter is simply a struggle over who will be forced into the position of It, this will not be ultimately redemptive. It is only when the subject is brought to a recognition of the other's damaged but never totally destroyed subjectivity as equal to his/her own, having basically the same potential and aspiration to transcendence, that a qualitatively new way of being in the world and toward God can emerge. What is perceived in this new way of being is the Eternal Thou, the creative divine word that always has *more* to say to us. This is the meaning of the women's movement as the new *way of eminence*.

New Space: New Time

The unfolding of God, then, is an event in which women participate as we participate in our own revolution. The process involves the creation of new space, in which women are free to become who we are, in which there are real and significant alternatives to the prefabricated identities provided within the enclosed spaces of patriarchal institutions. As opposed to the foreclosed identity allotted to us within those spaces, there is a diffused identity—an open road to discovery of the self and of each other. The new space is located always "on the boundary." Its center is on the boundary of patriarchal institutions, such as churches, universities, national and international politics, families. Its center is the lives of women, whose experience of becoming changes the very meaning of center for us by putting it on the boundary of all that has been considered central. In universities and seminaries, for example, the phenomenon of women's studies is becoming widespread, and for many women involved this is the very heart of thought and action. It is perceived as the core of intellectual and personal vitality, often as the only part of the "curriculum" which is not dead. By contrast, many male adminis-trators and faculty view "women's studies" as peripheral, even trivial, perhaps hardly more serious than the "ladies' page" of the daily news-paper. Most "good" administrators do sense that there is something of vitality there, of course, and therefore tolerate or even encourage women's studies—but it remains "on the boundary." So too, the coming together of women on the boundary of "the church" is the center of spiritual community, unrecognized by institutional religion.

The new space, then, has a kind of invisibility to those who have not entered it. It is therefore inviolable. At the same time it communicates power which, paradoxically, is experienced both as power of presence and power of absence. It is not political power in the usual sense but rather a flow of healing energy which is participation in the power of being. For women who are becoming conscious, that participation is made possible initially by casting off the role of "the Other" which is the nothingness imposed by a sexist world. The burst of anger and creativity made possible in the presence of one's sisters is an experience of becoming whole, of overcoming the division within the self that makes nothingness block the dynamism of being. Instead of settling for being a warped half of a person, which is equivalent to a self-destructive non-person, the emerging woman is casting off role definitions and moving toward androgynous being. This is not a mere "becoming equal to men in a man's world"—which would mean settling for footing within the pa-triarchal space. It is, rather, something like God speaking forth God-self in the new identity of women.[54] While life in the new space may be "dangerous" in that it means living without the securities offered by the patriarchal system for docility to its rules, it offers a deeper security that can absorb the risks that such living demands. This safety is participation in *being*, as opposed to inauthenticity, alienation, nonidentity—in a word, nonbeing.

The power of presence that is experienced by those who have begun to live in the new space radiates outward, attracting others. For those who are fixated upon patriarchal space it apparently is threatening. Indeed this sense of threat is frequently expressed. For those who are thus threatened, the presence of women to each other is experienced as an absence. Such women are no longer empty receptacles to be used as "the Other," and are no longer internalizing the projections that cut off the flow of being. Men who need such projection screens experience the power of absence of such "objects" and are thrown into the situation of perceiving nothingness. Sometimes the absence of women that elicits this anxiety is in fact physical. For example, when women deliberately stay away from meetings, social gatherings, etc., in order to be free to do what is important to ourselves, there is sometimes an inordinate response of protest. Sometimes the absence is simply non-cooperation, refusal to "play the game" of sex roles, refusal to flatter and agree, etc. This too hints at presence of another space that women have gone off to, and the would-be users are left with no one to use. Sometimes, of course, the absence of women takes the form of active resistance. Again, it throws those who would assume the role of exploiters back into their sense of nothingness.

In this way then, women's confrontation with the experience of nothingness invites men to confront it also. Many of course respond with hostility. The hostility may be open or, in some cases, partially disguised both from the men who are exercising it and from the women to whom it is directed. When disguised, it often takes seductive forms, such as invitations to "dialogue" under conditions psychologically loaded against the woman, or invitations to a quick and easy "reconciliation" without taking seriously the problems raised. Other men react with disguised hostility in the form of being "the feminist's friend," not in the sense of really hearing women but as paternalistic supervisors, analysts, or "spokesmen" for the movement. Despite the many avenues of nonauthentic response to the threat of women's power of absence, some men do accept the invitation to confront the experience of nothingness that offers itself when "the Other" ceases to be "the Other" and stands back to say "I am." In so doing men begin to liberate themselves toward wholeness, toward androgynous being. This new participation in the power of being becomes possible for men when women move into the new space.

Entry into the new space whose center is on the boundary of the institutions of patriarchy also involves entry into new time. To be caught up in these institutions is to be living in time past. This is strikingly evident in the liturgies and rituals that legitimate them. By contrast, when women live on the boundary, we are vividly aware of living in time present/future.

Participation in the unfolding of God means also this time breakthrough, which is a continuing (but not ritually "repeated") process. The center of the new time is on the boundary of patriarchal time. What it is, in fact, is women's *own* time. It is our *life-time*. It *is* whenever we are living out of our own sense of reality, refusing to be possessed, conquered, and alienated by the linear, measured-out, quantitative time of the patriarchal system. Women, in becoming who we are, are living in a qualitative, organic time that escapes the measurements of the system. For example, women who sit in institutional committee meetings without surrendering to the purposes and goals set forth by the male-dominated structure, are literally working on our own time while perhaps appearing to be working "on company time." The center of our activities is organic, in such a way that events are more significant than clocks. This boundary living is a way of being in and out of "the system." It entails a refusal of false clarity. Essentially it is being alive now, which in its deepest dimension is participation in the unfolding of God.

It should be apparent, then, that for women entrance into our own space and time is another way of expressing integrity and transformation. To stay in patriarchal space is to remain in time past. The appearance of change is basically only separation and return—cyclic movement. Breaking out of the circle requires anger, the "wrath of God" speaking God-self in an organic surge toward life.[55] Since women are dealing with demonic power relationships, that is, with structured evil, rage is required as a positive creative force, making possible a breakthrough, encountering the blockages of inauthentic structures. It rises as a reaction to the shock of recognizing what has been lost—before it had even been discovered—one's own identity. Out of this shock can come intimations of what human being (as opposed to half being) can be. Anger, then, can trigger and sustain movement from the experience of nothingness to recognition of participation in being. When this happens, the past is changed, that is, its significance for us is changed. Then the past is no longer static: it too is on the boundary. When women take positive steps to move out of patriarchal space and time, there is a surge of new life. I would analyze this as participation in God the Verb who cannot be broken down simply into past, present, and future time, since God is form-destroying, form-creating, transforming power that makes all things new.

CHAPTER TWO

Exorcising Evil from Eve:
The Fall into Freedom

You are the devil's gateway. . . . How easily you destroyed man, the image of God. Because of the death which you brought upon us, even the Son of God had to die.
                    —TERTULLIAN

All witchcraft comes from carnal lust, which is in women insatiable.
                    —SPRENGER AND KRAMER in
                    MALLEUS MALEFICARUM

I believe . . . that in the rejection, or transcending, of the scapegoat principle lies the greatest moral challenge for modern man [sic].
                    —THOMAS S. SZASZ

The story of the Fall of Adam and Eve is not given serious weight in the modern consciousness, it would seem. Of course it is the focus of many threadbare jokes and cartoons but many, perhaps most, people would insist that they do not take it seriously. Among some theologians there is a tendency to "demythologize" the biblical story, that is, to remove the "shell" of myth while retaining some alleged content (Bultmann and some of his followers). Others have attempted to "break the myth," that is, to retain it while recognizing it *as myth* and not taking it literally (Tillich). Its meaning has been rendered by theologians into abstract and universal terms, such as "universal alienation" and "existential estrangement." One could get the impression that the vision of the man-woman relationship portrayed is unimportant for modern consciousness, religious or secular.

The fact is, however, that the myth has projected a malignant image of the male-female relationship and of the "nature" of women that is still deeply imbedded in the modern psyche. In the Christian tradition it continues to color the functioning of the theological imagination. Berdyaev found it possible to write the amazing comment that "there is something base and sinister in the female element."[1] What is equally amazing (verified by this author's experience) is that theological students, confronted with such a passage, frequently are unable to see anything remarkable or significant about it. The myth has in fact affected doctrines and laws that concern women's status in society and it has contributed to the mind-set of those who continue to grind out biased, male-centered ethical theories—a point to be developed in a later chapter. The myth undergirds destructive patterns in the fabric of our culture. Literature and the mass media repeat the "temptress Eve" motif in deadly earnest, as do the rationalizations for social customs and civil laws, such as abortion legislation, which incorporate punitive attitudes toward women's sexual function.[2]

In view of the fact that the destructive image of women that was reflected in and perpetuated by the myth of the Fall retains its hold over the modern psyche—even though in a disguised and residual manner—it is not adequate for theologians simply to intellectualize and generalize the alleged content of the myth as an expression of a universal state of alienation. Indeed this approach is intellectually bankrupt and demonic. It amounts merely to abandoning the use of explicitly sexist theological imagery while failing to acknowledge its still persistent impact upon society. Such silence about the destructiveness of the myth's specific content is oppressive because it conveys the message—indeed *becomes* the message—that sexual oppression is a nonproblem. It is not good enough to talk about evil abstractly while lending implicit support to traditional images that legitimate specific social evils.

The Myth Revisited

The story of the Fall was an attempt to cope with the confusion experienced by human beings trying to make sense out of the tragedy and absurdity of the human condition. Unfortunately, as an exclusively male effort in a male-dominated society, it succeeded primarily in reflecting the defective social arrangements of the time. The myth was both symptom and instrument of further contagion. Its great achievement was to reinforce the problem of sexual oppression in society, so that woman's inferior place in the universe became doubly justified. Not only did she have her origin in the man; she was also the cause of his downfall and all his miseries. Humorless treatises on the subject of Eve's peculiar birth and woeful sinfulness written by the indefatigable fans of Adam down through the millennia are their own best parodies. Yet a hoax of cosmic proportions took a few thousand years to be seen through. Having at last noticed the incongruity, theologians have dismissed it from their attention. Few have even barely begun to glimpse the significance of the tragedy of sexual injustice that was inadvertently "revealed" by the story of the Fall.

The fact that the myth cultivated a backward-looking consciousness and, taken as an overall perspective on the world, constituted an obstacle to progress, was noted by Teilhard de Chardin as early as 1933 (in an essay entitled "Christologie et évolution"). The story conveys to the popular imagination the idea that the best has already been; paradise seems to be located in the past. The *specific* nature of the backward-looking vision which Teilhard failed to acknowledge is fixation upon a one-sided and distorted Image of half the human species—and also of the other half (Adam is pictured as a servile and arrogant dunce)—which prevents the becoming of psychically whole human beings.

Other critics of the tradition such as Hesnard, looking at it from a psychoanalytic point of view, have pointed out that it encourages an all-pervasive guilt feeling that condemns life and its instinctive joys. The refusal of life is experienced as frustration, which becomes self-accusation and aggression against the self. Logically, this would appear to lead to self-annihilation, but what usually happens is that it is at least partially transformed into aggression against others. In this way, the self-hatred encouraged by Christianity becomes a perversion of the basic desire and need to communicate with others and so fosters hatred, oppression, and even war.[3] The *specific* form of aggression which such critics fail to take adequately into account is that which makes women into objects. They do not really deal with the fact that the projection of "the Other"—easily adaptable to national, racial, and class differences—has basically and primordially been directed against women.

To summarize: Theologians and scholars generally have failed to confront the fact that in the myth of the Fall the medium is the message. Reflection upon its specific content and the cultural residues of this content leads to the conviction that, partially through this instrument, the Judeo-Christian tradition has been aiding and abetting the sicknesses of society. In a real sense the projection of guilt upon women *is* patriarchy's Fall, the primordial lie. Together with its offspring—the theology of "original sin"—the myth reveals the "Fall" of religion into the role of patriarchy's prostitute. This is not to say, of course, that religion was ever in a true paradise, dispensing pure revelation, free of idolatry and of servitude to unjust social arrangements. The point is simply that by its built-in bias and its blind reinforcement of prejudice the myth does express the "original sin" of patriarchal religion. The message that it unintentionally conveys—the full implications of which we are only now beginning to grasp—is that in patriarchy, with the aid of religion, women have been the primordial scapegoats.

The Fall and False Naming

The myth of the Fall can be seen as a prototypic case of false naming. Elizabeth Cady Stanton was indeed accurate in pointing out the key role of the myth of feminine evil as a foundation for the entire structure of phallic Christian ideology.[4] As I have indicated, the myth takes on cosmic proportions since the male's viewpoint is metamorphosed into God's viewpoint. It amounts to a cosmic false naming. It misnames the mystery of evil, casting it into the distorted mold of the myth of feminine evil. In this way images and conceptualizations about evil are thrown out of focus and its deepest dimensions are not really confronted. Implied in this colossal misnaming of evil is the misnaming of women, of men, of God. Consequent upon this dislocation of the mystery of evil has been a dislocation of the Christian "solution"—a point to be developed in the next chapter.

Out of the surfacing woman-consciousness is coming the realization that the basic counteraction to patriarchy's false naming of evil has to come primarily from women. By dislodging ourselves from the role of "the Other," that is, by saying inwardly and outwardly our own names, women are dislodging the mystery of evil from this false context and thus clearing the way for seeing and naming it more adequately.

Effects of the Myth

As one author puts it: "The fall of man should rightly be called the fall of woman because once more the second sex is blamed for all the trouble in the world."[5] The attitude of negativity on the part of the male is directed against women. This, clearly, was the prevailing psychological climate which engendered the myth and sustained its credibility. However, there is more to the problem than this. The myth has provided legitimation not only for the direction of the self-hatred of the male outward against women, but also for the direction of self-hatred inward on the part of women. As long as the myth of feminine evil is allowed to dominate human consciousness and social arrangements, it provides the setting for women's victimization, by both men and women.

It is now quite commonly known that it is characteristic of any oppressed group that its members suffer from a divided consciousness. Freire has described this phenomenon:

The oppressed suffer from the duality which has established itself in their innermost being. They discover that without freedom they cannot live authentically. Yet, although they desire authentic existence, they fear it. They are at one and the same time themselves and the oppressor whose consciousness they have internalized.[6]

As contradictory, divided beings, the oppressed do not fully grasp the paralyzing fact that the oppressor, having invaded the victims' psyches, now exists within themselves. They are caught in a web of self-defeating behavior.

This problem, which has been perceived as the dilemma of all oppressed groups, is most tragically the case with women—divided beings *par excellence* (a point unacknowledged in Freire's book, which does not even allude to the condition of women). Having been divided against the self, women want to speak, but remain silent. The desire for action is by and large reduced to acting vicariously through men. Instead of living out the dynamics of the authentic self, women generally are submerged in roles believed to be pleasing to males. When a rebel tries to raise up her own identity, that is, to create her own image, she exposes herself to threatened existence in sexist society. This is partly because both women and men identify with the goals of the superordinate group and therefore see the rebellious female as "the enemy."

It may also be that, in attacking her, women are also attacking the male in the sense that she is a surrogate victim, a more vulnerable object for repressed resentment. It seems that sexist society generates a chronic inability to realize the location of the problem, to ferret out the cause of the destruction.

Patriarchal religion adds to the problem by intensifying the process through which women internalize the consciousness of the oppressor. The males' judgment having been metamorphosed into God's judgment, it becomes the religious duty of women to accept the burden of guilt, seeing the self with male chauvinist eyes. What is more, the process does not stop with religion's demanding that women internalize such images. It happens that those conditioned to see themselves as "bad" or "sick" in a real sense become such. Women who are conditioned to live out the abject role assigned to the female sex actually appear to "deserve" the contempt heaped upon "the second sex."

The "Original Sin" of Women

The first salvific moment for any woman comes when she perceives the reality of her "original sin," that is, internalization of blame and guilt. In naming women's enforced complicity in oppression our "original sin," it is important, of course, not to fall into the trap of "blaming the victim." It is all too easy and basically misleading to say that it is women's *fault* that society is sexist. This is as fallacious as suggesting that it is the fault of blacks that society is racist, or the fault of the poor that poverty exists. It is dishonest to use the example of exceptional great women to support the idea that any woman who "has what it takes" can succeed. When I write of women's complicity I mean a complicity that has in large measure been enforced by conditioning. The phrase "original sin" is then torn from its original semantic context. The new sense retains the connotation of an inherited defect. However, it is understood that the "sin" is inherited through socialization processes. It is the inherited burden of being condemned to live out the role of "the Other." The fault should not be seen as existing primarily in victimized individuals, but rather in demonic power structures which induce individuals to internalize false identities.

Honest recognition of what has happened means making oppression in a sense even more oppressive, by adding to the simple fact the *realization* of oppression.[7] This entails refusal of the false transcendence that sometimes comes with not seeing the problem and acceptance of the pain that accompanies insight. Moreover, having glimpsed the way things are is not enough. Real insight implies commitment to changing the destructive situation, and the implications of this are not comfortable. For the person who has learned to *see* sexism, nothing can ever be the same again. Yet there is hope involved in the insight into sexism. This hope has its basis in the fact that those who are oppressed live in dialectical relationship with the privileged group. The status of the latter requires the consent of the former to the oppressive situation. Recognition of this is redemptive and revelatory knowledge, pointing the way to "salvation" from the dehumanizing situation. The beginning of an adequate response is a will to integrate and transform the heretofore divided self.

Healing

The healing process demands a reaching out toward completeness of human being in the members of both sexes—that is, movement toward androgynous being. For women, this means exorcism of the internalized patriarchal presence, which carries with it feelings of guilt, inferiority, and self-hatred that extends itself to other women. It means recognition that women are in a real sense possessed by a demonic power within the psyche—the masculine subject ("male chauvinist pig") within—that reduces the self to an object. Ejection of this alien presence means affirming that "female is beautiful," not in the sense of accepting patriarchy's models and imposed standards for evaluating females, but in the sense that women are discovering and defining ourselves.

It would be naïve to think that the healing of the divided self can take place in one act. A truly healing insight involves a will to change that externalizes itself in continually unfolding action, so that the insight grows and action becomes more meaningful.

It would also be naïve to think that healing can take place in isolation. The individual's sense of reality depends upon some kind of communal consent. It would be absurd to think that singly a woman can win the struggle for psychic wholeness. The sense of reality that such an individual is trying to sustain would be pitted against a system with enormous resources for persuading her of her error, sinfulness, or mental illness. As a noted sociologist remarked: "At best, a minority viewpoint

is forced to be defensive. At worst, it ceases to be plausible to anyone."[8]
A minority of one has little chance of survival. The "bonding" phenomenon among women, expressed by the word "sisterhood," is therefore
essential to the battle against false consciousness. Only women hearing
each other can create a counterworld to the prevailing sense of reality.

Universally Redemptive Quality of the Struggle

Women's eradication of the "sin" of complicity in self-destruction is basically redemptive for the whole society, since oppression is dehumanizing
for both the subordinate and the superordinate groups. For the most
part, however, those in the oppressive group, though they may wish
to be "fair" and to be humanists, cannot allow themselves to see the
full implications of this. The psychology of vested interests works in subtle
ways and the institutions of sexist society support these interests. At the
same time, women are plagued with insecurity and guilt feelings over
opposing men—feelings which are part of the "original sin" syndrome of
complicity in sexism. This suffering in "conscience" on the part of wom-
en trying to break out of the alienated identity institutionalized in our society, even when it is recognized as "bad faith," remains a formidable
obstacle to be overcome. For this reason it is important to keep in focus
the fact that in self-liberation women are performing the most effective
action possible toward universal human liberation, making available to
men the fullness of human being that is lost in sexual hierarchy. To oppose the essential lovelessness of the sexually hierarchical society is
the radically loving act. Seen for what it is, the struggle for justice opens
the way to a situation in which more genuinely loving relationships are
possible.

Eradicating the Side Effects of "Original Sin"

Among the side effects of women's internalization of identity as "the
Other" is *psychological paralysis*. This arises from a general feeling
of hopelessness, guilt, and anxiety over social disapproval. Such anxiety
is well founded, for women attempting to express new consciousness
do live in conflict with the mechanisms of social control, which include
ridicule, insults, instant pschoanalysis expressed in such comments as
"penis-envy," "man-hater," or "unfeminine." The beginning of overcom-

ing this paralysis is outward action. This may mean participation in a discussion group or a consciousness-raising group, standing up to challenge a speaker who has expressed biased opinions about women, writing an article, a "letter to the editor" or simply a letter to a friend, expressing new insights. It may mean taking part in the action of a task force working against discrimination in laws, communications media, organized religion, educational institutions. Whatever the action chosen, it can open the way to a new pattern of activity, and it is the process itself of engaging in such activity that engenders hope. It brings opposition into the open, which means that aggressive energy can be turned outward instead of inward. Such action may reveal opponents (but, after all, this was already known and dreaded), but it also reveals allies and potential friends. The self-confidence that comes with this breakthrough to self-affirmation is qualitatively new, not to be confused with the confidence which comes with being "popular" socially, or with being a competent writer, musician, or tennis player. It is the self-esteem that comes with affirming an undivided self.

Another side effect of feminine complicity is, of course, *feminine antifeminism*. This, unlike masculine antifeminism, rarely takes the form of physical violence. The part of the antifeminist woman that identifies with the power structure looks upon a woman who threatens that structure as a threat to herself. She expresses disapproval and hostility. This divisiveness among women is an extension of the duality existing within the female self. It lashes out at unexpected moments and from unexpected sources. Often it happens that the woman who has achieved outstanding success in a "masculine" field openly discourages other women from following her example. Having accepted her role as token in the higher echelons of the professional establishment, she adopts the attitudes of her male colleagues toward women who would aspire to follow the same road. Her words of discouragement and her lack of supportive sisterhood confuse and present a kind of "double bind" situation to women who look to her for encouragement. On the one hand, they see in her the authentic self—acting, speaking, creating. On the other hand, they see that this self is acting, speaking, and creating on behalf of "the system" and in opposition to their own aspirations. Only a minority of women are able to see that such behavior is self-contradictory and that the successful token who behaves in this way is acting as patriarchy's puppet, giving out the message she has been programmed to give out: "Listen, even I, your would-be self, say you shouldn't try." Perhaps it isn't too surprising that most women follow the line of least resistance and listen to the words rather than the actions of such successful women, whose achievement is thus prostituted. Just as overcoming the paralysis of the divided self begins with perception carried out into concrete action, so triumph over feminine antifeminism will begin through conscious efforts at "bonding" supportively with other women and affirming collectively as well as individually the will to liberation. Ultimately only women can eradicate the psychological violence done by and through women to members of our own sex, by giving support and by making each other conscious of what is in large measure an unconscious duplicity.

A third effect of women's original sin is *false "humility,"* which is an internalization of masculine opinion in an androcentric society. This means never aspiring "too high"; imposing on the self a strangely ambivalent fear of success, as Matina Horner has shown.[9] This avoidance of success is rooted partially in guilt feelings over being a "rival" to males or "threatening the male ego." Such false humility is expressed not only individually but collectively, as when women's organizations publicly espouse such attitudes of self-depreciation and even act politically to impose them upon other women. A striking example of such an organization is the National Council of Catholic Women, which opposed the Equal Rights Amendment. Some of its spokeswomen expressed fear that the amendment was "a threat to the nature of woman."[10] Such organizations function as a kind of super-ego, saying "No" to personal achievement and pride.

Self-depreciation on an organizational level is evident also when women are deeply involved in liberal and even radical causes of all sorts except our own cause, even openly repudiating "independent" women's liberation. The basic fallacies in this attitude were analyzed in *The Fourth World Manifesto*. The authors of the *Manifesto* have shown that it is self-defeating for women to allow ourselves to be submerged in one male-dominated cause as opposed to another. Referring especially to nationalism, they point out that one nation versus another is in fact one male-dominated society versus another. The righteous indignation of Frantz Fanon against the French, coupled with his obstinate refusal to see the dehumanizing conditions imposed upon Algerian women by Algerian men for what they are, illustrates the problem. The fact that

French colonialism was seen as oppressive did not deter him from defending colonialism toward women, nor his countrymen from practicing it. Nationalist movements do not liberate women as such because national freedom is identified with male freedom.[11]

The self-depreciation which inclines women individually and collectively to find every cause more important than our own is deeply connected with the myth of feminine evil. Women have been conditioned to see any act that affirms the worth of the female ego as blameworthy. Female ambition can "pass" only when it is diluted into vicarious ambition through the male or on behalf of patriarchal values.

To counteract this mass-produced self-depreciation, women will have to build female pride, raising up our own standards of how it is good to be a woman. Our failure has consisted in not actively affirming the female ego. If we must feel shame, it should be for this. The raising up of women's new image and pride means giving prime energy to our own cause and refusing to see this as an illegitimate rival to other causes. It is not a rival to any truly revolutionary movement, but goes to the root of the evils such movements are trying to eradicate.

A fourth by-product of women's complicity in our own mutilation is *emotional dependence*. This is closely related to self-depreciation and is rooted in low self-images. Specifically it manifests itself in various ways. It is to be seen in housewives who never go out for an evening without their husbands, in young women who become depressed if they do not have dates every weekend or who are embarrassed to go to the movies or a restaurant alone or even with other women. It can be seen in nuns who seek the advice of priests rather than make their own decisions. In working women who have the jobs of subordinates, such as secretaries, it is sometimes manifested in a rigid attitude of following rules and orders blindly. When such women are also in superordinate positions, as in the case of some schoolteachers and principals, they are often inflexible in applying rules to their subordinates. This emotional dependence extends also into the intellectual life, hindering free thought and creativity. Few women, even among the gifted, have managed to challenge the society's prevailing vision of the "nature of reality" with vigor, consistency, and persistence. It would be difficult to overestimate the damaging effect of anxiety and dependence upon women's creativity.[12]

Clearly, there is no simple "one-shot" cure for a lifetime of conditioning to dependency. Women can raise each other's consciousness of it, and encourage each other to take the risks necessary to become free. The process of discovering and analyzing the social mechanisms that reinforce this state is itself liberating and opens the way to creativity of a radical sort. There is an unmistakable excitement in the air when women get together to analyze "the problem," generating a burst of creativity. At least implicitly, there is understanding that *here*, among women, is the source of independent challenge to "the way things have always been." This beginning to be together is the beginning of the end of female dependence.

Some Norms for Noncooptation

The work of "unveiling" and actively repudiating the myth of feminine evil will require a corporate redemptive action by women. That is, it will demand a collective refusal of all cooptation of women's energies to reinforce the structures and ideologies of patriarchy. This refusal will be most effective if it is *active* and *positive*, that is, not merely a negative withdrawal but creative existence on the boundary of these structures. I would hasten to add that such creative living on the boundary should not be confused with having one's cake and eating it too—a subtle perversion of "the real thing" which may resemble it superficially. Real boundary living is a refusal of tokenism and absorption, and therefore it is genuinely dangerous.

As a general normative basis for action, I propose that institutions and/or movements that coopt women can be classified into several categories and that decisions about how to relate to them can be based upon this analysis and classification. The divisions proposed here are intended as general guidelines, and applications to particular situations will have to be made according to specific circumstances.

In the first category belong antifeminine organizations and movements whose ideologies, policies, and goals not only are directly and explicitly sexist, but even are exclusively or primarily defined by sexism. It is obvious that women should not only reject any identification with such an organization but should actively oppose it, setting up channels to work for the liberation of women precisely in the areas it attacks.[13]

The second category includes institutions whose sexism is direct and explicit (e.g., written into rules or by-laws) but whose ideologies, policies, and goals are not defined exclusively or primarily by sexism. Decisions about such cases will involve weighing such factors as the positive merits that the institution may have in spite of its sexism, and judging how strong are the possibilities of changing and/or using it without losing a disproportionate amount of creative energy in the effort. Obviously an important factor to be considered in deciding whether or not to expend energy on the organization is the value and potential of the nonoppressive ideas and goals that it promotes. It might well be that in many cases women would do better to decide that it is not worth the effort. In other cases, it might be worthwhile to remain *on the boundary* of the organization, in the manner that I have already described, transferring the center of activity to our new space on the edge of such patriarchal space. When making this kind of decision, it would be well to keep in mind that in a patriarchal world nearly all organizations and movements are to some degree patriarchal, so that the imperative to live always on the boundary is a constant. There are, however, choices to be made about the *specific* boundary areas that one will inhabit. That is, the question arises: On the edge of which institutions should my energies be focused?

The third category of coopting institutions, organizations, and movements includes those whose sexism is indirect and implicit. That is, these do not usually have stated policies and ideologies of sexism, but it is a hidden agenda. Women are denied full equality even though this denial is not in the written rules and is simply enforced in practice and approved in the general climate of opinion. The same criteria would apply here as those described in the second category. However, the factors in favor of electing this kind of boundary situation will sometimes tend to be stronger, since there will be a greater flexibility and maneuverability, and more chances for using the resources of this form of patriarchal space for anti-sexist purposes.

In the fourth category are political, humanist, religious, and generally "countercultural" movements which have liberation as their stated goal but which fix all their attention upon some deformity *within* patriarchy—for example, racism, war, poverty—rather than patriarchy itself, without recognizing sexism as root and paradigm of the various forms of oppression they seek to eradicate. At this point in history these can be judged to coopt women insofar as they fail to work in some significant way for women's liberation as such and look upon women merely as included incidentally in other oppressed groups. Basically the same criteria apply here as in the second and third categories. The authentic place for women in relation to such movements is on the boundary. Although there are obvious reasons in favor of electing this kind of boundary situation it should also be recognized that there is a kind of seductiveness about a movement which is revolutionary, but not revolutionary enough.

The fact that giving priority to racial identification does not serve women's own best interests is illustrated by the eruptions of conflict between the black liberation movement and the women's movement. Black women are urged to stand behind and take orders from their men and are called disloyal if they give priority to the cause of their sisters. This contemporary phenomenon in American life is one more manifestation of the deep connection between sexism and racism. In the South, Negro women are sexually exploited by white men. Black men have often raped white women in revenge for their own degradation. Yet it was not women who brought slaves to America. Women have been pawns in the racial struggle, which is basically not the struggle that will set them free as women. If, as a result of black liberation, the prize achieved by black women is the same status as that of their white sisters, they will have an empty victory. Moreover, there is some question as to whether even this "same status" is attainable. The race problem is inextricably connected with sex.[14] It is most unlikely that racism will be eradicated as long as sexism prevails. Outstanding black women scholars such as Pauli Murray and Angela Davis have pointed to the conflict situation in which black women have been placed. Davis has shown that the myth of the black "matriarch" is an ideological weapon designed to impair the capacity of blacks for resistance by foisting upon them the ideal of male supremacy. It was the weapon of the infamous "Moynihan report," a cruel fabrication that inhibits blacks from seeing the real roots of racism.[15] Pauli Murray suggests that by asserting a leadership role in the growing feminist movement, the black woman can keep it allied to the objectives of black liberation while simultaneously advancing the interests of all women.[16]

Moreover, ideologists and leaders of the peace movement fail to recognize the deep connections between militarism and sexism. Indicative of lack of consciousness concerning the meaning of sexism are some statements issued by leading symbol-model figures of the movement, notably the Berrigan brothers. They make it clear that they see women's liberation (if indeed they see it at all) as something that will just happen in the course of working for the peace movement and "larger" causes in general. The fact of sexism in society is barely acknowledged, or if so, it is nullified by an ambiguous attitude of "blaming the victim." Meanwhile it infects the peace movement itself.[17]

It is understandable, then, though it may seem paradoxical, that some women find that living on the boundary of such movements is not always the most radical option. Indeed, some find this to be a less radical choice for themselves than accepting the full absurdity of living on the edge of a more overtly oppressive block of patriarchal space. For black women, of course, there may be compelling reasons for choosing to work with the black movement. Nevertheless, for others with less complex situations to deal with, the advantages of overtly oppressive organizations are an important consideration. Since the situation within such "space" is blatantly unjust, there is less chance of confusion and seduction. Also, there are opportunities to crack the monolithic image that the hierarchies of such institutions present by exposing and fostering independent thinking on the part of the silent majority who are falsely represented.

The categories suggested above are distinct but decisions about particular cases may be complex. This complexity is evident in the case of hybrid institutions such as a church-related university. A decision about locating on its boundary should take into consideration its complicated identity. Again, a revolutionary movement could have characteristics of both the third and the fourth categories, if in fact women are denied leadership roles. It may be that in some cases it will be difficult to judge in the concrete under which classification a given institution or movement should be considered. Still, it is important to try to judge the situation as accurately as possible. For example, some women might find it difficult to judge whether such an institution as the Catholic Church belongs in the first or the second category. On the one hand, it claims to be on the side of justice, human freedom, and peace. On the other hand, it is committed to patriarchal symbols and formulations of doctrine and to sexist policies, such as refusal of official ministerial power to women and opposition to birth control and abortion. Those whose hopes had

been raised during the Vatican II years have experienced a gradual erosion of these hopes beginning in the 1960s and increasingly in the '70s.
The intransigent opposition of the Catholic Church to the repeal of abortion laws has been blatantly obvious. Many who still had hopes for participation of women in the official ministry of the Catholic Church became
totally disillusioned when the press gave wide attention to the *motu pro-
prio* of Pope Paul VI in September 1972, in which he barred them even
from installation in the ministries of lector and acolyte. This is in effect
an accumulation of evidence that the hierarchy itself of the Catholic
Church have clearly placed their institution in the first category.

In dealing with the problem of cooptation, women can start with
the basic principle that our own liberation, seen in its fullest implications,
is primary in importance. When sexual caste is seen as the "original
sin" upon which other manifestations of oppression are modeled, it
becomes eminently unreasonable to feel guilt over according it priority.
If there *is* a place for guilt, it is for not recognizing that a male-dominated
"liberation" movement cannot essentially change the situation of the
more than 50 percent female membership of all down-trodden, poor,
and oppressed races and minority groups. Recognizing this, women may
well decide that independent "bonding" with each other and cooperation
on this basis with male-governed groups is the better choice.

Sisterhood Means Revolution

The positive refusal of cooptation means in effect the becoming of the
sisterhood of women, which is necessary to overcome paralysis, self-
hatred extended to women as a caste, self-depreciation, and emotional
dependence upon men for a feeling of self-esteem. It would be a mistake
to think that this is merely the feminine counterpart to "brotherhood,"
basically the same in meaning, but applied to females. Sisterhood is
the bonding of those who are oppressed by definition. Although males
in oppressed classes and groups have often called each other "brother,"
there is nothing inherent in the term that signals bonding against oppression, since men are not victimized *as men*. In fact, as a term for relationship of males to each other, signifying the higher caste in sexually
hierarchical society, the term really points to the phenomenon of male
bonding which Lionel Tiger has analyzed as a way of keeping men always

on top.[18] By contrast, sisterhood does point directly to the revolutionary phenomenon of the bonding of those who have been conditioned to be divided against each other—a bonding that signals revolt and is in itself the beginning of liberation. The new sisterhood is not mere incorporation into a brotherhood, as for example religious "sisters" have been incorporated in a particular way into the brotherhood of the church.[19] In contrast to this, it is an active effort to heal the duality within the female self. Rather than meaning delusory incorporation into the "brotherhood of man," it implies standing apart. It provides the only realistic basis for accepting fraternity, since without it women are thrown back into the emotional dependence upon men which the prevailing social arrangements demand. This is a fact that women in the Radical Left discovered in the sixties.[20] Since the new bonding says No to a social order that has prevailed from time immemorial, the word "sisterhood" *says* revolution.

The Scapegoat Syndrome

Society as we know it has a perverse need to create "the Other" as object of condemnation so that those who condemn can judge themselves to be good. This point has been made by scholars as different in outlook as Thomas Szasz and Erich Neumann.[21] Eve was such a production. She represents the category into which the Christian tradition has tended to place all women who have not managed to imitate the rather puzzling model of the virgin who is also a mother.

Insight into how the creation and scapegoating of "bad" women has served sexist society can be gleaned from the theological utterances on the subject of prostitution. Augustine wrote:

What can be called more sordid, more void of modesty, more full of shame than prostitutes, brothels, and every other evil of this kind? Yet remove prostitutes from human affairs and you will pollute all things with lust; set them among honest matrons, and you will dishonor all things with disgrace and turpitude.[22]

Embellishing upon this bit of male wisdom, Thomas Aquinas remarked that:

. . . prostitution in the world [is] like the filth in the sea or the sewer in a palace. Take away the sewer and you will fill the palace with pollution; and likewise with the filth [in the sea]. Take away prostitutes from the world and you will fill it with sodomy . . . wherefore Augustine says . . . that the earthly city has made the use of harlots a lawful immorality.[23]

The fact is that prostitutes—"the greatest guardians of virtue," to use a phrase of Lecky, historian of morals—have been allotted the privilege of serving as venereal safety valves for men. Interesting questions that arise are: Just *whose* lust would pollute all things without them? And *whose* virtue was being guarded? Surely not the virtue of the prostitutes nor of the men who used them. Then, seemingly, it is the "virtue" of the honest matrons, who of course had no such venereal outlet and whose "virtue" would seem to consist in being less likely to be called upon to function as sewers for men who were not their husbands and consequently bear illegitimate children. That is, they remained the unsullied private property of their husbands (or fathers, in the case of virgins). Society as structured, then, has required this wretched caste. The existence of "good" women—according to male standards of being unmolested private property—has required the existence of "bad" women, who have been scapegoats for male sexual guilt.

Even today, laws reveal the same bias. In the United States, in most states males cannot be punished directly for patronizing a prostitute. Even in states where such crimes do exist, restrictive interpretations often lead to exoneration of male customers of prostitutes.[24] In modern times the definitions themselves of prostitution continue to reveal the double standard. It has been defined, for example, as "the practice of a female in offering her body to an indiscriminate intercourse with men for money or its equivalent"; as "indiscriminate sexual intercourse with men for compensation"; and as "common lewdness of a woman for gain."[25] The evidently one-sided view of the problem reflected in these definitions sees the act of the woman as criminal while ignoring the responsibility of the male second party.

It appears to have been the case, then, that the primordial casting of women into the role of "the Other" spawned a second dichotomizing into good and bad women. This may appear puzzling in view of the fact that other oppressed groups are seemingly not dichotomized so drastically. In the United States, blacks who are "Uncle Toms" are praised and well treated, but not placed upon a pedestal and exalted. The striking dichotomization of women may be understood when one reflects upon the fact that this is the only case in which an oppressed group is dispersed among the superordinate group and intimately bound to the "master" by ties that are biolgical, emotional, social, and economic. Because there is this identification of men with "their" women, as well as otherness, it would be dysfunctional to proclaim unambiguously that all women are all bad.

At the same time, the otherness of women as such, that is, as a caste, supersedes the identification that men feel with some women as possessions who reflect their accomplishments and serve their interests. As a consequence, the "goodness" attributed to the few is not the goodness of a self-actualizing person but of an impotent creature, lacking in knowledge and experience. In this respect there is an analogy with the idolization of black children in the South, who become objects of contempt when they reach adulthood and become threatening. In the case of the ideal of goodness foisted upon women, however, there is a special aura of glorification of the ideal, as symbolized in Mary, for example. This impossible ideal ultimately has a punitive function, since, of course, no woman can really live "up" to it. (Consider the impossibility of being both virgin and mother.) It throws all women back into the status of Eve and essentially reinforces the universality of women's low caste status.

Destroying the Victim: From Witch-burning to Lobotomy

Women as a caste, then, are "Eve" and are punished by a cohesive set of laws, customs, and social arrangements that enforce an all-pervasive double standard. However, given the ambiguous identification of men with "their own" women, who are kept in a state of powerlessness, the myth of feminine evil cannot be lived out to its completely logical conclusion, which would be total destruction. Society as we know it fears and tries to destroy "the Other." In the case of the Jews in Nazi Germany, these dynamics were worked out to the logical "final solution" in an effort at complete extermination. In the case of women, while all are mutilated outrageously, the "privilege" of complete destruction is reserved for a segment of the female population who are called upon to bear the brunt of a wholly consistent logic. This has been the case with poor and ignorant women under the prevailing legal system who, driven by the total situation of their lives into the condition of unwanted or literally unbearable pregnancy, have died from the barbarities of back-alley abortions or desperate attempts at self-abortion, or in childbirth, or from pregnancy-related debilities.

A most striking example of the selective total destruction of a large number of women was the torturing and burning of women condemned by the church as witches. The most important medieval work on the subject, the *Malleus Maleficarum*, written by two Dominican priests (Sprenger and Krämer) in the fifteenth century, proclaims that "it is women who are chiefly addicted to evil superstitions." This is, after all, only to be expected, for "all witchcraft comes from carnal lust, which is in women insatiable."[26] According to the authors, men are protected from such a horrible crime because Jesus was a man.[27] Unlike the mythical Eve, the witches were real living persons condemned by the church's hierarchy, which was threatened by their power. Indeed, "power" is a key word in understanding why some and not others were selected for this horrible fate. The authors of *Malleus Maleficarum* asserted that among women, midwives surpass all others in wickedness.[28] As Michelet points out, there is reason to believe that women who were midwives and who healed were greatly feared by the Church, for their power threatened the supremacy of the clerics.[29]

Scholars such as Margaret A. Murray point out that in examining the records of the witches we are dealing with the remains of a pagan religion which Christianity was determined to stamp out.[30] Scholars' estimates of the number of witches who were burned vary greatly — from 30,000 to several million. Given the inadequacy of the records, it is impossible to demand accuracy. Despite the statements of Sprenger and Krämer, it is certain that there were also male witches, that is, adherents of the Old Religion. However, it is also clear that women were special targets of the church's hatred. It is certain that the frenzy of the struggle against witchcraft began to grow in intensity in the fifteenth century and petered out early in the eighteenth century. We also know that the methodology of witch hunting had as a basic premise (though not always admitted in these terms) that the person accused could not win. One test was to fling the accused bound into water, for a witch, having denied her baptism, would in turn be repelled by the water so she would float and not sink into it. If she was innocent, she would sink. Clearly, the "test" took care of the accused, one way or the other. Another infallible sign of guilt was the witch's inability to shed tears during torture and before the judges. The historian Henry Charles Lea tells us:

In such a case the inquisitor was instructed to adjure her to weep by the loving tears shed for the world by Christ on the cross, but the more she was adjured, we are told, the drier she would become. Still, with the usual logic of the demonologist, if she did weep it was a device of the devil and was not to be reckoned in her favor. [31]

The role of witch, then, was often ascribed to social deviants whose power was feared. All women are deviants from the male norm of humanity (a point emphasized by the "misbegotten male" theory of Aristotle and Aquinas, the "penis-envy" dogma of the Freudians, and other psychological theories such as the "inner space" doctrine of Erikson and the "anima" theory of Jung). However, those singled out as witches were frequently characterized by the fact that they had or were believed to have power arising from a particular kind of knowledge, as in the case of "wise women" who knew the curative powers of herbs and to whom people went for counsel and help. Defined as evil, they became the scapegoats of society, and in this process, the dominant ethos was reinforced. The Inquisitor functioned as the protector of society against deviance—against deviant behavior which was threatening because powerful.

In modern times psychiatric ideology has to a large extent replaced theology as custodian of society's values. Clearly, the semantics of "good" and "evil" have been replaced partially by "health" and "mental illness." In our times, a woman who is defined as unhealthy because she wants power over her own life can't win according to the rules of the psychiatrists' games. As Szasz has shown, the tortures are more subtle but the pattern is the same. Szasz's analysis is a development of an analogy between institutional psychiatry and the Inquisition which was earlier made by Elizabeth Packard, a woman who was psychiatrically imprisoned for "madness" in the nineteenth century by her husband, who disagreed with her theological views. [32] Women, particularly, although of course not exclusively, are victimized by the barbarities of modern psychiatry, especially psychosurgery. As a result of the efforts of Dr. Peter Breggin's investigations, it is now well known that there has emerged a second wave of psychosurgery, which, interestingly, is contemporaneous with the second wave of feminism. This includes operations in which healthy brain tissue is mutilated in order to change a person's emotions and conduct. The current wave of psychosurgery is aimed not only at state hospital patients, but especially at relatively well-functioning "neurotics," particularly women. On February 24, 1972, Dr. Breggin's article, "The Return of Lobotomy and Psychosurgery," was read into the Congressional Record. Discussing the remarkably large proportion of women who are being lobotomized, Dr. Breggin explains that it is more socially acceptable to lcbotomize women because creativity, which the operation totally destroys, is in this society "an expendable quality in women." A famous psychosurgeon (Freeman, the "dean of lobotomists") is quoted as saying that lobotomized women make good housekeepers. Concerning this phenomenon, Dr. Barbara Roberts, a feminist, observes that psychosocial conditioning is no longer as effective as it once was in suppressing female anger:

But, ever resourceful, patriarchal class society is developing what could prove to be the "final solution" to the "woman problem" (and for the "problems" caused by all other oppressed groups). That weapon is psychosurgery.[33]

The weapons that modern technology is developing for social control of deviants, particularly women, are more subtle than burning at the stake. They merely destroy minds—the capacity for creativity, imagination, and rebellion—while leaving hands and uteruses intact to perform the services of manual work and breeding.

Beyond Good and Evil

The beginning of liberation comes when women refuse to be "good" and/or "healthy" by prevailing standards. To be female is to be deviant by definition in the prevailing culture. To be female and defiant is to be intolerably deviant. This means going beyond the imposed definitions of "bad woman" and "good woman," beyond the categories of prostitute and wife. This is equivalent to assuming the role of witch and madwoman. Though this might be suicidal if attempted in isolation (not less self-destructive, however, than attempting to live within the accepted categories), when done in sisterhood it amounts to a collective repudiation of the scapegoat syndrome. It is then tantamount to a declaration of identity beyond the good and evil of patriarchy's world, and beyond sanity and insanity.

It cannot be claimed that such a declaration of identity will cause the mystery of evil to disappear automatically from human existence. What it amounts to, however, is a massive exorcism. Repudiation of the scapegoat role and of the myth of the Fall by the primordial scapegoats may be the dawn of real confrontation with the mystery of evil.

Margaret Murray pointed out that the word "witch" is allied with "wit," basically meaning *to know*. The witch's knowledge has always been that of one who foretells. In addition, Murray indicated that when this is done in the name of one of the established religions it is called prophecy, but when divination is done in the name of a pagan god it is called "mere" witchcraft. This kind of prophetic knowing is characteristic of the women's movement. The knowledge that women are now acquiring is an experiential knowledge that drives beyond the inane "goodness" of the victimized "honest matron" (or respectable suburban housewife or docile nun). It also drives beyond the projected "wickedness" of the equally victimized whore whose options have been so few that the "evil" is less a choice than a forced limitation. This knowledge that drives beyond the unreal goodness and wickedness imposed upon women is both experiential and reflective. It is not reducible to "knowing" only in the sense of sexual experience. It is, rather, a knowing that comes with discovery of the self's potential in all areas of endeavor, in a way that has been denied to women not only by external deterrents, such as restrictive laws and rules, but also by internal deterrents, which are the result of upbringing. It brings with it an ability to assess and evaluate experiences independently of and in the face of the culture's imposed valuation. It is therefore prophetic knowledge, pointing beyond "things as they are."

In going beyond the imposed innocence which both the good woman and the bad woman have in common (i.e., lack of valuation and choice of identity by the self) women are gaining the psychological freedom required to challenge the destructive false innocence that is characteristic of our age. Albert Camus wrote of the contrast between the unabashed and honest crimes of earlier times and the hypocrisy of our age:

But slave camps under the flag of freedom, massacres justified by philanthropy or by the taste for the superhuman, in one sense cripple judgment. On the day when crime dons the apparel of innocence —through a curious transposition characteristic of our times —it is innocence that is called upon to justify itself.[34]

This "innocence" is characteristic of the phallic morality that identifies good with "us" and bad with "them," particularly when such an attitude is carried to its logical conclusion. It can be seen through when those most victimized by it begin to come of age, that is, to find our integrity beyond such "good" and "evil."

This movement beyond patriarchy's good and evil can be seen mythically as "the Fall"—the dreaded Fall which is now finally beginning to occur, in which women are bringing ourselves and then the other half of the species to eat of the forbidden fruit—the knowledge refused by patriarchal society. This will be a Fall from false innocence into a new kind of adulthood. Unlike the old adulthood that required the arresting of growth, this demands a growing that is ever continuing, never completed.

In writing this way, I am tearing the image of "the Fall" from its context in patriarchal religion. I have suggested that the original myth revealed the essential defect or "sin" of patriarchal religion—its justifying of sexual caste. I am now suggesting that there were intimations in the original myth—not consciously intended—of a dreaded future. That is, one could see the myth as prophetic of the real Fall that was yet on its way, dimly glimpsed. In that dreaded event, women reach for knowledge and, finding it, share it with men, so that together we can leave the delusory paradise of false consciousness and alienation. In ripping the image of the Fall from its old context we are also transvaluating it. That is, its meaning is divested of its negativity and becomes positive and healing.

Rather than a Fall *from* the sacred, the Fall now initiated by women becomes a Fall *into* the sacred and therefore into freedom. Mircea Eliade, at the close of his book *The Sacred and the Profane*, suggests that in the modern mind religion and mythology have been "eclipsed" in the darkness of the unconscious: "Or, from the Christian point of view it could also be said that nonreligion is equivalent to a new 'fall' of man."[35] I am proposing a different interpretation of the contemporary situation, arising from the new women's experience of liberation. That is, if the symbols and myths of patriarchal religion are dying, this is hardly a total tragedy, since they have perpetuated oppression. To the extent that they have done this, they have represented a pseudo-sense of the sacred. The Fall beyond the false dichotomy between good and evil has the potential to bring us away not only from the false paradise of the pseudo-sacred symbols of patriarchy but also from the banal nonreligious consciousness that Eliade deplores. It can bring us into a new meeting with the sacred.

In his insightful foreword to Montague Summers' *The History of Witchcraft*, Felix Morrow points out that Summers' justifications of the church's persecution of the witches spring from a concept of the supernatural in which God is inconceivable without the devil.[36] The Fall from this schizoid image of the supernatural can come when women refuse the schizoid identity foisted upon *us*. As we overthrow the unreal "good" and "evil" projected upon us, we will be overthrowing the unreally good "God" whose existence requires an incarnate devil to be persecuted (and to do the persecuting).

In a real sense the symbols of patriarchal religion deserved to "die." What women's becoming can mean is something beyond their death and beyond their rebirth. It is not a mere cyclic return or resurrection of the sacred into profane consciousness that is at stake. Rather, women's becoming is something more like a new creation. As I will attempt to show in the next chapter, it can mean the arrival of New Being.

CHAPTER THREE

Beyond Christolatry:
A World Without Models

Take the snake, the fruit-tree and the woman from the tableau, and we have no fall, nor frowning Judge, no Inferno, no everlasting punishment—hence no need of a Savior. Thus the bottom falls out of the whole Christian theology. Here is the reason why in all the Biblical researches and higher criticisms, the scholars never touch the position of women.

—ELIZABETH CADY STANTON

Historical Christianity has fallen into the error that corrupts all attempts to communicate religion. . . . It has dwelt, it dwells, with noxious exaggeration about the person of Jesus.

—RALPH WALDO EMERSON

The distortion in Christian ideology resulting from and confirming sexual hierarchy is manifested not only in the doctrines of God and of the Fall but also in doctrines concerning Jesus. A great deal of Christian doctrine has been docetic, that is, it has not seriously accepted the fact that Jesus was a limited human being. A logical consequence of the liberation of women will be a loss of plausibility of Christological formulas which reflect and encourage idolatry in relation to the person of Jesus.

As the idolatry and the dehumanizing effects of reifying and therefore limiting "God" become more manifest in women's expanded consciousness, it will become less plausible to think of Jesus as the "Second Person of the Trinity" who "assumed" a human nature in a unique "hypostatic union." Indeed, it is logical that the prevalent emphasis upon the total uniqueness and supereminence of Jesus will become less meaningful. To say this is not at all to deny the charismatic and revelatory power of the personality of Jesus (or of other persons). The point is, rather, to attempt a realistic assessment of traditional ways of looking at and using his image.

It is still not unusual for Christian priests and ministers, when confronted with the issue of women's liberation, to assert that God "became incarnate" uniquely as a male and then to draw arguments for male supremacy from this. Indeed the Christological tradition itself tends to justify such conclusions. The underlying—and often explicit—assumption in the minds of theologians down through the centuries has been that the divinity could not have deigned to "become incarnate" in the "inferior" sex, and the "fact" that "he" did not do so of course confirms male superiority. The erosion of consent to male dominance on the part of women is undermining such assumptions of the tradition.

It might indeed seem logical that the widely publicized phenomenon of "the death of God" would have entailed also a "death of Jesus" in the twentieth century, at least in the sense of transcending the Christian fixation upon the person of Jesus. Obviously this did not happen within the mind-set of such Christologically oriented thinkers as Bultmann, Barth, Brunner, Reinhold Niebuhr, Bonhoeffer. Even so universalist a theologian of the past generation as Tillich, who seemingly was profoundly in accord with Nietzsche's proclamation of God's death, found it necessary to write: "The ultimate concern of the Christian is not Jesus but the Christ Jesus who is manifest as the crucified."[1] A young black theologian, Henry Nicholson, in his book *Jesus Is Dead*, pointedly asks: "Why does *ultimate concern*, which Tillich described as faith, have to be concerned with accepting Jesus at all, crucified or not?"[2]

It is not necessary to look to the past generation of theologians to see the almost universal pervasiveness of this fixation upon Jesus and the seemingly compulsive need to baptize and legitimate religious thinking, even of the most "radical" type, as "Christian." The attitude is almost all-pervasive in seminaries and theological schools, and certainly among those undertaking to write theology. Among the more colorful manifestations of the phenomenon is the work of Thomas J. J. Altizer, who, as a radical "death of God" theologian, proposed a "gospel of Christian atheism." For Altizer and many others less forthright in expressing their views, God is dead but Jesus is alive.[3]

I am proposing that Christian idolatry concerning the person of Jesus is not likely to be overcome except through the revolution that is going on in women's consciousness. It will, I think, become increasingly evident that exclusively masculine symbols for the ideal of "incarnation" or for the ideal of the human search for fulfillment will not do. As a uniquely masculine image and language for divinity loses credibility, so also the idea of a single divine incarnation in a human being of the male sex may give way in the religious consciousness to an increased awareness of the power of Being in all persons.

Seeds of this awareness are already present in the traditional doctrine that all human beings are made to the image of God and in a less than adequate way in the doctrine of grace. Now it should become possible to work out with increasing realism the implications in both of these doctrines that human beings are called to self-actualization and to the creation of a community that fosters the becoming of women and men. This means that no adequate models can be taken from the past.

It may be that we will witness a remythologizing of religion. Symbolism for incarnation of the divine in human beings may continue to be needed in the future, but it is highly unlikely that women or men will continue to find plausible that symbolism which is epitomized in the image of the Virgin kneeling in adoration before her own son. Perhaps this will be replaced by the emergence of imagery that is not hierarchical. The point is not to deny that a revelatory event took place in the encounter with the person Jesus. Rather, it is to affirm that the creative presence of the Verb can be revealed at every historical moment, in every person and culture.

New Being

Since the mystery of evil has been dislocated in patriarchal religious consciousness, it is logical to ask whether the Christian idea of salvation suffers from a comparable and consequent dislocation. The idea of a unique male savior may be seen as one more legitimation of male superiority. Indeed, there is reason to see it as a perpetuation of patriarchal religion's "original sin" of servitude to patriarchy itself. To put it rather bluntly, I propose that Christianity itself should be castrated by cutting away the products of supermale arrogance: the myths of sin and salvation that are simply two diverse symptoms of the same disease.

It is evident, I think, that the growing woman-consciousness is in conflict with fundamentalist and orthodox doctrines concerning Jesus. Even Tillich's conception of the Christ as the New Being presents the usual enigma of a partial truth. It may be claimed with justification that Tillich's Christology has some advantages. It is to some extent free of the static categories both of strictly "biblical" thought and of hellenic formulas. It stresses the humanity of Jesus (as opposed to a "high" Christology) and recognizes the Christ as a symbol. However, as in the case of his analysis of the Fall, Tillich abstracts from the specific content of the symbol, which in fact functions to justify oppressive societal structures. Once again there is no notice taken of the fact that the medium is the message. Defenders of this method argue that the symbol "can be used oppressively" or that it "has been used oppressively" but insist that it need not function in this way. This kind of defense is understandable but it leaves a basic question unanswered: If the symbol *can* be "used" that way and in fact has a long history of being "used" that way, isn't this an indication of some inherent deficiency in the symbol itself?

It is indeed true that our psyches cry out for New Being. However, it is most improbable that under the conditions of patriarchy a male symbol can function exclusively or adequately as bearer of New Being. Inevitably such a symbol lends itself to reinforcement of the prevailing hierarchies, even though there may be some ambivalence about this. I think, rather, that the bearers of New Being have to be those who live precariously on the boundary of patriarchal space—the primordial aliens: women. The story of Adam and Eve has been described as the hoax of the millenia. So now also the idea of the God-Man (God-Male, on the imaginative level)—the dogma of the hypostatic union—is beginning to be perceived by some women as a kind of cosmic joke. Under the conditions of patriarchy the role of liberating the human race from the original sin of sexism would seem to be precisely the role that a male symbol *cannot* perform. The image itself is one-sided, as far as sexual identity is concerned, and it is precisely on the wrong side, since it fails to counter sexism and functions to glorify maleness.

When one has grasped this problem, it is natural to speculate that the doctrine of the Second Coming might be a way to salvage tradition—whether this be conceived as appearing in the form of a woman or a group of women or in terms of so-called "feminine" charac-teristics.[4] Seen in this way, the awakening of women to our human poten-tiality through creative action would be envisaged as having the potential-ity to bring about a manifestation of God which would be the second appearance of God incarnate, fulfilling the latent promise in the original revelation that male and female are made to the image of God. While this would appear to have the advantage of maintaining some continuity with the Christian tradition while radicalizing it, I would point out that before moving too quickly into acceptance of this kind of language it would be important to be well aware of what we are about. If it is under-stood to mean that a First Coming has occurred in the person of Jesus, then feminism would appear to be restricted to being seen as a kind of continuum, as a completion of what has essentially already happened within the context of Christianity. This might be in some ways a comfort-able position for those from a Christian background to assume. It would enable us to call ourselves Christians without putting any great strain upon conscience. Yet this kind of "continuum thinking" can dull percep-tion and inhibit us from developing fully the insights of radical feminism. It is easy to find means of relief from the burden of acknowledging with consistency the fact that patriarchal religion *is* patriarchal. Later in this chapter I will suggest an entirely different manner in which the symbol of a Second Coming may be emerging genuinely in the psyches of women.

Jesus Was a Feminist, But So What?

In an admirable and scholarly article Leonard Swidler has marshaled historical evidence to show convincingly that Jesus was a feminist.[5] The response that appears to be forthcoming from many women goes some-thing like this: "Fine. Wonderful. But even if he wasn't, *I am*." Professor Swidler's work has the advantages of striving for historical accuracy and of maintaining continuity with tradition. At the same time, there are inherent difficulties in this approach. First, his assumption that one can extract "religious truth" from "time-conditioned categories" seems to mean that we can shuck off the debris of a long history of oppressiveness and get to the pristine purity of the original revelation. This is problematic in that it tends to be backward-looking, assuming at least implicitly that past history (that is, some peak moments of the past) has some sort of prior claim over present experience, as if recourse to the past were necessary to legitimate experience now. A second difficulty with the "Jesus was a feminist" approach to feminism is interrelated with the first: Implicit in this approach is the notion that there *are* adequate models that can be extracted from the past. The traditional idea of *imitatio Christi* is the not-so-hidden agenda of this method.

In contrast, women have the option of giving priority to what we find valid in our own experience without needing to look to the past for justification. I suggest that this is the more authentic approach to our problems of identity. Moreover, the contemporary situation has a qualitative newness about it that can be recognized even in abstraction from the insights of feminism. Margaret Mead wrote of this dramatic difference as a new and unique "generation gap." She points out that those born and bred before World War II are immigrants in time. We no longer live in a postfigurative culture, in which children can look to their grandparents and parents as models for their own future. What is happening cannot even be described accurately as a cofigurative culture, in which the elders are still dominant, while the prevailing models for members of the society are contemporaries. According to Mead, it is time for asking wholly new questions, for the becoming of a *prefigurative* culture. She writes:

If we are to build a prefigurative culture in which the past is instrumental rather than coercive, we must change the location of the future. . . . So, as the young say, The Future is Now.[6]

Although Mead affirms the need for asking "wholly new questions" she herself does not appear to ask or to hear the new questions that radical feminism is raising. However, her recognition that it is a time for openness to radical newness is an important insight that we can share.

Aside from the impossibility of looking to the *past* for adequate guidance, I propose that there are inherent difficulties in looking to Jesus, or to anyone else, as a model. The very concept of model, as commonly understood, is one of those conceptual products that either should be rejected as not applicable to persons or else made into a new word by being lifted out of its old context. The same term may be retained, materially speaking, but what we are about is breaking models in the old sense of the term. It seems to have been part of the patriarchal mind-set to imitate slavishly a master or father-figure with an almost blind devotion and then to reject this figure in order to be oneself. It is perhaps significant that the Latin term *modulus* means a small measure: it is necessary to shrink the self in order to imitate a model in this sense. This imitation-rejection syndrome is not what is going on with women now. Those who have come far enough in consciousness to break through the destructive conditioning imposed through "models" offered to the female in our culture are learning to be critical of all ready-made models. This is not to say that strong and free women do not have an influence, but this is transmitted rather as an infectious freedom. Those who are really living on the boundary tend to spark in others the courage to affirm their own unique being. It may be, as Paul Van Buren contends, that Jesus had such an effect upon his followers.[7] The important thing, then, was the freedom and power of being in which they participated, which enabled them to be their unique selves. The point was not blind imitation of Jesus' actions and views. If reading the Gospels—or anything else —sparks this kind of freedom in some persons today, this is hardly to be disparaged. But then Jesus or any other liberated person who has this effect functions as model precisely in the sense of being a model-breaker, pointing beyond his or her own limitations to the potential for further liberation.

Jesus and the Scapegoat Syndrome

There are other problems, particularly for women, inherent in the Christian fixation upon the person of Jesus, as that person is depicted through tradition. These problems center around an aspect of Jesus' image that in large measure negates the possibility of communicating the contagious freedom that I have just discussed. This aspect is his role as "mankind's most illustrious scapegoat," to use Szasz's expression.[8] In order to imitate such a lifestyle, it is necessary to live "sacrificially." The complex web of inauthenticity and hypocrisy that this evokes in the behavior of Christians has been recognized. Nicholson protests: "One does not live for the sole purpose of fulfilling others."[9] As Szasz analyzes the problem:

The moral aim of Christianity is to foster identification with Jesus as a model; its effect is often to inspire hatred for those who fail—because of their origins or beliefs—to display the proper reverence toward him. The Judeo-Christian imagery of the scapegoat—from the ritual of Yom

Kippur to the Crucifixion of Jesus as the Redeemer—thus fails to engender compassion and sympathy for the Other.[10]

While the image of sacrificial victim may inspire saintliness in a few, in the many the effect seems to be to evoke intolerance. That is, rather than being enabled to imitate the sacrifice of Jesus, they feel guilt and transfer this to "the Other," thus making the latter "imitate" Jesus in the role of scapegoat. It appears that what happens is that those under the yoke of Christian imagery often are driven to a kind of reversal of what this imagery ostensibly means. Unable to shoulder the blame for others, they can affirm themselves as "good" by blaming others.[11]

Discussing the problem of scapegoat psychology from a Jungian standpoint, Erich Neumann observes that for "mass man," as for primitives, evil cannot be acknowledged as one's own evil, since consciousness is too weakly developed to deal with such an internal conflict. Therefore, evil is experienced as something alien. The outcast role of the alien is important as an object for the projection of the "shadow" (our own unconscious counterpersonality), so that this can be exteriorized and destroyed. "It is our subliminal awareness that we are actually not good enough for the ideal values which have been set before us that results in the formation of the shadow . . ."[12] Neumann points out also that the shadow element from which the collective is trying to liberate itself through scapegoat psychology has its fling once again in the very cruelty which attends the destruction of the scapegoat.[13]

Both Szasz and Neumann recognize that minority groups and those in marginal positions are the usual candidates for the role of scapegoat. Szasz is far more aware of the implications of this mechanism for the oppression of women. However, the full import of this problem, especially vis-à-vis Christianity, is just now beginning to become explicit in the consciousness of women. The fact that women's role as scapegoats has been fostered by Christianity, especially in connection with the myth of feminine evil, has already been discussed in the preceding chapter. The point here is to recognize some interconnections between this and Christianity's fixation upon Jesus, particularly as a model.

It is significant that it is not only the *negative* qualities of a victim that have been projected upon women: the propensity for being temptresses, the evil and matter-bound "nature" of the female, the alleged shallowness of mind, weakness of will, and hyper-emotionality.

The qualities that Christianity *idealizes*, especially for women, are also those of a victim: sacrificial love, passive acceptance of suffering, humility, meekness, etc. Since these are the qualities idealized in Jesus "who died for our sins," his functioning as a model reinforces the scapegoat syndrome for women. Given the victimized situation of the female in sexist society, these "virtues" are hardly the qualities that women should be encouraged to have. Moreover, since women cannot be "good" enough to measure up to this ideal, and since all are by sexual definition alien from the male savior, this is an impossible model. Thus doomed to failure even in emulating the Victim, women are plunged more deeply into victimization.

It is also important to remember that in medieval theology Jesus came to be understood as the priest *par excellence*, who offered the supreme sacrifice of himself on the cross. The priestly caste in the church then came to be understood as those set apart and enabled in a special way by their ordination to participate in this sacrifice, identifying with Jesus in the act of offering his body and blood in the Mass. Women universally have been excluded from this role on the basis of sex. This imposed incapacity to identify ritually with the supreme scapegoat, in the sense of officially and actively "offering the sacrifice of the Cross" (or in fact participating officially in any ministry in Roman Catholicism) may at first seem inconsistent with women's victimized role within Christianity. However, a closer analysis reveals a basic consistency. As the powerless victims of scapegoat psychology, women are deprived of the "credit" for sacrifice and the dignity of taking an active role. Women are not the "innocent" victims offering the self in immolation for the sins of others, as Christian theology has imagined Jesus. In fact, the blame is never lifted from the female sex. Those in the official priesthood share in the "innocence" and active dignity of the Christ. Women, though encouraged to imitate the sacrificial love of Jesus, and thus willingly accept the victim's role, remain essentially identified with Eve and evil. Salvation comes only through the male.

Fallacies Involved in Not Facing the Christological Problem

For a number of reasons it is difficult for theologians to face the full import of the growing feminist consciousness vis-à-vis the Christological tradition. First of all, the vast majority are men and not sensitized to the problem of patriarchal conditioning. Second, there are problems of guilt feelings attached to any challenge of orthodoxy. Although the sanctions of medieval society no longer prevail (for example, burning at the stake for heresy), to a large extent these sanctions have been internalized as guilt or self-disapproval. Third, there are in fact still negative sanctions in seminaries, churches, and theological schools, such as loss of the esteem of authorities and of one's peers, which could result in professional disadvantages for those who do not "think right." Finally, and perhaps most subtly, there are positive sanctions for remaining or appearing to remain orthodox—the rewards that society confers upon those who are considered safe, such as promotions and administrative posts. The orthodox or semi-orthodox who are academics can hope to be called "scholarly." Those who are clergy can be called "well-balanced" by colleagues and superiors, and "inspiring" by parishioners.[14]

Given the enormous influence of sanctions, much of which is not openly recognized or acknowledged, a challenge to a central image of the tradition coming from a cognitive minority can expect to encounter defensive responses. Those who are asking the questions are arguing out of the experience of patriarchal religion's oppressiveness. Radical feminist insight is experienced as stronger than the sanctions of orthodoxy. By contrast, those who have a vested interest in institutional religion as it presently exists—whether this interest be economic or psychological or both—find it difficult to confront the problem or in fact even to recognize its existence. This factor of resistance usually is not expressed blatantly. It may well be disguised even from those who are inhibited from facing the problem and who believe that they are being open and fair-minded. It is important, then, to see the devices used to avoid facing the fact that the awakening consciousness of women is revealing inherent deficiencies in the Christian symbols and specifically in the fabric of Christology itself.

I have pointed out in the Introduction to this book that methods of avoiding insight into the conflict between feminism and Christianity can be analyzed into four categories. This analysis applies specifically and *par excellence* to the problem of Christolatry.

One method of avoiding the issue, then, is *universalization* of the problem. It is argued, for example, that along with not being a woman Jesus was not black, not elderly, not Chinese, et cetera. The implication would seem to be that women are not the only "outsiders." This is a kind of universalization of negatives in regard to the person of Jesus, and while it is, of course, true, it completely misses the point. The problem is not that the Jesus of the Gospels was male, young, and a Semite. Rather, the problem lies in the exclusive identification of this person with God, in such a manner that Christian conceptions of divinity and of the "image of God" are all objectified in Jesus. The tactic of defensively universalizing "what Jesus was not" generally accompanies the supposition that Jesus was the God-man, that is, the divinity who assumed this and only this particular human nature. For it is precisely this supposition that engenders the problem. The basic premise of this kind of orthodoxy is that "God came" in the man (male) Jesus, and only in Jesus—hence the difficulty, which is described by its advocates as "the scandal of particularity" (meaning all forms of particularity). This position equates religious experience with a kind of "leap of faith"—a "leap" which many have come to recognize as inauthentic and even idolatrous.

The universalization process is characterized by refusal to recognize the evident fact that the "particularity" of Jesus' maleness has not functioned in the same way as the "particularity" of his Semitic identity or of his youth. Non-Semites or persons over, say, thirty-three, have not been universally excluded from the priesthood on the basis that they do not belong to the same ethnic group or age group as Jesus. By contrast, the universal exclusion of women from the priesthood, and until recently from the ministry in most Protestant churches, has been justified on this basis. The functioning of the Christ image in Christianity to legitimate sexual hierarchy has frequently been blatant.

A second way of avoiding the Christological issue is *particularization*. This is done by attempting to limit the fact of oppression to particular times, places, or institutions, or to specific areas of activity. Thus a Protestant will frequently argue that the problem is peculiar to Catholicism. A Catholic may argue that it is peculiar to the Middle Ages but not to the modern period, or that the only theological bias against women concerns their exclusion from the hierarchy, but that this bias is not reflected in any other aspect of life. In all of these instances the basic impact of the Christological issue is dodged by shifting the emphasis to a specific set of conditions while refusing to see the universality of the conditioning process. This argument reduces the problem of patriarchal myth to one of dysfunctional application. The particularization fallacy basically is a failure to come to grips with the fact that sexist bias is endemic to and therefore perpetuated by Christianity.

A third way of shifting focus away from the patriarchal implications of Christolatry is *spiritualization*. I have already pointed out that the Pauline text: "In Christ there is neither . . male nor female" functions in this manner, for it simply and blatantly ignores the fact that *this is a male symbol* and therefore on this level *does* exclude the female. Among Christian intellectuals there has been some tendency to release "Christ" from rigid and exclusive identity with the historical Jesus, but these efforts often reveal insensitivity to the problem of female identity. Sociologist Peter Berger, for example, claims that he finds it difficult to see "how the discovery of Christ as the redeeming presence of God in the world can be exclusively linked to the figure of the historical Jesus." Berger goes on to conclude that "while Christ can be and has been 'named,' He is not identical with any name—an affirmation close to those Christian heresies that de-emphasized the historical Jesus as against the cosmic Christ . . ."[15] What Berger does not notice, apparently, is that Christ *is* identical with a name, and that name is "Male"—a fact which he himself unwittingly acknowledges by the exclusive use of the masculine pronoun, *"He,"* capitalized. This "He"—whether "He" refers to the particular "Jesus of the Gospels" or to the "cosmic Christ" —whatever else "He" may be, is *not* female and *not* truly "generic."

Spiritualization sometimes takes the form of a "futurizing" fallacy. When presented with the problem of women vis-à-vis Christ, theologians sometimes actually argue that when women finally do attain equality "it won't matter that God came as a man." Whether the future is envisaged in this-worldly or other-worldly terms, such eschatologizing distracts from the fact of present oppression and the obligation to do something about it. Instead of confronting the problem, it insists upon clinging to a myth that perpetuates it. It assumes that projections spawned out of patriarchal society will survive in a diarchal society—an unverifiable and implausible assumption.

A fourth method of evading the problem is *trivialization*. This is a tactic that is implied in and generally accompanies those already described. It is possible to universalize, particularize, and spiritualize away the conflict between women's becoming and Christolatry precisely because female aspirations to humanity are not being taken seriously.

Women who raise the problem are frequently told to turn their minds to "more serious questions." Women will learn to see through such tactics precisely to the degree that we do take our humanity seriously.

The Divided Self: Christ-Mary

The religious experience is an encounter with a power beyond the appearances of things, persons, and events. This power, seen as the ultimate ground of existence, is experienced as sacred and elicits awe. Religious organizations through their symbols and practices attempt to establish and sustain a relationship with the ultimate ground. Whatever else the symbols thus employed may be, they are first of all human projections. Feuerbach expressed the situation correctly though not adequately when he wrote that "God" is the highest subjectivity of "man" abstracted from "himself." This judgment is also applicable, correctly though inadequately, to the symbolization of Christ and Mary. The psychological acrobatics of Christians surrounding the symbolizations of Christ and Mary have little to do with the historical Jesus. They have even less to do with the historical person Mary, the mother of Jesus, and are devastating to the fifty percent of the human race whose lot she shared. The task at hand is healing of the divided self, which means breaking the idols that have kept it torn apart.

Compensatory Glory: The Image of Mary as Model

In the preceding chapter I have indicated that total identification of women with evil would be dysfunctional. Catholicism has offered women compensatory and reflected glory through identification with Mary. The inimitability of the Virgin-Mother model (literally understood) has left all women essentially identified with Eve. At the same time, it has served to separate the "feminine" ideal of good from the active role attributed to Jesus. The vicarious, derivative, and passive ideal of feminine good is *partially* identified with the Jesus model (insofar as Jesus is seen as victim). Yet it is also split off from the latter through reification in the symbol of Mary. This "makes sense" when one realizes that, as the real scapegoats of patriarchy, women cannot effectively be identified with the savior image. On one level, then, the Mary symbol functions to perpetuate the façade of semi-identification (by relation) of females with the Christ, deflecting female outrage and inhibiting insight and hope.

As symbolically portrayed, then, Mary is "good" only in relation to Jesus. This "fact" was reinforced on one level of perception by the doctrine of the Immaculate Conception—the doctrine that Mary was conceived without original sin—although the dogma gives also a contradictory message, as I will later show. This doctrine "officially" sets her apart from all other women as utterly unique, an impossible "model." It may be objected that this also sets her apart from men, but when the symbolism is seen in its full context (as expressed in Catholic doctrine) it can be seen as intending to reinforce sexual hierarchy, for the Immaculate Conception "occurred" in anticipation of Christ's divinity. That is, Mary was said to have been "immaculately conceived" in order to be worthy to become the Mother of Jesus, who was divine. Once again, the Marian doctrine reinforces sexual caste. The inimitability of "Mary conceived without sin" ensures that all women as women are in the caste with Eve. At the same time it reflects and reinforces duality of status. Women who are related to men have to be seen by "their men" as exceptions in some way, just as Mary is good by reason of her relationship with Jesus. It would be intolerable for men to view as entirely evil those who are related to them more or less as "private property." In sharp contrast to this, women who are "public property"—notably prostitutes—can be "all woman" (Eves) without the precarious identification with Mary that the privileged "good" women have had superimposed upon femaleness as such.

Prophetic Dimensions of the Image of Mary

The quasi-obliteration of Mary in Protestantism is well known. Tillich summarized the situation succinctly: "The Virgin Mother Mary reveals nothing to Protestants."[16] Some might claim that this signals a kind of advance for women, but the hypothesis is dubious.

Protestant thinkers such as Robert McAfee Brown have observed that Mariology is the area of greatest theological division between Protestants and Catholics. Still, there seems to be harmonious accord on the "fact" of her subordinate role in "Redemption." The difference often seems to amount only to a matter of the extent of subordination or de-emphasis. Possibly this "agreement" on the matter of subordination could be considered a sort of symbolic ecumenical message to the women of the world. It was reaffirmed in Chapter 8 of *Lumen Gentium*: *The Constitution on the Church* from Vatican Council II.[17]

If one looks at common objections of Protestants to the Catholic stress upon Mary, some important insights emerge. It is sometimes objected that she has been made almost equal to or even perhaps more important than Jesus—that she appears somewhat as a goddess. It is occasionally also objected that the stress upon Mary as Virgin detracts from women's role in marriage as wife and mother.[18] I suggest that both of these objections strike precisely at elements in the Mary symbol which, when "selectively perceived," have broken out of the stranglehold of Christian patriarchalism and managed to convey a message (partial and blurred) of women's becoming. I suggest that such a process of selective perception has indeed taken place in the psyches of many people, and that this fact has to be understood if one is to grasp the import of the tremendous power that the image of Mary has wielded in the human imagination. This power has been operative despite all the efforts to tame and domesticate it—despite the simpering plaster statues, the saccharine prayers, sermons, poems, and hymns, and the sexist theology that has "explained" it.

The following analysis is *not* an attempt to reinstate Mariology. It is not an effort to extract religious "truth" from "time-conditioned categories." My method contains no built-in assumption that we should direct our efforts toward salvaging anything from the patriarchal past. I do not think that we should try to "go back" to an alleged pristine revelation within Christianity, nor do I assume that the history of the Mary symbol has any demonstrable connection with the historical mother of Jesus. The burden of my analysis is to show that the symbol has been a two-edged sword, despite the single-minded intentions of its male promoters, and to raise some questions about its origin, about the reason for its power, and about the fact that the most oppressive of the Christian churches has captured and used this power.

The sometimes God-like status of Mary (always officially denied in Roman Catholicism, of course) may be, as Simone de Beauvoir suggests, a remnant of the ancient image of the Mother Goddess, enchained and subordinated in Christianity, as the "Mother of God."

Yet, if it is a leftover, it may also be a foretelling image, pointing to the future becoming of women "to the image of God." This point will be developed later in this chapter.

The image of Mary as Virgin, moreover, has an (unintended) aspect of pointing toward independence for women. This aspect of the symbol is of course generally unnoticed by theologians. Gordon Kaufman, for example, noting (rightly) that the church is responsible for many confused and even absurd opinions on Christological questions, then goes on to say that the doctrine of the virgin birth is "one of the earliest, and most unfortunate, of these confusions." He adds that the doctrine is an attempt to understand the theological fact that for faith Jesus Christ is Son of God.[19] One significant point about this interpretation is the fact that, typically, even a progressive Christian theologian finds the virgin birth doctrine more absurd than the idea that Jesus Christ is the Son of God. What is more interesting and more to the point here is the fact that he sees the virgin birth doctrine *as significant only in relation to Christ*. The prophetic aspect of the virgin symbol is precisely what he does not see. Another respected contemporary theologian, John Macquarrie, although he is somewhat more flexible on the virgin birth doctrine, exhibits the same propensity to perceive this in purely relational terms. He writes: "The question to be considered is whether this doctrine helps to explicate the person of Christ, whether it enables us better to see Jesus as the incarnate Word."[20] Later he adds: "The doctrine of the virgin birth is meant to point to Christ's origin in God."[21] So also Karl Barth wrote that the doctrine of the virgin birth upholds the divine initiative in the Incarnation.[22] The point of interest here is the fact that even what would seem to be the most nonrelational aspect of the symbol of Mary, the idea of her virginity, is comprehended by male theologians only in a relational way, having significance only as tied to the male savior and the male God.

In contrast to this contextual understanding of the Virgin symbol in Christianity, the symbol itself, taken out of this context, could be heard (and sometimes has been heard) to say something else: The woman who is defined as virgin is not defined exclusively by her relationships with men. Of course, if this is taken on a biological level, one could say that she is being defined merely by what she does *not* do sexually—which is still a kind of inverse sexual and relational definition. However, even the Mariological tradition works against this biological and "inverse-relational" interpretation. Mary was said to have been a virgin "before, during, and after" the birth of Jesus. This can be heard in such a way that by its very absurdity it literally screams that biology and abstinence from sexual activity are *not* the essential dimensions of the symbol of Mary as virgin. Sprung free of its Christolatrous context, it says something about female autonomy. The message of *independence* in the Virgin symbol can itself be understood apart from the matter of sexual relationships with men.[23] When this aspect of the symbol is sifted out from the patriarchal setting, then "Virgin Mother" can be heard to say something about female autonomy within the context of sexual and parental relationships. This is a message which, I believe, many women throughout the centuries of Christian culture have managed to take from the overtly sexist Marian doctrines.

On a functional level, Protestant obliteration of the Virgin ideal has to some extent served the purpose of reducing "women's role" exclusively to that of wife and mother, safely domesticated within the boundaries of the patriarchal family. Within Catholicism, the actual living out of the Virgin model has of course been less than totally liberating. Nuns have in a limited sense been removed from male domination. That is, the domination has been from a distance and often indirect. Yet, they have been cloistered by patriarchal power, often physically and nearly always psychologically and socially. In spite of this, some strong independent women have emerged within Catholicism, perhaps partially because of the sort of mental screening process I have described. Aided by such screening mechanisms, some women have managed to absorb from the Mary image a vision of the free and independent woman who stands alone. Thus the relational aspect of the symbol has been minimized, though seldom totally discarded.[24]

In contrast to this, women in Protestant Christianity appear to have been thrown back into the ambiguous situation of having only Jesus as a symbol-model—an impossible model especially for women, as I have attempted to show. Concretely, instead of having "the nun" as religious ideal, Protestant women have been offered the picture of "the minister's wife." Clearly, this has hardly been a liberating image.

It is evident, then, that women can look neither to Catholicism nor to Protestantism for adequate models of liberation. Yet it is important to be aware of "sub-intended" dimensions in Marian dogmas, since an analysis of these reveals the dynamics of cooptation of female power.

I will briefly examine two major Marian dogmas that have been proclaimed officially in modern times: the dogmas of the Immaculate Conception and of the Assumption.

I have already pointed out that the doctrine of the Immaculate Conception of Mary, as it became formulated, reinforced the imagery of sexism to the extent that it was seen in the context of preparing her to become the Mother of Jesus, who "saved" her, so to speak, in advance. However, when the idea itself of Mary's being conceived free of "original sin" is "selectively perceived," it can convey an entirely different meaning. It can be understood as a negation of the myth of feminine evil, a rejection of religion's Fall into servitude to patriarchy. It then functions as a prophetic intimation of the *Fall* that is yet on its way, that I have pointed to in the preceding chapter. This is the feared Fall beyond patriarchy's "good and evil," in which women no longer bear the burden of the scapegoat's role. Seen outside its "normal" context, the symbol of the Immaculate Conception foreshadows the coming Fall into the sacred, in which women are "conceived" as free from the crippling burden of submersion in the role of "the Other," and therefore are able to bring the human psyche beyond the pseudo-sacred of oppressive symbols and values.

In connection with the dogma of the Immaculate Conception, it is important to note its slowness in becoming "official" doctrine in Catholicism. Thomas Aquinas, a fairly consistent patriarch in this matter, rejected the doctrine. He insisted that if the Blessed Virgin had never incurred the stain of original sin, "she would not have needed redemption and salvation which is by Christ. . . . But this is unfitting, *through implying that Christ is not the savior of all men*" (italics mine).[25] Yet Aquinas taught that the Virgin was sanctified in her mother's womb, "after animation." This way he could assert her "specialness," while at the same time claiming that she was "cleansed" by the grace of Christ: "If the soul of the Blessed Virgin had never incurred the stain of original sin, this would be derogatory to the dignity of Christ, by reason of His being the universal savior of all."[26] This position coincides with that of St. Bernard, Peter Lombard, Alexander of Hales, Albert the Great, and St. Bonaventure. There was, however, a movement in progress at the time, chiefly in England, in favor of the doctrine of the Immaculate Conception. Due to the influence of St. Anselm, the doctrine was maintained by Eadmer, Nicolas of St Albans, Osbert of Clare, Robert Grosseteste

(Bishop of Lincoln) and William of Ware, who was the master of Duns Scotus. For centuries the question remained unresolved. Many continued to fear that it would place Mary on a par with Jesus. Finally the doctrine was made official by Pope Pius IX's bull *Ineffabilis*, on December 8, 1854.[27] The resistance of some Catholics and the shocked horror of Protestants indicates that they dimly glimpsed the unintended threat to male supremacy. The defenders of the doctrine, having no conscious intention whatever of relinquishing Christ's supremacy, claimed that this was not contradicted, since the grace of redemption might at the same time be one of preservation and prevention. It can be seen, then, that the doctrine has given out contradictory messages. *As doctrine* it reinforces sexual caste, as I have pointed out in the preceding section. *As free-wheeling symbol*, however, it can be read in another light. It can be seen as reflecting the power and influence of the Mother Goddess symbol which Christianity was never able to wipe out entirely. Sprung free from its Christolatrous context it says that, conceived free of "original sin," the female does not need to be "saved" by the male. The symbol then can be recognized as having been an infiltrator into sexist territory, an unrecognized harbinger of New Being.

The doctrine of the Assumption also can be seen as having a prophetic content interwoven with its sexist content. The doctrine was officially proclaimed by Pope Piux XII, in the apostolic constitution *Munificentissimus*, on November 1, 1950.[28] It was taught that the Virgin was taken up body and soul into heavenly glory upon completion of her earthly sojourn. Of course, the doctrine was encased in a Christocentric context. It was reaffirmed in Chapter 8 of *Lumen Gentium*, with the comment that: "She was exalted by the Lord as Queen of all, in order that she might be the more thoroughly conformed to her Son, the Lord of lords (cf. Apoc. 19:16) and the conqueror of sin and death."[29] Catholic theologians have maintained that the use of the term "Assumption" for Mary, as opposed to "Ascension" for Jesus, is significant, for the latter term is active, suggesting that Jesus "went up" under his own power, whereas "assumption" is passive: Mary was "taken up." While this jargon supports sexual hierarchy, there is another message in the symbol, not consciously recognized by its proponents.

Some insight on the prophetic aspect of the Assumption can be gained from C. G. Jung who, years before the dogma was proclaimed, wrote:

But since the woman, as well as evil, is excluded from the Deity in the dogma of the Trinity, the element of evil would also form a part of the religious symbol, if the latter should be a quaternity. It needs no particular effort of imagination to guess the far-reaching spiritual consequences of such a development.[30]

Jung was acutely aware of the phenomenon of the extreme dichotomizing of good and evil in the human psyche in Western society. A reflection of this is the concept of the supernatural that I have already described, in which the "good" God requires the existence of a devil. The "devil," of course, is projected upon others. Jung observes that "it is highly moral people, unaware of their other side, who develop peculiar irritability and hellish moods which make them insupportable to their relatives."[31] On a massive scale, he recognized the violent eruption of unacknowledged unconscious forces in the massacre of the Jews in Nazi Germany. He saw that the split requires a healing, for "evil has us in its grip." In his "Late Thoughts" he wrote:

The only ray of light is Pius XII and his dogma. But people do not even know what I am referring to when I say this.[32]

Jung, of course, was referring to the image of Mary (woman) *rising* toward incorporation in the divinity, which for him implied "bringing up" matter and evil.

Essentially, the insight of Jung here is acknowledgment of the destructiveness caused by the degradation of women in the religious imagination. The "ray of hope" that he saw was nowhere to be found in Judaism or Protestantism, for "in the Protestant and Jewish spheres the father continues to dominate as much as ever."[33] While it would be unfortunate and incongruous for radical feminism to espouse a dogmatic Jungian ideology, the insights of Jung on such matters as the dogma of the Assumption are sometimes helpful. Jung, of course, was not free from the biases of patriarchy himself, and his language can reinforce stereotypic thinking. In spite of this, his intuitions and clues deserve careful attention.

The Assumption symbol, as is the case with the Immaculate Conception, presents itself in a context that ensures the subordination of the female. It could hardly be otherwise in an institution so determinedly sexist as Roman Catholicism. Yet, the fact of the double message is not entirely lost upon women, and certainly not upon the most vigorous opponents, both Protestant and Catholic, of such "Marian excesses." Apparently the only group totally immune to insight into its ambivalent character is the official body of Catholic ecclesiastical orthodoxy—and this immunity is very likely only on the level of explicit conscious "rationality." In itself, the image of Mary "rising" says something.[34]

Jung thought that the dogma of the Assumption suggested a kind of "rounding off" of the problematic Trinitarian symbol, so that Mary becomes the "fourth person" of the Trinity. Although this interpretation obviously would be rejected by ecclesiastical proponents of the dogma, Jung is probably right in his belief that symbols have a kind of life of their own. He thought that the Assumption was a hopeful sign of the collective psyche's effort to overcome a shallow and rigid dichotomizing of good and evil. Symbolically and socially, women have been identified with matter, sex, and evil. Jung saw the Assumption as saying No to these assumptions, challenging the false innocence of the God and the godly whose identity depends upon nonidentification with women.

While the Jungian insight concerning the dogma in relation to the Trinitarian symbol is interesting, it leaves us, so to speak, up in the air. For it seems not to take into account the fact that it was the most oppressive and sexist of the Christian churches, at one of the most oppressive times in its history and under one of its most oppressive popes, that presented us with this symbolic solace. The same Pope Pius XII was simultaneously pouring forth voluminous utterances on the rightful place of "woman" in society, that is, having an uncontrollable number of babies and serving her male master in dutiful submission. To this a Jungian would no doubt answer that the Pope's unconscious, which generated the symbol, had a sort of will of its own. That is, the answer would be that the Pope literally did not know what he was saying. I see no reason to disagree with that. However, the analysis needs further development.

The extreme dichotomy between quasi-prophetic symbolic exaltation and social degradation of women by the Roman Catholic church can of course be analyzed in terms of compensation mechanisms —compensation for the women being held down and compensation for a celibate all-male clergy seeking "the spiritual essence" of their undiscovered other halves. However, I think the most important aspect of the phenomenon has to do with the *harnessing* of women's power by this quintessentially hierarchical and sexist institution.[35] Especially in its periods of greatest desperation it has tried to capture female presence and power in a symbol, *using* this to capitivate the psyches of women and men, mesmerizing them, binding them in unquestioning loyalty to itself. For is it not the owner and manipulator of the Marionette that is so attractive to the masses, casting its spell upon them, luring them into the churchly fathers' suffocating embrace?

The embarrassed reluctance of contemporary thinkers of Catholic background to confront the fact and meaning of "Marian excesses"—especially in a Protestant or "ecumenical" environment—is hardly indicative of great progress in courage and insight. In fact, this amounts to failure to confront an extremely important phenomenon, the understanding of which would be profoundly threatening to Christolatrous religion, pointing to a distant past that such religion has never been able to destroy completely, and to a future that may witness its death and burial.

Mary and the Great Mother

Claiming that revelation through the Virgin Mother Mary has come to an end, ceasing to create a revelatory situation, at least for Protestants (and comparing her to Apollo in this regard), Tillich poses the question: How can a real revelation come to an end? His response is that only the idolatrous side is destroyed, and "that which was revelatory in it is preserved as an element in more embracing and more purified revelations . . ."[36] For Tillich, of course, the most embracing revelation is what he calls the "final revelation" which is in the Christ. But the question I must raise is *why* must *that* revelation (or for that matter any particular revelation) be the "final revelation"? What if there has been another manifestation of transcendence whose history preceded the advent of Christianity by many thousands of years, which appeared under different names and forms, which survived in a covert way within Christianity and gave it its power over the human psyche? And what if this now is beginning to come into its own again, foretelling a future of spiritual expansion beyond the scope of the Christian imagination's ability to envisage?

Christians who have been aware of the ancient cults of the Great Mother have been most anxiously insistent that these should not be confused with worship of Mary. Berdyaev wrote:

The cult of the Mother of God, of the Most Holy Virgin, is essentially distinct from the pagan worship of the female principle; it is worship of the womanhood which is entirely illumined and serene, which has achieved victory over the base element in femaleness.[37]

The text is of course interesting for its frank claim that there is a "base element in femaleness"—a point discussed already in the preceding chapter. What is to the point here, however, is the insistence that the "serene" womanhood of Mary has achieved "victory" over this. One may ask what sort of victory the subordinated role of Mary in Christianity can possibly be? The logical conclusion is that the "serenity" of the Mary symbol, since it is always officially submerged in Christianity, has its source in this submersion and subordination that is required to purify the female "element." The victory is that of the male. Many will testify that it is the oatmeal quality of serenity imposed upon Mary in Christianity that has partially blinded them to the significance of the symbol in itself. Even more to the point is Berdyaev's unproved assumption, hardly peculiar to himself, that the cult of the "Mother of God" *is* "essentially distinct" from the "pagan" worship of the Great Mother, which, presumably, contains a base and sinister element, essential to femaleness, that is purified by Christianity.

In regard to the insistence that Mary is essentially distinct from the Great Mother, it should be noted that countless persons have intuited something else. Typical of those who have experienced the amazing discovery of the autonomous power of Mary's image (often in spite of themselves) was Henry Adams, who when traveling in Europe at the turn of the century, observed that the great cathedrals were built not to "God" but to Mary. Admiring their magnificence, he was conscious of the force that created it all.

Symbol or energy, the Virgin had acted as the greatest force the Western world ever felt, and had drawn men's activities to herself more strongly than any other power, natural or supernatural, had ever done.[38]

The identity between the image of Mary (despite all the official attempts to domesticate her) and something more ancient and universal than Christianity need not be left to the realm of "unverifiable" intuition, however. Elizabeth Gould Davis, in her well-documented and ground-breaking book *The First Sex*, writes:

The church seemed doomed to failure, destined to go down to bloody death amidst the bleeding corpses of its victims, when the people discovered Mary. And only when Mary, against the stern decrees of the church, was dug out of the oblivion to which Constantine had assigned her and became identified with the Great Goddess was Christianity finally tolerated by the people. [39]

Davis claims that it was the discovery, attributed to Saint Patrick, that the pagans would accept Christ only if they could have Mary that changed the official policy toward Mary in the church. In the people's minds this was the Great Goddess who, as E. O. James writes, is "of many names but one personality."[40] She has had a power which Davis contrasts with the "artificiality and rootlessness of the Olympian gods, as of the Jewish and Christian God" whose artificiality derives from the fact that they are *"contrived*—deliberately invented by patriarchs to replace the ancient Great Goddess." For Davis, "the only reality in Christianity is Mary, the Female Principle, the ancient goddess re-born."[41]

The Great Silence

The universal and irrational belief that there is a "base element" in femaleness reflects "man's underlying fear and dread of women" to which Karen Horney referred, pointing out that it is remarkable that so little attention is paid to this phenomenon.[42] More and more evidence of this fear, dread, and loathing is being unearthed by feminist scholars every day, revealing a universal misogynism which, in all major cultures in recorded patriarchal history, has permeated the thought of seemingly "'rational" and civilized "great men"—"saints," philosphers, poets, doc-tors, scientists, statesmen, sociologists, revolutionaries, novelists.[43] A quasi-infinite catalog could be compiled of quotes from the male leaders of "civilization" revealing this universal dread—expressed sometimes as loathing, sometimes as belittling ridicule, sometimes as patronizing contempt.

What has not received enough attention, however, is the *silence* about women's history. I do not refer *primarily* to the "Great Silence" concerning the acts of women under patriarchy, the failure to record or even to acknowledge the creative activity of great women and talented women. However, this is extremely significant and should be attended to. A typical case was Thomas More's brilliant daughter, Margaret. Men simply refused to believe that she was the author of her own writings. It was supposed that certainly she could not have done it without the help of a man. There were the women authors (e.g., George Eliot, George Sand, the Brontës) who could only get acceptance for their writings by disguising their sex under the pen name of a man. A reasonably talented woman today need only reflect honestly upon her *own* personal history in order to understand how the dynamics of wiping women out of history operate. Women who give cogent arguments concerning the oppression of women before male audiences repeatedly hear reports that "they were not able to defend their position." Words such as "flip," "slick," or "polemic" are used to describe carefully researched feminist writings. I point to this phenomenon of the wiping out of women's contributions within the context of patriarchal history, because it means that we must consciously develop a new sense of pride and confidence, with full knowledge of these mechanisms and of the fact that *we cannot believe* the history books that tell us implicitly that women are nothing. I point to it also because we have to overcome the hyper-cautiousness (not to be confused with striving for accuracy) that keeps us from strongly affirming our own history and thereby re-creating history.

I refer to the silence about women's historical existence *since* the dawn of patriarchy also because this opens the way to overcoming another "Great Silence," that is, concerning the increasing indications that there was a universally matriarchal world which prevailed before the descent into hierarchical dominion by males. Having experienced the obliterating process in our own histories and having come to recognize its dynamics within patriarchal history (which is pseudo-history to the degree that it has failed to acknowledge women), we have a basis for suspecting that the same dynamics operate to belittle and wipe out arguments for and evidence of the matriarchal period. Erich Fromm wrote:

The violence of the antagonism against the theory of matriarchy arouses the suspicion that it is . . . based on an emotional prejudice against an assumption so foreign to the thinking and feeling of our patriarchal culture. [44]

While of itself such violence of antagonism obviously does not *prove* that the position so despised is correct, the very force of the attacks should arouse suspicions about the source of the opposition. It is important not to become *super*-cautious and hesitant in looking at the evidence offered for ancient matriarchy. It is essential to be aware that we have been conditioned to fear proposing any theory that supports feminism.

The writings supporting the matriarchal theory produced many decades ago are receiving new attention. These early contributions included the works of Bachofen (*Das Mutterrecht*, 1861), Louis Henry Morgan (*Ancient Society*, 1877), Robert Briffault (*The Mothers*, 1927), and Jane Harrison (*Prolegomena to the Study of Greek Religion*, 1903). They point not only to the existence of universal matriarchy, but also to evidence that it was basically a very different kind of society from patriarchal culture, being egalitarian rather than hierarchical and authoritarian. Bachofen claimed that matriarchal culture recognized but one purpose in life: human felicity. The scholarly proponents of the matriarchal theory maintain that this kind of culture was not bent on the conquest of nature or of other human beings. In brief: It was not patriarchy spelled with an "m." This is an important point, since many who are antagonistic to women's liberation ignorantly and unimaginatively insist that the result will be the same kind of society with women "on top." "On top" thinking, imagining, and acting is essentially patriarchal.

Elizabeth Gould Davis points out that recent archaeological discoveries support these early theories to a remarkable extent. She shows that archaeologists have tended to write of their discoveries that women were predominant in each of their places of research as if this must be a unique case. She maintains that "all together these archaeological finds prove that feminine preeminence was a universal, and not a localized, phenomenon."[45] Davis further comments upon detailed reports that have been made on three prehistoric towns in Anatolia: Mersin, Hacilar, and Catal Huyuk. She concludes that "in all of them the message is clear and unequivocal: ancient society was gynocratic and its deity was feminine."[46] There is an accumulation of evidence, then, in support of Bachofen's theory of our gynocentric origins, and for the primary worship of a female deity.

The Second Coming of Women and the Antichrist

The absurd story of Eve's birth is an excellent example of a process that is prevalent in men's treatment of women and their accomplishments throughout the history of patriarchy. I shall simply call this phenomenon *reversal*. In some cases it is blatantly silly, as in this case of insistence that a male was the original mother, and that "God" (a male) revealed this. In other instances it has been pseudo-biological, as in the centuries-long insistence that women are "misbegotten males"—a notion refuted by modern genetic research, which demonstrates that it would be far more accurate to designate the male (produced by a Y chromosome, which is an incomplete X chromosome) as a misbegotten female. Very commonly, it consists simply in stealing women's ideas and assuming credit for them, that is, denial by men that the ideas ever came from their female originators. Many women are aware of this happening in their own lives, and many have consciously allowed it to happen, in the belief that this was the only way of getting acceptance for an idea or a plan, and that the latter was more important than credit for its authorship. I suggest that it is time not only to become conscious of this phenomenon but also to end complicity in its continuance. The *idea and actualization of feminism* is far more important than any idea that could succeed through such self-abnegating and humiliating tactics.

We should also consider the possibility that the reversal phenomenon has taken place in assertions that Christianity "has raised the status of women" and affirmed our "dignity." Women who have attempted to be feminists and at the same time Christians have generally gone along with this, believing that Christianity did advance the cause of women in the past but that it now (oddly) lags behind. However, the record of barbarous cruelty to women in Christendom hardly gives unequivocal support to this kind of apologetic. Christian theology widely asserted that women were inferior, weak, depraved, and vicious. The logical consequences of this opinion were worked out in a brutal set of social arrangements that shortened and crushed the lives of women.[47]

I propose that another form of reversal has been the idea of redemptive incarnation uniquely in the form of a male savior, for, as already indicated, this is precisely what is impossible. A patriarchal divinity or his son is exactly *not* in a position to save us from the horrors of a patriarchal world. Does this mean, then, that the women's movement points to, seeks, or in some way constitutes a *rival* to "the Christ"? On another, but related, level Michelet wrote that the priest has seen in the witch "an enemy, a menacing *rival*."[48] In its depth, because it contains a dynamic that drives beyond Christolatry, the women's movement *does* point to, seek, and constitute the primordial, always present, and future Antichrist. It does this by breaking the Great Silence, raising up female pride, recovering female history, healing and bringing into the open female presence.

I suggest that the mechanism of reversal has been at the root of the idea that the "Antichrist" must be something "evil." What if this is not the case at all? What if the idea has arisen out of the male's unconscious dread that women will rise up and assert the power robbed from us? What if it in fact points to a mode of being and presence that is beyond patriarchy's definitions of good and evil? The Antichrist dreaded by the patriarchs may be the surge of consciousness, the spiritual awakening, that can bring us beyond Christolatry into a fuller stage of conscious participation in the *living* God.

Seen from this perspective the Antichrist and the *Second Coming of women* are synonymous. This Second Coming is not a return of Christ but a new arrival of female presence, once strong and powerful, but enchained since the dawn of patriarchy. Only *this* arrival can liberate the memory of Jesus from enchainment to the role of "mankind's most illustrious scapegoat." The arrival of women means the removal of the primordial victim, "the Other," because of whom "the Son of God had to die." When no longer condemned to the role of "savior," perhaps Jesus can be recognizable as a free man. It is only female pride and self-affirmation that can release the memory of Jesus from its destructive uses and can *free* freedom to be contagious.

The Second Coming, then, means that the prophetic dimension in the symbol of the Great Goddess—later reduced to the "Mother of God"—is the key to salvation from servitude to structures that obstruct human becoming. Symbolically speaking, it is the Virgin who must free and "save" the Son. Anthropologically speaking, it is women who must make the breakthrough that can alter the seemingly doomed course of human evolution. Unlike the so-called "First Coming" of Christian theology, which was an absolutizing of men, the women's revolution is not an absolutizing of women, precisely because it is the *overcoming* of dichotomous sex stereotyping, which is the source of the absolutizing process itself. To the degree that it is true to its ontological dynamics, feminism means refusal to be captured again in a stereotypic symbol. It means the freeing of women and men from the sexist ethos of dichotomizing and hierarchizing that is destroying us all. Far from being a "return" to the past, it implies a qualitative leap toward psychic androgyny. The new arrival of female presence is the necessary catalyst for this leap.

As marginal beings who have no stake in a sexist world, women—if we have the courage to keep our eyes open—have access to the knowledge that neither the Father, nor the Son, nor the Mother *is* God, the Verb who transcends anthropomorphic symbolization. Such knowledge will entail a transvaluation of values undreamed of by Nietzsche or any other prophet whose prophecy was dwarfed by secret dread of the Second Coming. This event, still on its way, will mean the end of phallic morality. Should it not occur, we may witness the end of the human species on this planet.

CHAPTER FOUR

Transvaluation of Values:
The End of Phallic Morality

If the first woman God ever made was strong enough to turn the world upside down, all alone—these together ought to be able to turn it back and get it rightside up again: and they is asking to do it. The men better let 'em.
—SOJOURNER TRUTH (1851)

> *See*
> *That no matter what you have done*
> *I am still here.*
> *And it has made me dangerous, and wise.*
> *And brother,*
> *You cannot whore, perfume, and suppress*
>   *me anymore.*
> *I have my own business in this skin*
> *And on this planet.*
> *—GAIL MURRAY (1970)*

A transvaluation of values can only be accomplished when there is a tension of new needs, and a new set of needy people who feel all old values as painful—although they are not conscious of what is wrong.
—FRIEDRICH NIETZSCHE

In order to understand the potential impact of radical feminism upon phallocentric morality it is important to see the problem of structures of alienation on a wide social scale. Some contemporary social critics of course have seen a need for deep psychic change. Herbert Marcuse, for example, encourages the building of a society in which a new type of human being emerges. He recognizes that unless this transformation takes place, the transition from capitalism to socialism would only mean replacing one form of domination by another. The human being of the future envisaged by Marcuse would have a new sensibility and sensitivity, and would be physiologically incapable of tolerating an ugly, noisy, and polluted universe.[1] Norman O. Brown, recognizing that the problem of human oppression is deeply linked with the prevalence of the phallic personality, quotes King James who in 1603 said: "I am the husband and the whole island is my lawful wife."[2] The statement calls to mind the traditional insistence of ecclesiastics that the church is "the bride of Christ." For Theodore Roszak, such imagery poses a dilemma:

Does social privilege generate the erotic symbolism? Does the erotic symbolism generate social privilege? . . . Politically, it poses the question of how our liberation is to be achieved. How shall we rid ourselves of the king or his dominating surrogates?[3]

The point is not missed by any of these authors that the desired psychic change is related to overcoming sexual alienation. What is lacking is adequate recognition of the key role of women's becoming in the process of human liberation. When this crucial role is understood and experienced, it can be seen that there are ways of grappling with the problems of psychic/social change that are concrete and real. As distinct from the speculations of Marcuse, Brown, and other social philosophers, the analysis developing out of feminism has a compelling power deriving from its concreteness and specificity. It speaks precisely out of and to the experience of the sexually oppressed and has an awakening force that is emotional, intellectual, and moral. It changes the fabric of lives, affecting also the consciousness of the men related to the women whose consciousness it is changing.

The dynamics of the psychic/social revolution of feminism involve a two-fold rejection of patriarchal society's assumptions about "women's role." First, there is a basic rejection of what Alice Rossi calls the pluralist model of sex roles, which involves a rigid "equal but different" ideology and socialization of the sexes.[4] The assumption of such "pluralism" is that there is and should be "complementarity," based not upon individual differences but upon sex stereotyping. Feminists universally see through the fallaciousness and oppressiveness of the "complementarity" theme at least to some degree. However, there are "levels and levels" of perception of this, and permitting oneself to have deep insight is threatening to the self. Thus, it is possible to stop at a rather surface level of denying this stereotypic pluralism, by reducing the problem to one of "equal pay for equal work," or (in the past) acquisition of the right to vote, or passage of the Equal Rights Amendment. In the present wave of feminism, a second and deeper rejection of patriarchal assumptions is widespread. This is rejection of what Rossi calls the "assimilation model." Radical feminists know that "50/50 equality" within patriarchal space is an absurd notion, neither possible nor desirable. The values perpetuated within such space are seen as questionable. When the myth of the eternal feminine is seen through, then the brutalization implied in the eternal masculine also becomes evident. Just as "unveiling" the eternal feminine logically entails revealing the true face of the eternal masculine, the whole process, if carried through to its logical conclusion, involves refusal of uncritical assimilation into structures that depend upon this polarization. The notion of a fifty percent female army, for example, is alien to the basic insights of radical feminism.

Intrinsic to the re-creative potential of the women's movement, then, is a new naming of values as these have been incarnated in society's laws, customs, and arrangements. This means that there will be a renaming of morality which has been false because phallocentric, denying half the species the possibility not only of naming but even of *hearing* our own experience with our own ears.

Hypocrisy of the Traditional Morality

Much of traditional morality in our society appears to be the product of reactions on the part of men—perhaps guilty reactions—to the behavioral excesses of the stereotypic male.[5] There has been a *theoretical* one-sided emphasis upon charity, meekness, obedience, humility, self-abnegation, sacrifice, service. Part of the problem with this moral ideology is that it became accepted not by men but by women, who hardly have been helped by an ethic which reinforces the abject female situation. Of course, oppressed males are forced to act out these qualities in the presence of their "superiors." However, in the presence of females of the oppressed racial or economic class, the mask is dropped. Basically, then, the traditional morality of our culture has been "feminine" in the sense of hypocritically idealizing some of the qualities imposed upon the oppressed.

A basic irony in the phenomenon of this "feminine" ethic of selflessness and sacrificial love is the fact that the qualities that are *really* lived out and valued by those in dominant roles, and esteemed by those in subservient roles, are not overtly held up as values but rather are acted out under pretense of doing something else. Ambitious prelates who have achieved ecclesiastical power have been praised not for their ambition but for "humility." Avaricious and ruthless politicians often speak unctuously of sacrifice, service, and dedication. Not uncommonly such pronouncements are "sincere," for self-deceit is encouraged by a common assumption that the simple fact of having an office proves that the incumbent truly merits it. The Judeo-Christian ethic has tended to support rather than challenge this self-legitimating facticity, by its obsession with obedience and respect for authority. Since the general effect of Christian morality has been to distort the real motivations and values operative in society, it hinders confrontation with the problems of unjust acquisition and use of power and the destructive effects of social conditioning. Since it fails to develop an understanding and respect for the aggressive and creative virtues, it offers no alternative to the hypocrisy-condoning situation fostered by its one-sided and unrealistic ethic.

A mark of the duplicity of this situation is the fact that women, who according to the fables of our culture (the favorable ones, as opposed to those that stress the "evil" side of the stereotype) should be living embodiments of the virtues it extols, are rarely admitted to positions of leadership. It is perhaps partial insight into the inconsistency of this situation that has prompted Christian theologians to justify it not only by the myth of feminine evil but also by finding a kind of tragic flaw in women's natural equipment. Commonly this flaw has been seen as an inherent feebleness of the reasoning power, linked, of course, to emotional instability. Typically, Thomas Aquinas argued that women should be subject to men because "in man the discretion of reason predominates."[6] This denial of rationality in women by Christian theologians has been a basic tactic for confining them to the condition of moral imbecility. Inconsistently, women have been blamed for most of the evil in the world, while at the same time full capacity for moral responsibility has been denied to females.

Feminism Versus the "Feminine" Ethic

While Christian morality has tended to deny responsibility and self-actualization to women by definition, it has also stifled honesty in men. I have pointed out that the pseudo-feminine ethic—which I will also call the passive ethic—conceals the motivations and values that are actually operative in society. While it is true that there has been an emphasis upon some of the aspects of the masculine stereotype, for example, control of emotions by "reason" and the practice of courage in defense of the prevailing political structure or of a powerful ideology (the courage of soldiers and martyrs), these have been tailored to serve mechanisms that oppress, rather than to liberate the self. The passive ethic, then, whether stressing the so-called feminine qualities or the so-called masculine qualities does not challenge exploitativeness but supports it. This kind of morality lowers consciousness so that "sin" is basically equated with an offense against those in power, and the structures of oppression are not recognized as evil.

Feminism has a unique potential for providing the insight needed to undercut the prevailing moral ideology. Striving for freedom involves an awakening process in which layer upon layer of society's deceptiveness is ripped away. The process has its own dynamics: after one piece of deception is seen through the pattern can be recognized elsewhere, again and again. What is equally important, women build up a refusal of self-deception. The support group, which is the cognitive minority going through the same process, gains in its power to correlate information and refute opposing arguments. Nietzsche, the prophet whose prophecy was short-circuited by his own misogynism, wanted to transvaluate Judeo-Christian morality, but in fact it is women who will confront patriarchal morality *as patriarchal*. It is radical feminism that can unveil the "feminine" ethic, revealing it to be a phallic ethic.

Existential Courage and Transvaluation

The Aristotelian theory of moral virtue, which was assumed into Christian theology, centered around the virtue of prudence, the "queen" of the moral virtues. Prudence presumably is "right reason about things to be done," enabling one to judge the right and virtuous course.[7] Since moral virtue was understood as the mean between two extremes, prudence was understood as a virtue in the intellect which enabled one to steer between two opposed vices.

As Sam Keen and others have pointed out, a theory of moral virtue so dominated by the motif of prudence is basically Apollonian. It presupposes a view of human life in which the emotions are considered inferior to "reason," which is at the summit of the hierarchy of human faculties. Aquinas, following Aristotle, believed that prudence involved a kind of practical knowledge by which one was enabled to judge in a particular set of circumstances what would be the best course of action. Since prudential knowledge was understood to be connatural and nonideological, it would seem that there should have been hope for an ethic thus envisaged to be free of subservience to authoritarian structures. However, it did not work out this way. In the opinion of Aquinas and of all "main line" Catholic moralists the prudent person would accept guidance from the moral teachings of the church and attempt to apply these in the given situation. Ecclesiastical ideology, then, did work itself into one's prudential decisions about how to act.[8]

A major difficulty with all of this arises from the fact that the moral teachings designed to guide the Christian in making prudential decisions have to a large extent been the products of technical reason, that is, the capacity for "reasoning" about means for achieving ends, cut off from the aesthetic, intuitive, and practical functions of the mind. As Tillich realized, when the reasoning process about means is cut off from the deep sources of awareness in the human mind (ontological reason), then the ends to which the means are uncritically directed are provided by other nonrational forces external to the self.[9] These may be traditions or authoritarian structures or ideologies that have become so embedded in the psyche that they have rendered themselves invisible. In any case the result is blindness concerning the ends or goals which are actually behind the whole reasoning process and which are motivating the selection of certain premises that will determine the course of the reasoning. These hidden purposes also determine what other data, that is, what other possible premises, will be excluded from consideration in the reasoning process.

It is precisely this unconsciousness of ends and motivations which makes so much of Christian doctrine about morality suspect. While Tillich and others have seen the problem of heteronomy conflicting with autonomy in a general way, it is feminist women who now are gaining insights about *specific* ways in which prudential ethics has lent itself to the service of patriarchal power and about *specific* issues that have been clouded by this. Patriarchal systems demand precisely this: cautious execution of means on the part of those who are in bondage to such systems, without application of the mind's powers to the work of criticizing their purposes. This blotting out of critical power involves a desensitizing to elements in human experience which, if heeded, would challenge the "reasonableness" of the dominant ethic.

Classical and medieval moralists did of course put a great deal of emphasis upon the role of the end or goal in determining the morality of a human act. However, in Christian scholastic ethics especially, the greatest attention was paid to the *ultimate* end of human acts, that is, "eternal happiness." Intermediate ends did not receive the kind of scrutiny that a revolutionary morality requires. The built-in assumption was that these goals should be determined by authority and receive unquestioning assent from subordinates. Such assumptions still dominate a great deal of "modern" ethical theory, as I will show later in this chapter in discussing specific issues. The potential that radical feminism has for breaking their demonic power has its source in the awakening of existential courage in women, which can give rise to a Dionysian feminist ethic.

Although repudiation of the passive and Apollonian ethic of authoritarian religion Is not entirely new, there is a qualitative newness arising from the fact that women are beginning to *live* this repudiation personally, corporately, and politically. Those who have been socialized most profoundly to live out the passive ethic are renouncing it and starting to affirm a style of human existence that has existential courage as its dominant motif.

It may be asked what this qualitative newness means. In what does it consist? Aren't there "situation ethicists" around already challenging the Old Morality? I have already answered this question in part by pointing out that the women's revolution is a *communal* phenomenon. The insights coming from this corporate experience—a collective refusal to be "the Other"—may be expressed in theoretical terms by some individuals. But this theorizing, insofar as it does genuinely express feminist experience, is qualitatively distinct from the individual musings—however erudite and sincere they may be—of male situation ethicists who by definition belong to patriarchy's dominant elite.

Clues to fundamental differences between the Dionysian feminist ethic that is beginning to be lived and spoken about by some women and the "New Morality" of situation ethics can be found in the work of Joseph Fletcher, author of *Situation Ethics*. Fletcher insists upon labeling what he is doing as "Christian situation ethics."[10] One may well ask why the label "Christian" is necessary. What does it add to "situation ethics"? Fletcher himself responds to this question by saying that what makes it different from other moralities is a theological factor, "the faith affirmation that God himself suffered for man's sake to reconcile the world in Christ."[11] This means that, however valuable many of the author's insights may be, there is here a basic affirmation of sacrificial love morality. Fletcher feels constrained to give priority to "the desire to satisfy the neighbor's need, not one's own."[12] As the primordial victims of this kind of unrealistic and destructive moral ideal, women—once consciousness has been liberated—can see that this kind of "New Morality" is very much like the old. It does not move us beyond the good and evil of patriarchy because it does not get us out of the bind of scapegoat psychology. Those who have actually been scapegoats and have said No to being victims any longer are in a position to say No to this modernized Christolatrous morality, in which "love" is always privatized and lacking a specific social context, and in which the structures of oppression are left uncriticized.[13]

Out of this "No" to the morality of victimization, which women share with all the oppressed, comes a "Yes" to an ethic which transcends the most basic role stereotypes, those of masculine/feminine. Janice Raymond points out that this ethic upholds as its ideal "a dynamic metaphysical process of becoming, in which what has been traditionally circumscribed as masculine and feminine is divested of its sex-typing and categorization and is brought together into a new reality of being, a new wholeness of personhood." Far from being "unisex," in the sense of universal sameness, it involves a revolt against standardization.[14] As another feminist writer has pointed out, terms such as "masculinize" or "feminize" would then come to mean a process of warping children to develop only half of their potentialities. In these terms a man of our culture now seen as "masculine" would be seen to have been masculinized, that is, to have lost half of himself.[15]

Before the androgynous world can begin to appear, however (a world in which even the term "androgynous" itself would be rendered meaningless because the word reflects the archaic heritage of psycho-sexual dualism), women will have to assume the burden of castrating the phallic ethic (which "appears" as a feminine ethic or a passive ethic) by calling forth out of our experience a new naming in the realm of morality. To do this it will be necessary to understand the dynamics of the false naming in the realm of ethics that has been encased in patriarchy's definitions of good and evil. In order to illustrate these prevalent mechanisms I will examine their operation in relation to a specific problem that has been debated endlessly by male ethicists: the problem of abortion.

Abortion and the Powerlessness of Women

In panels and discussions on religion and abortion I have frequently cited the following set of statistics: one hundred percent of the bishops who oppose the repeal of anti-abortion laws are men and one hundred percent of the people who have abortions are women. These thoroughly researched "statistics" have the double advantage of being both irrefutable and entertaining, thereby placing the speaker in an enviable situation vis-à-vis the audience. More important than this, however, is the fact that this simple juxtaposition of data suggests something of the context in which positions and arguments concerning the morality of abortion and the repeal of anti-abortion laws should be understood. To be comprehended adequately, they must be seen within the context of sexually hierarchical society. It is less than realistic, for example, to ignore the evidence suggesting that within Roman Catholicism the "official" opposition to the repeal of anti-abortion laws is profoundly interconnected —on the level of motivations, basic assumptions, and style of argumentation—with positions on other issues. Such interconnected issues include birth control, divorce, the subordination of women in marriage and in convents, and the exclusion of women from the ranks of the clergy. The fact that all of the major ethical studies of the abortion problem, both Catholic and Protestant, have been done by men is itself symptomatic of women's oppressed condition.

Since the condition of sexual caste has been camouflaged so successfully by sex-role segregation, it has been difficult to perceive anti-abortion laws and anti-abortion ethical arguments within this context. Yet it is only by perceiving them within this total environment of patriarchal bias that it is possible to assess realistically how they function in society.

If, for example, one-sided arguments using such loaded terminology as "the *murder* of the unborn *child*" are viewed as independent units of thought unrelated to the kind of society in which they were formulated, then they may well appear plausible and cogent. However, once the fact of sexual caste and its implications have been unveiled, such arguments and the laws they attempt to justify can be recognized as consistent with the rationalizations of a system that oppresses women but incongruous with the experience and needs of women.

A number of male-authored essays on abortion that have appeared recently in liberal publications have been praised for their "clarity" and "objectivity." Yet in many cases, I suggest, such articles give the illusion of clarity precisely because they concentrate upon some selected facts or data while leaving out of consideration the assumptions, attitudes, stereotypes, customs, and arrangements which make up the fabric of the world in which the problem of abortion arises. Moreover, upon closer examination, their "objectivity" can be seen as the detachment of an external judge who first, does not share or comprehend the experience of the women whose lives are deeply involved and second, has by reason of his privileged situation within the sexual caste system a built-in vested interest opposed to the interest of those most immediately concerned.

Illustrative of this problem is an article by Professor George Huntston Williams of Harvard, in which he proposes as model for the politics of abortion a "sacred condominium" in which the progenitors and the body politic "share sovereignty in varying degrees and in varying circumstances." As he develops his thesis, it becomes evident that the woman's judgment is submerged in the condominium, and that the theory's pretentions to offer reasonable solutions are belied by the realities of sexual politics in the society in which we actually live. Basically, Professor Williams' theory ignores the fact that since men and women are not social equals, the representatives of the male-dominated "body politic" cannot be assumed to judge without bias. It also overlooks the fact that the "progenitors" do not have equal roles in the entire reproductive process, since it is obviously the woman who has the burden of pregnancy and since under prevailing social conditions the task of upbringing is left chiefly and sometimes solely to the woman. It disregards the fact that the male sometimes deserts his wife or companion (or threatens desertion) in a situation of unwanted pregnancy.

The inadequacies of Professor Williams' approach are evident in his treatment of the problem of abortion in the case of rape. He writes:

Society's role . . . would be limited to ascertaining the validity of the charge of rape. Here the principals in the condominium could be at odds in assessing the case and require specialized arbitration. If this were the case, the medical and legal professions could be called upon together with that of social work. But even if rape is demonstrable [emphasis mine] *the mother may surely assent to the continuance of the misplaced life within her. . . .*[16]

What is left out in this eloquent, multisyllabic, and seemingly rational discussion? First, it does not take into consideration the bias of a society which is male-controlled and serves male interests. Second (and implied in the first point), it leaves out the fact that it is very difficult to prove rape. In New York State, for example, for many years corroborating evidence has been required to convict a man of rape. In some states, if the man accused of rape was known previously by the woman, this fact can be used in his defense. According to the laws of many states, it is impossible for a man to rape his wife. Moreover, women who have been raped and who have attempted to report the crime to the police frequently have reported that the police treated them with ridicule and contempt, insinuating that they must have worn provocative clothing or invited the attack in some way. Little or no attention is given to the fact that rapists often force their victims into disgusting and perverted acts, under threat of death. The whole mechanism of "blaming the victim" thus works against women, adding to the trauma and suffering already endured. Nor are the police alone in taking this view of the situation. Their judgment reflects the same basic attitude of sexist society which is given physical expression in the rapist's act.[17]

The kind of spiritual counseling that women frequently receive within the "sacred condominium" is exemplified in an article by Fr. Bernard Häring. Writing of the woman who has been raped, he says:

We must, however, try to motivate her [emphasis his] *to consider the child with love because of its subjective innocence, and to bear it in suffering through to birth, whereupon she may consider her* enforced maternal obligation fulfilled [emphasis mine] *and may give over the*

*child to a religious or governmental agency, after which she would try
to resume her life with the sanctity that she will undoubtedly have
achieved through the great sacrifice and suffering.*[18]

Fr. Häring adds that if she has already "yielded to the violent temptation" to rid herself of the effects of her experience, "we can leave
the judgment of the degree of her sin to a merciful God." Those who
are familiar with "spiritual counseling" have some idea of what could
be implied in the expression "try to motivate her." Despite Fr. Häring's
intention to be compassionate, his solution is not adequate. The paternalistic and intimidating atmosphere of "spiritual counseling" is not
generally conducive to free and responsible decision-making, and can
indeed result in "enforced maternal obligation." The author does not
perceive the irony of his argument, which is visible only when one sees
the environment of the woman's predicament. She lives in a world in
which not only the rapist but frequently also the priest view her as an
object to be manipulated—in one case physically, and in the other case
psychologically. *Machismo* religion, in which only men do spiritual
counseling, asks her to endure a double violation, adding the rape of
her mind to that of her body. As Mrs. Robinson of the once popular hit
song knew: "Every way you look at it, you lose."

Feminist ethics—yet to be developed because women have yet to
be free enough to think out our *own* experience—will differ from all of
this in that it will refuse to give attention merely to the isolated physical
act involved in abortion, and will insist upon seeing this within its social
context. Christian moralists generally have paid attention to context
when dealing with such problems as killing in self-defense and in war.
They have found it possible to admit the existence of a "just war" within
which the concept of "murder" generally does not apply, and have per-
mitted killing in self-defense and in the case of capital punishment. They
have allowed to pass unheeded the fact that by social indifference a
large proportion of the earth's population is left to die of starvation in
childhood. All of these situations are viewed as at least more complex
than murder. Yet when the question of abortion is raised, frequently it
is only the isolated material act that is brought into focus. The traditional
maxim that circumstances affect the morality of an action is all but forgotten or else rendered nonoperative through a myopic view of the circumstances. Feminists perceive the fact of exceptional reasoning in the

case of abortion as related to the general situation. They ask the obviously significant (but frequently overlooked) question: Just *who* is doing the reasoning and *who* is forced to bear unwanted children?

Feminist ethics will see a different and more complex human meaning in the act of abortion. Rather than judging universally in fixed categories of "right" and wrong" it will be inclined to make graded evaluations of choices in such complex situations as those in which the question of abortion concretely arises. It will attempt to help women to orchestrate the various elements that come into play in the situation, including the needs of the woman as a person, the rights of women as an oppressed class, the requirements of the species in adapting to changing conditions, such as over-population, the positive obligations of the woman as the mother of other children or as a professional, the negative aspects of her situation in a society which rewards the production of unwanted children with shame and poverty. It will take into consideration the fact that since the completely safe and adequate means of birth control does not yet exist, women are at the mercy of our reproductive systems.

At this moment in history the abortion issue has become a focal point for dramatic conflict between the ethic of patriarchal authoritarianism and the ethic of courage to confront ambiguity. When concrete decisions have to be made concerning whether or not to have an abortion, a complex web of circumstances demands consideration. There are no adequate textbook answers. Essentially women are saying that because there is ambiguity surrounding the whole question and because sexually hierarchical society is stacked against women, abortion is not appropriately a matter of criminal law. In our society as it is, no laws can cover the situation justly. Abortion "reform" generally works out in a discriminatory way and is not an effective deterrent to illegal abortions. Thousands of women who have felt desperate enough to resort to criminal abortions have been subjected to psychological and physical barbarities, sometimes resulting in death. The emerging feminist ethic has as its primary emphasis not self-abnegation but self-affirmation in community with others. The kind of suffering that it values is that which is endured in acting to overcome an oppressive situation rather than that which accompanies abject submission to such a situation.

Some of the essentially unjust mechanisms operative in the arguments of phallic ethicists on abortion have already been illustrated in the passages from Williams and Häring. These include arguing out of the hidden false assumptions that women and men have equal roles in the entire reproductive process, that women and men have an equal voice in the "body politic," that women have completely free choice in the matter of sexual behavior and its consequences, that women have an adequately safe means of birth control, and that passive acceptance of suffering in the victim's role is the better choice.

There are also other devices. Among these is the domino theory or "wedge argument": If the fetus can be destroyed, who will be the next victim? Professor Ralph Potter writes:

When a fetus is aborted no one asks for whom the bell tolls. No bell is tolled. But do not feel indifferent and secure. The fetus symbolizes you and me and our tenuous hold upon a future here at the mercy of our fellow men.[19]

To this argument Jean MacRae has appropriately responded that if no bell tolls for the fetus perhaps this is because the death of the fetus is significantly different from that of a more actualized human being. She also makes another observation that is very much to the point, namely that the question of abortion has to do with a *unique* struggle between two living beings, for it is only in the case of unwanted pregnancy that the *body* and the whole well-being of a person is controlled by another being.[20]

Yet another device is what we might call "the unanswerable argument." This consists in posing such a question as: "When does human life begin?" Since no unanimous response is forthcoming, the conclusion drawn is that women with unwanted pregnancies must passively submit to the situation until they can produce the impossible answer. Still another tactic is that employed by John Noonan in asserting that the moral condemnation of abortion has been an almost absolute value in history.[21] The question that is unasked is: Whose history? The fact that history written by men has ignored the historical experience of women is not taken into account. Indeed it is clear that even within Christian societies multitudes of women have by their actions repudiated the assumption that the life of the fetus is an absolute value. The argument that all or most of these women have suffered great guilt feelings is first of all false as an alleged statement of fact, and second it is dishonest in not recognizing that even if such guilt feelings exist in some cases, they may be explained by social conditioning.[22] Moreover, there are societies in which abortion is accepted without question by both women and men.[23]

As the movement for the repeal of anti-abortion laws began to gain momentum in the United States it became evident that a situation of open warfare was developing between the upholders of religious and civil patriarchal power and feminism in this country. This has a tragic aspect, since fixation upon the abortion issue represents neither the epitome of *feminist consciousness* nor the peak of *religious consciousness*.

As for *feminist consciousness*: abortion is hardly the "final triumph" envisaged by all or the final stage of the revolution. There are deep questions beneath and beyond this, such as: Why should women be in situations of unwanted pregnancy at all? Some women see abortion as a necessary measure for themselves but no one sees it as the fulfillment of her greatest dreams. Many would see abortion as a humiliating procedure. Even the abortifacient pills, when perfected, can be seen as a protective measure, a means to an end, but hardly as the total embodiment of liberation. Few if any feminists are deceived in this matter, although male proponents of the repeal of abortion laws tend often to be shortsighted in this respect, confusing the feminist revolution with the sexual revolution.[24] I will discuss this confusion later in this chapter.

In regard to *religious consciousness*, surely lobbying to prevent the repeal of unjust laws cannot be its highest manifestation. A community that is the expression of authentic spiritual consciousness, that is, a living, healing, prophetic religious community, would not cut off the possibility for women to make free and courageous decisions, either by lobbying to prevent the repeal of anti-abortion laws or by psychological manipulation. It would try to *hear* what women are saying and to support demands for the repeal of unjust laws. Women did not arbitrarily choose abortion as part of the feminist platform. It has arisen out of the realities of the situation. On its deepest level, the issue is not as different from the issue of birth control as many, particularly liberal Catholics, would make it appear. There are deep questions involved which touch the very meaning of human existence. Are we going to let "nature" take its course or take the decision into our own hands? In the latter case, who will decide? What the women's movement is saying is that decisions will be made affecting the processes of "nature," and that women as individuals will make the decisions in matters most intimately concerning ourselves. I think that this, on the deepest level, is what authoritarian religion fears. Surely its greatest fear is not the destruction of life, as its record on other issues reveals.

As Lawrence Lader has shown, the lobbying power employed by the Catholic church against abortion has been tremendous. It has available vast economic resources—untaxed funds used for propagandizing, despite the illegality of using tax-free money for campaigning. Lader refers to it as the most powerful tax-deductible lobby in history. It has used the Catholic school system and such organizations as the Knights of Columbus to channel opposition against abortion law repeal. Lader points out that it has made political alliances—pointing specifically to the alliance between Richard Nixon and Cardinal Cooke of New York on the issue. Among the instruments used by the church in this religious war has been language. There has been a planned and concerted tactic on the part of the hierarchy to use inflammatory language such as "murder" rather than "abortion," and "child" rather than "fetus," and to make the sort of odious comparisons that call to mind the massacre of the Jews by the Nazis.[25] A predictable effect of such activity, when it is seen in combination with other sexist policies, is a relocation of women's spiritual energy outside the domain of hierarchical established religion.

If by a kind of reductionism one could imagine the essential goal of feminism to be the repeal of anti-abortion laws, the struggle might be simplified to the dimensions of women's liberation versus the official Catholic church. Then it might appear that liberal Protestantism would offer an alternative channel for female religious activity. However, since feminism cannot be reduced to an isolated "issue," and since the very issue of abortion is revelatory of the fact that feminism is not merely an issue but rather a new mode of being, it is becoming more and more clear to feminist consciousness that the faded authoritarianism of the liberal churches is hardly more acceptable to free women than the pomp and power of the more obvious enemy. For a community really expressive of authentic religious consciousness would coincide with the women's movement in pointing beyond abortion to more fundamental solutions, working toward the development of a social context in which the problem of abortion would be unlikely to arise. As catalyst for social change, it would foster research into adequate and safe means of birth control. As educative force, it would make available information about the better means now in existence, for example, vasectomy. Most fundamentally, as a prophetic and healing community it would work to eradicate sex role socialization and the sexual caste system itself, which in many ways works toward the entrapment of women in situations of being burdened with unwanted pregnancies. I think it should be clear that authentic religion would point beyond abortion, not by instilling fear and guilt, but by inspiring the kind of personal, social, and technological creativity that can, in the long run, make abortion a nonproblem.

Patriarchal power structures, whether civil or ecclesiastical, of course do not operate in this humanizing way. The blindness induced by them is revealed in the incongruous and biased statements of those who serve them—many of whom are in highly responsible positions and are "well-educated." A Massachusetts legislator argued that "those who play must pay." Richard Nixon stated:

Further, unrestricted abortion policies, or abortion on demand, I cannot square with my personal belief in the sanctity of human life—including the life of the yet unborn.[26]

Writing in the Boston *Globe*, a physician made comparisons between abortion and the German mass murders of Jews.[27] Similar comparisons have been made by Brent Bozell of the Catholic *Triumph* magazine. A poignant response to this comparison was made by Regina Barshak, a Jewish woman who as a teenager was incarcerated in Auschwitz and then became the sole survivor of a large, mass-murdered family. Ms. Barshak wrote of the "callous exploitation of these ignoble events." In temperate terms she reminded readers of the differences between "a safe medical procedure on fertilized zygotes and, on the other hand, the deliberate sadism performed upon fully formed bodies and souls of active, fully conscious, loving human beings." She pointed out that the voices of the prestigious Vatican leaders were not heard "on behalf of these tortured lives."[28]

The Most Unholy Trinity: Rape, Genocide, and War

The first dimension of what I have baptized as The Most Unholy Trinity is rape. It is clear that there has always been a connection between the mentality of rape and the phenomenon of war, although there is much unseeing of this connection when the war is perceived as "just." An example within recent times was the horrible treatment of the women of Bangladesh. Many horrendous stories came out at the time of the civil war between East and West Pakistan, but scant reference was made to "the heartbreaking reports that as many as 200,000 Bengali women, victims of rape by West Pakistani soldiers, had been abandoned by their husbands, because no Moslem will live with a wife who has been touched by another man."[29] Joyce Goldman, a writer who discovered such a reference buried in a postwar "return to normality" article, decided that if male reporters would not investigate, she would attempt to do so. The experience of reading her account is unforgettable. A Pakistani officer is quoted as saying: "We used the girls until they died." Many of the women imprisoned in barracks (to be used by soldiers as "cigarette machines," as one government official described it), tried to commit suicide. Goldman cites reports of a town named Camilla, near Dacca, where women were raped and then thrown from the rooftops like rubbish. "One eight-year-old girl who was found too child-small for the soldiers' purposes was slit to accommodate them, and raped until she died."[30] Goldman points to the obvious cruel irony in the fact that these victims were then abandoned by their husbands as unclean, which is an obvious corollary of looking upon women as objects and possessions, for then they must have only one possessor. Most significantly she shows that the concept of a raped woman as damaged is only a morbid exaggeration of "our" own attitudes, for the women of Bangladesh have suffered "collectively, exaggeratedly what individual women in this and other 'advanced' countries know from their own experience."[31]

One way of unseeing this is to protest that it happened in another culture, in a Moslem country. Readers who react in this way should be interested in an article that appeared in the New York Times, November 19, 1972 (L, p. 47). The item reports the death of a seven-year-old girl who, together with her nine-year-old sister, was lured by three teenaged boys to the roof of a South Bronx tenement by a promise of pizza. The younger girl was raped and thrown off the roof to her death. The older sister was sexually molested but escaped. Police described her as "hysterical." Most of the rest of the same page of the New York Times was occupied by an enormous advertisement for the Saks Fifth Avenue Men's Store. The ad is a picture of three very cock-sure males in stylish sport clothes accompanied by three bulldogs. The words of the ad:

There is something about an S.F.A. man. You can spot him anywhere. . . . Even his idlest comments are eminently commanding. . . .

It does not require too surrealistic a leap of the imagination to associate the three "eminently commanding" males and their three bulldogs with the three teenaged males who raped the seven-year-old girl and threw her to her death. After all, the latter, too, were "eminently commanding." In a rapist culture, this quality expresses itself in a variety of ways.

"Informed" Christians and Jews may protest that rape and brutality are alien to our own heritage. The reader, then, should refer to biblical passages which tell a different story, namely that there is precedent for looking upon women as spoils of war. In the Book of Numbers, Moses, after the campaign against Midian, is described as enraged against the commanders of the army for having spared the lives of all the women:

So kill all the male children. Kill also all the women who have slept with a man. Spare the lives only of the young girls who have not slept with a man, and take them for yourselves. (Numbers 31:17–18)

The story continues:

Moses and Eleazar the priest did as Yahweh had ordered Moses. The spoils, the remainder of the booty captured by the soldiers, came to six hundred and seventy-five thousand head of small stock, seventy-two thousand head of cattle, sixty-one thousand donkeys, and in persons, women who had never slept with a man, thirty-two thousand in all. (Numbers 31:31–35)

In Deuteronomy, the advice given to the Hebrews is that when they go to war and Yahweh delivers the enemy into their power, they may choose a wife from among them.

Should she cease to please you, you will let her go where she wishes, not selling her for money: you are not to make any profit out of her, since you have had the use of her. (Deuteronomy 21:14)

Even outside the context of war (if such a context is imaginable in a patriarchal world), the value placed upon women in the Old Testament is illustrated in the story of the crime of the men of Gibeah. A man who was giving hospitality to a Levite and his concubine was having dinner with them. Scoundrels came to the house demanding to have the guest, in order to abuse him. The response of the host was to offer them his daughter as substitute for the guest. The devoted father is reported to have said:

Here is my daughter; she is a virgin; I will give her to you. Possess her, do what you please with her, but do not commit such an infamy against this man. (Judges 19:24)

Since the visitors refused this offer, the guest gallantly offered them his concubine as a replacement for himself. They raped her all night and she died. Tastefully the guest, when he had returned home with her, cut her into twelve pieces and sent these around Israel with a message about the crime. The text offers no negative judgment upon the host or his guest. The crime was seen as an offense against men, not against their female property.

The second dimension of The Most Unholy Trinity is genocide. It should require no great imaginative leap to perceive a deep relationship between the mentality of rape and genocide. The socialization of male sexual violence in our culture forms the basis for corporate and military interests to train a vicious military force. It would be a mistake to think that rape is reducible to the physical act of a few men who are rapists. This ignores the existence of the countless armchair rapists who vicariously enjoy the act through reading pornography or news stories about it. It also overlooks the fact that all men have their power enhanced by rape, since this instills in women a need for protection. Rape is a way of life. Since this is the case, police do not feel obliged to "believe" women who report rape. Typical of police attitudes was the statement of Police Captain Vincent O'Connell of Providence, Rhode Island, concerning women who attempt to report rape: "We are very skeptical when we first interview them. We feel there's a tendency for women not to tell the truth."[32]

The politics of domination are everywhere. E. Ionesco wrote:

*The world of the concentration camps . . . was not an exceptionally
monstrous society. What we saw there was the image, and in a sense
the quintessence, of the infernal society into which we are plunged
every day.*[33]

This "everyday world" is fundamentally a world of sexual dominance
and violation.

The logical extension of the mentality of rape is the objectification
of all who can be cast into the role of victims of violence. Rape is the
primordial act of violation but it is more than an individual act. It is expressive of a basic alienation within the psyche and of structures of alienation
within society. Rape is an act of group against group: male against
female. As I have pointed out, it is also an act of male against male,
in which the latter is attacked by the pollution of his property. Rape
is expressive of group-think, and group-think is at the core of racial prejudice whose logical conclusion and final solution is genocide.

Writing of Vietnam, Paul Mayer pointed out that the United States
is conducting the same kind of genocide against the Indochinese as
the Nazis once ordered against European Jewry. "The method has
changed from the gas chambers of Auschwitz to those crematoria that
rain burning death and terror from the skies, particularly on civilians."[34]
Mr. Mayer's dismay that American Catholics and Jews do not see the
parallel appears to spring from his not seeing the fundamental patriarchal
character of these traditions. The record of the church in Nazi Germany
is well known. Guenter Lewy writes:

*When thousands of German anti-Nazis were tortured to death in Hitler's
concentration camps, when the Polish intelligentsia was slaughtered,
when hundreds of thousands of Russians died as a result of being
treated as Slavic Untermenschen, and when 6,000,000 human beings
were murdered for being "non-Aryan," Catholic Church officials in Germany bolstered the regime perpetrating these crimes.*[35]

With characteristic insight, Lewy points out that the hold of the church
upon the faithful is precarious and that this prevents it from risking confrontation with a state that tramples upon human dignity and freedom.
Lewy asserts that the situation is worsened when the clergy are infected

with an alien creed. I would point out that the creed of totalitarian governments is not at all that "alien." As Lewy himself notes, theologians such as Michael Schmaus and Joseph Lortz saw basic similarities between the Nazi and the Catholic *Weltanschauung*.[36] At any rate, whether one wishes to call the affinity an infection or a recognition of some dimension of secret sameness, the alliance of hierarchical Catholicism with the demonic forces is a familiar pattern.

In the 1960s and '70s, rather than acknowledge the genocidal policies of the United States in Southeast Asia, the American Catholic bishops turned the full force of their concern to the protection of fetuses. Feeble efforts have been made to answer the objections to this obsessive and exclusive identification with fetuses by inserting timid and vague laudatory remarks about "peace." When plans for the "Respect Life Week" (read: fetal life) held in October 1972 were beginning to be formulated, the body of American bishops rejected a proposal to link the Vietnam war to abortion. A 32-page handbook was put together for the October "Respect Life Week," in which the only mention of the war in Indochina was a scant bibliographical reference. Questioned about this, Msgr. James McHugh explained that "it was decided to keep the presentation brief and let the people fill in the specifics."[37]

Catholic silence about the genocidal war is appalling to Catholic pacifists such as Gordon Zahn. What does not seem to occur to men of such unquestionable integrity as Professor Zahn is the idea that "Catholic pacifism" may involve a contradiction in terms. Significantly, Professor Zahn himself holds the position that abortion is immoral even in the case of rape.[38] A more differentiated perspective would perhaps allow him to consider the possibility that there is a logical link between the willingness to impose upon a woman the effects of rape, that is, unwanted pregnancy, and silence about and even open support of the rape of Indochina.

Silence in the face of genocide or open support of this is hardly foreign to Protestant Christianity. In Nazi Germany, there was the Nazi-approved National Church, or *Reich* church, coopted by Hitler. This fact is not obliterated by the compensatory fact that there existed also the "Confessing Church," which refused to cooperate with the Nazis, nor is it wiped out by the lives of Protestant heroes such as Dietrich Bonhoeffer, who was hanged by the Nazis.[39] For that matter, there were also Catholic heroes and martyrs such as Franz Jägerstätter, the peasant who was beheaded, and Alfred Delp, a priest killed by the Nazis. The fact is that the United States, at the peak of its genocidal mania, was a predominantly Protestant nation. Nor should it be forgotten that Christianity, Catholic and Protestant, has deep roots in the Judaic tradition, in which the people of Yahweh were able to see themselves as different from "the Other"—the worshippers of "false gods." If, then, many American Jews have allowed themselves not to see the parallels between American genocide and Auschwitz, this phenomenon is not totally contradictory, for the mentality of rape is also embedded in the Hebrew tradition itself.

The third dimension of The Most Unholy Trinity is war. Theodore Roszak writes of "the full and hideous flowering of the politics of masculine dominance" which from the late nineteenth to the mid-twentieth centuries became more candid than ever before.[40] Such diverse figures as Teddy Roosevelt, General Homer Lea, Patrick Pearse, and the Spanish political philosopher Juan Donoso-Cortés agreed in associating war with "the manly and adventurous virtues" and the civilized horror of war with loss of manhood.[41] This masculine metaphysical madness was lived out in Nazism and Fascism. It is being lived out today to an even greater extent, but the language of violence has become disguised, mathematized, and computerized. There are occasional linguistic lapses that are gross enough to make tragic absurdity visible, as when a military officer made the famous statement that it was necessary to destroy a (Vietnamese) village in order to save it. Such lapses briefly jolt the consciences of a few, but the majority, drugged by the perpetual presence of the politics of rape on the TV screen, sees it all but sees nothing. The horrors of a phallocentric world have simultaneously become more visible and more invisible.

The translation of metaphysical madness into mathematics is illustrated in the writings of Paul Ramsey, a noted ethicist, who calmly defends the thesis "that counterforce nuclear war is the upper limit of rational, politically purposive military action."[42] Ramsey deplores the fact that "so far public opinion in this country seems to ignore the difference between 25 million dead as the probable result of all-out counterforce warfare and 215 million dead as a result of all-out countercity warfare between the great powers."[43] For him, this is not merely a quantitative but a "qualitative moral distinction." Significantly, this megadeath ethicist claims to be articulating "the principles effective in Christian conscience in regard to participation in war."[44] Significantly also, the same ethicist asserts that he is one of those "who believe that morally abortion is, or sometimes is, a species of the sin of murder."[45]

It is clear that not all Christian ethicists so markedly illustrate the peculiarities of phallic morality as Ramsey, whose cerebral verbalizations accurately reflect the myopia of the hierarchical ethos. However, more complex and thus dimmer reflections are to be found in the writings of moralists recognized as sane, urbane, and humane, for example, James Gustafson, who writes:

As the morally conscientious soldier fighting in a particular war is convinced that life can and ought to be taken, "justly" but also "mournfully," so the moralist can be convinced that the life of the defenseless fetus can be taken, less justly, *but* more mournfully [*emphasis mine*].[46]

The comparison is misleading, disproportionate, and—some might say—grotesque. Translated into blunt terms, his message is that abortion (though sometimes permissible) is a more serious aberration than war, and that fetuses are more to be mourned than adult human beings.

It is important to be attuned to the simplicity behind the stage setting of complexity in the war games defended by phallic morality. Governor Ronald Reagan, speaking at one of the 1972 one-thousand-dollars-a-plate Nixon campaign dinners, was reported to have said: "When you go to a John Wayne movie, when you buy the ticket, you know he's going to clobber the bad guy, but it's pretty exciting."[47] This kind of unseeing appears incredible to those with at least one eye still partly open. A kind of insight into the mechanism that produces this incredible phenomenon may be gleaned from a statement of legal philosopher Edmond Cahn, who, when writing in the context of analyzing a legal problem, asserted: "It is characteristic of the male, when an incident or event is sufficiently disagreeable, to pretend that in point of fact it never actually happened."[48] While this statement in itself could be misused as identifying some innate characteristic of "all males as such"—a device obviously to be excluded—it does say something about the phallic mentality into which the dominant elite in our world have been socialized. Reflection upon this mechanism of "pretending that it never happened" would perhaps be helpful to such sincere religious thinkers as Paul Mayer who expressed his pain at the fact of sizable Catholic and Jewish support for the reelection of Nixon, seeing a bitter contradiction in the fact that these two communities now were standing "at the side of the man who is overseeing the obliteration of the people and the land of Vietnam."[49] I would point to two dimensions of unseeing that are at work here: first, there is failure on the part of these religious groups to admit that this obliteration has in fact been taking place in Vietnam; second, there is failure on the part of those who bemoan such unseeing to recognize that the alleged "bitter contradiction" between the stance of members of these religious groups and their traditions is not so totally contradictory after all. If religious pacifists were less unseeing of the Christian past, even its relatively recent past in Nazi Germany—knowledge of which is surely available—they perhaps would not see the presence of Cardinal Krol on the presidential yacht and in Miami blessing the Republican convention as wholly out of keeping with "tradition."

The Most Unholy Trinity of Rape, Genocide, and War is a logical expression of phallocentric power. These are structures of alienation that are self-perpetuating, eternally breeding further estrangement. The circle of destruction generated by the Most Unholy Trinity and reflected in the Unwhole Trinitarian symbol of Christianity will be broken when women, who are by patriarchal definition objects of rape, externalize and internalize a new self-definition whose compelling power is rooted in the power of being. The casting out of the demonic Trinities *is* female becoming.[50]

The Women's Revolution and the "Sexual Revolution"

Female becoming is *not* the so-called "sexual revolution." The latter has in fact been one more extension of the politics of rape, a New Morality of false liberation foisted upon women, who have been told to be free to be what women have always been, sex objects. The difference is simply that there is now social pressure for women to be available to any male at the beckon of a once-over, to be a nonprofessional whore. The Old Morality was an ethic of the double standard. The New Morality has not essentially changed this, for male behavior and attitudes toward women have not changed in any basic way. The social context is still one in which women are without power, without outlets for or encouragement to the higher levels of creativity.

Women's liberation is profoundly antithetical to the "sexual revolution," and the second wave of feminism was energized into being largely because of the profound realization of betrayal that the "sexual revolution" engendered. This realization, which many women have shared, has been expressed by Anselma Dell'Olio:

Men have poured their creative energies into work; we have poured ours into love, and an unequal social and sexual relationship was the inevitable result. And because this was the situation the Sexual Revolution failed to correct, feminists are moving into an area they have won by default.[51]

Women have been trapped once again into dissipating energies that should be used creatively, raising our individual and collective self-esteem.

The sexual freedom that recently has been forced upon women leaves no freedom to refuse to be defined by sex. As feminist theoretician Dana Densmore has put it:

Sex is everywhere. It's forced down our throats. It's the great sop that keeps us in our place. The big lift that makes our dreary worlds interesting.[52]

In a spirit of perceptive irony, Densmore continues:

Spiritual freedom, intellectual freedom, freedom from invasions of privacy and the insults of degrading stereotypes—these are appropriate only to men, who care about such things and can appreciate them. . . . For such a creature [woman] to presume upon the territory of transcendence is horrifying, unthinkable, polluting the high, pure realms of the will and spirit, where we rise above *the flesh.*[53]

The draining of women's energies by obsession with genital sexuality, then, is a currently popular form of rape. Instead of being physically violated, women are given the privilege of giving literally everything away. This is the rape of mind and will that robs the female self of precious time, energy, and self-esteem. It is civilized technocracy's equivalent of what happened and essentially keeps happening to the women of Bangladesh.

Herbert Marcuse, studying technocracy under the regime of affluence, sees the root of psychic exploitation in repressive desublimation.

Desublimated sexuality, within a social context that cuts off the fuller possibilities of individual and communal human becoming, reinforces the status quo, keeping people "happy" with truncated, unrebellious existence. Our society limits the scope and need for sublimation. Sex is "free" (but also expensive) and the deep dynamic toward transcendence is under social control. Marcuse writes:

Institutionalized desublimation thus appears to be an aspect of the "conquest of transcendence" achieved by the one-dimensional society. Just as this society tends to reduce and even absorb opposition (the qualitative difference!) in the realm of politics and higher culture, so it does in the instinctual sphere. The result is the atrophy of the mental organs for grasping the contradictions and the alternatives. . . .[54]

Obviously Marcuse sees both men and women as caught in this web of one-dimensional existence, as indeed they are. I am proposing that women have the power of opposition to this reductionism. Women have been victimized both by false sublimation to the pedestal of do-nothingness and also by repressive desublimation as the quintessential victims—as sex objects who live only for the pleasure of being used by all men. The system will not work if women use our power to exorcise it by refusing both of these false identities. Self-actualizing women, who have reclaimed our precious energies both from the inane wastage of vicarious living and from the trap of obsessive fixation upon genital activity, are one "factor" that cannot be absorbed by the one-dimensional society. To recognize this is already to have the beginnings of knowledge that is beyond the inane and impotent "good" and self-destructive "evil" that characterize every option allowed to us by the phallic ethos. The women's revolution, then, is a sexual revolution in a genuine sense of recapturing the energy that has been wrested from us by sexual politics, including the politics of the male-centered "sexual revolution."

Heterosexuality-Homosexuality: The Destructive Dichotomy

Radical feminists are fundamentally agreed in the advocacy of total elimination of sex roles. As Anne Koedt points out:

Basic to the position of radical feminism is the concept that biology is not destiny, and that male and female roles are learned—indeed that they are male political constructs that serve to ensure power and status for men.[55]

The logical conclusion of this is that "the biological male is the oppressor not by virtue of his male biology but by virtue of his rationalizing supremacy on the basis of that biological difference."[56]

Radical feminism cannot be simply equated with the gay movement. One problem is that lesbians, as well as male homosexuals, frequently assume sex roles. The only difference from "normal" heterosexual role playing then becomes the fact that the parts are assumed by the "wrong" sex. Such standardization of persons into roles is antithetical to radical feminism, which is concerned with overturning the sex role system. Lesbians may also be radical feminists, but the fact of choosing women rather than men as sexual partners does not *of itself* necessarily challenge sexist society in an effective way, any more than choosing men as sex partners necessarily supports sexist society.

The categories of heterosexuality and homosexuality are patriarchal classifications. Because men in our society have been socialized to be destructive in their relationships with women, some women have come to the conclusion that authentic personal relationships with men under prevailing conditions are extremely difficult and perhaps impossible. However, doctrinaire insistence upon exclusive homosexuality fails precisely because it is not radical enough, for, as Anne Koedt shows, it lends support to the notion that it *does* matter what the sex of your partner may be.[57] At the same time, it would be unrealistic to abstract ourselves from the present historical situation. As Phyllis Chesler points out: "At this moment in history only women can (if they will) support the entry or re-entry of women into the human race."[58] Women in groups are repeatedly asking whether, given our conditioning as women, we can ever wage a feminist revolution as long as we are psychosexually bound to men. There are no easy answers to such a question. It is important to repudiate the old dogmas concerning sexual behavior and it is also important to avoid setting up new ones.

Male fear and hostility regarding "homosexuality" reflects anxiety over losing power that is based upon sex role stereotyping. The feminist transvaluation of values involves refusing to ascribe to such categorizations the validity that has falsely been bestowed upon them. By its sex role stereotyping, phallic morality has created the "problem" of homosexuality, which prevents us from seeing that two people of the same sex may relate authentically to each other. Having created the pseudo-problem, it also uses the label as a scare term to intimidate those who even appear to deviate from the norms dictated by role psychology, even when no genital activity is involved. As the authors of an article on lesbianism have pointed out:

Affixing the label lesbian not only to a woman who aspires to be a person, but also to any situation of real love, real solidarity, real primacy among women, is a primary form of divisiveness among women: it is the condition which keeps women within the confines of the feminine role. . . .[59]

The label, then, is an instrument of social control. Terrified, many women have modified behavior and even repressed genuine feelings of love (sexual or not) toward other women when this weapon has been brandished against them. The point should be not merely to deny that one is a lesbian, in the sense of withdrawing oneself from a category which remains uncriticized, or on the other hand merely to defiantly box oneself into this category, but rather to criticize and exorcise the label itself, which in fact makes sense only within the mad world of phallic categories.

On the level of an abstract semantic exercise, the process of exorcism is simple. It means taking such a term as "homosexual" out of the context of negative value judgments and allowing it to mean a deep and intimate relationship with a person of the same sex, with or without genital activity.[60] A value-free definition of "heterosexual" would be parallel to this. It should be clear that if value judgments are to be made about the relationship, these arise not from biological identity but from the quality of the relationship. If this much is seen, it also becomes obvious that the terms "homosexual" and "heterosexual" are irrelevant to the qualitative evaluation of a relationship.

Such a process is simple, of course, only on the level of "pure" logic. In fact the words "homosexual" and "lesbian" are burdened with a demonic archaic heritage of negative images. In a nonsexist society, in which sexual expression would not be classified according to stereotypic standards, the categories of homosexuality and heterosexuality would be unimportant. However, the archaic heritage will not be dispelled merely by one-dimensional refusal of sexist society's rules solely in the area of sexual behavior. They have to be perceived in the wide setting of patriarchal patterns of estrangement, which have ramifications in a vast array of problems, from the common experience of economic discrimination to the relatively rare but significant problem of transsexualism.[61] An effective refusal of the estrangement spawned by sexism will mean that we avoid fixating our attention upon one particular manifestation of it to the exclusion of others.

The Most Holy and Whole Trinity:
Power, Justice, and Love

Tillich has rightly shown that "all problems of love, power, and justice drive us to an ontological analysis."[62] What his analysis leaves out is the essential fact that division by socialization into sex roles divides the human psyche itself, so that love cut off from power and justice is pseudo-love, power isolated from love and justice is inauthentic power of dominance, and justice is a meaningless façade of legalism split off from love and real power of being. Without a perception of the demonic divisiveness of sex role socialization, an "ontological" analysis of these problems remains hopelessly sterile and removed from the concrete conditions of existence. It is not really ontological.

Given this multiple dividedness, "love " is restricted to the private sphere. The theory of the "two kingdoms," according to which "love" holds a prominent place in the private order whereas power reigns in the political order, has been a common idea in Lutheran theology. Expressed in other "language systems" than that of the "two kingdoms," this is a common idea in our whole culture. The idea that these realities can be separated and still be real is, of course, a mirage. Women's movement theorists have shown that "the personal is political," that the power structures get into the fabric of one's psyche and personal relationships: this is "sexual politics." Power split off from love makes an obscenity out of what we call love, forcing us unwillingly to destroy ourselves and each other. R. D. Laing has given us a terrible insight into the destructiveness of this privatized love which is ultimately public, reflecting the alienated consciousness shared by all. He writes of the menace to those trying to break out of alienated consciousness coming precisely from those who "love" them:

And because they are humane, and concerned, and even love us, and are very frightened, they will try to cure us, They may succeed. But there is still hope that they will fail.[63]

When extended outside the sphere of familial and personal relationships the "love" that serves patriarchal power sometimes is the impotent do-gooder quality that is conveyed by such expressions as "charity bazaar" or "charity case." Sometimes it is the mask of absolute violence, as in the case of the American "love" for the people of South Vietnam who are being "protected."

Genuine love, which is not blindly manipulable by political power of domination, seeks to overcome such power by healing the divided self. Sexist society maintains its grasp over the psyche by keeping it divided against itself. Through stereotyping it harnesses the power of human becoming. It is commonly perceived that on the deepest ontological level love is a striving toward unity, but the implications of this unity have not been understood by the philosophers of patriarchy. It means the becoming of new human beings, brought forth out of the unharnessed energy of psychically androgynous women, whose primary concern is not giving birth to others but to ourselves.

A qualitatively different understanding of justice also emerges when the peculiar rigidities of the stereotypic male no longer dominate the scene. Tillich has written of transforming or creative justice, which goes beyond calculating in fixed proportions. Unfortunately, he tries to uphold the idea that "the religious symbol for this is the kingdom of God."[64] I suggest that as long as we are under the shadow of a *kingdom*, real or symbolic, there will be no creative justice. The transforming and creative element in justice has been intuited and dimly expressed by the term "equity." Aristotle defined this as a correction of law where it is defective owing to its universality."[65] What this leaves out is the dynamic and changing quality of justice which does not presuppose that there are fixed and universal essences, but which is open to new data of experience.

The falsely universal and static quality of patriarchal thought which allows no breakthrough beyond "equity" reaches the ultimate state of sclerotic rigidity when the subject under consideration is the female half of the species. An example of this sclerosis which has prevented anything like creative justice in relation to women from emerging in Christian thought is the approach of renowned theologian Helmut Thielicke who, in his *The Ethics of Sex*, writes:

It is, so to speak, the "vocation" of the woman to be lover, companion, and mother. And even the unmarried woman fulfills her calling in accord with the essential image of herself only when these fundamental characteristics, which are designed for wifehood and motherhood, undergo a sublimating transformation, but still remain discernible. . . .[66]

Further on, Thielicke gets even worse, opining that "woman" is oriented monogamously because she is profoundly stamped by the sexual encounter, insisting that she is marked by the first man who "possesses" her:

One must go even further and say that even the first meeting with this first man possesses the faculty of engraving and marking the woman's being, that it has, as it were, the character of a <u>monos</u> *and thus tends toward monogamy.*[67]

For Thielicke, clearly, the male is God in relation to women. His language betrays him at every step. He claims that numerous psychopathological symptoms are "determined" by this "structure" of feminine sexuality. A woman's "frigidity" as well as the "vampire insatiability of the strumpet" are traced to her first sexual encounter. Creative justice, which could break through this dualistic sort of ethics, is not likely to come from those whose status benefits so totally from stereotypic rigidity.

The sterility and rigidity of noncreative justice that classifies and remains closed to change is reflected not only in ethics but also in legal systems as well as in the attitudes of those who interpret the law. Patriarchal rigidity expressed in law, moreover, carries over from women to other disadvantaged groups (and it is important to remember that over fifty percent of all of these segments of humanity—for example, blacks, the Third World—are women). Gunnar Myrdal, in his famous Appendix Five of *An American Dilemma*, wrote:

In the earlier common law, women and children were placed under the jurisdiction of the paternal power. When a legal status had to be found for the imported Negro servants in the seventeenth century, the nearest and most natural analogy was the status of women and children.[68]

Myrdal cites George Fitzhugh, who in his *Sociology for the South* (1854) categorizes together wives, apprentices, lunatics, and idiots, asserting that a man's wife and children are his slaves.

As marginal beings whose authentic personal interest is not served by the rigidities of patriarchal power, women have the potential to see through these. Some men have seen this, of course, but the tendency has been to capture the insight into stereotypes which reinforce the separation of love and justice and therefore support the demonic usages of political power. This can be seen in the cliche: "Man is the head, woman is the heart." At least one renowned legal authority, however, tried (very timidly) to suggest the possibility of overcoming the dichotomy by bringing more women into the legal profession. Justice Jerome Frank suggested that there might be a connection between the inflexibility of the Roman legal system and the fact that the power of the father (*patria potestas*) was a dominant characteristic of Roman society. He points out that in Greek society, in which the power of the father had diminished, the legal system was more flexible:

I suggest that it is barely possible that, as a result, the role of the mother emerged as an influence on Greek legal attitudes, so that equity, greater lenience, more attention to "circumstances that alter cases" in the application of rules, became an accepted legal ideal.[69]

Although Frank had tendencies to be both apologetic and stereotypic in his exposition of his opinion that women could bring flexibility into the legal system, his view is hardly totally bereft of insight. In support of it, he cited Henry Adams' passages about the role of Mary in the twelfth and thirteenth centuries. Adams saw Mary as functioning symbolically as the only court of equity capable of overruling strict law (symbolized in the Trinity):

*The mother alone was human, imperfect, and could love. . . . The
Mother alone could represent whatever was not Unity; whatever was
irregular, exceptional, <u>outlawed</u> [emphasis mine]; and this was the
whole human race. . . .*[70]

The church has harnessed (but not succeeded in destroying) this
power of diversity, irregularity, and exceptionality by standardizing it into
its bland and monolithic image of Mary. It has captured this power of
diversity and imprisoned it in a symbol. The real diversity and *insight*
into diversity is in existing rebellious women, whose awareness of power
of being is emerging in refusal to be cast into a mold. The primordial
experiencers of powerlessness and victims of phallic injustice, fixed in
the role of practitioners of servile and impotent "love," having been
aroused from our numbness, have something to say about the Most
Holy and Whole Trinity of Power, Justice, and Love.[71] Grounded in
ontological unity this Trinity can overcome Rape, Genocide, and
their offspring, the Unholy Spirit of War, which together they spirate
in mutual hate.

Women are beginning to be able to say this because of our con-
spiracy—our breathing together. It is being said with individuality and
diversity, in the manner of *outlaws* —which is exactly what radical feminists are. It is being said in the diverse words of our lives, which are
just now being spoken.

CHAPTER FIVE

The Bonds of Freedom:
Sisterhood as Antichurch

A woman must never be free of subjugation.
        —THE HINDU CODE OF MANU, V

I thank thee, O Lord, that thou has not created me a woman.
        —DAILY ORTHODOX JEWISH PRAYER

Creator of the heavens and the earth, He has given you wives from among yourselves to multiply you, and cattle male and female. Nothing can be compared with Him.
        —HOLY KORAN OF ISLAM

Wives, submit yourselves unto your husbands . . . for the husband is the head of the wife, even as Christ is the head of the church.
        —EPHESIANS 5:23–24

Religion legitimates so effectively because it relates the precarious reality constructions of empirical societies with ultimate reality.
        —PETER BERGER, IN THE SACRED CANOPY

As the victims of a planetary caste system whose very existence has been made invisible to us, women have been divided from each other by pseudo-identification with groupings which are androcentric and male-dominated. Among these are the various religions whose ideologies degrade and mystify women to such an extent that even the fact of this degradation is not perceived by its victims.

Despite deception, women are breaking through to awareness of sexual caste as a universal phenomenon. As women revolt against this, a new sense of reality is emerging. That is, a counterworld to patriarchy is coming into being which is by the same token counter to religion *as patriarchal*. Sisterhood, then, by being the unique bonding of women against our reduction to low caste is Antichurch. It is the evolution of a social reality that undercuts the credibility of sexist religion to the degree that it undermines sexism itself. Even without conscious attention to the church, sisterhood is in conflict with it. There are, of course, other movements in contemporary society that threaten organized religion. In the case of other movements, however, it is not sexism that is directly under attack. The development of sisterhood is a unique threat, for it is directed against the basic social and psychic model of hierarchy and domination upon which authoritarian religion *as authoritarian* depends for survival. This conflict arises directly from the fact that women are beginning to overcome the divided self and divisions from each other.

Aside from the general way in which the movement, simply by its own dynamics, conflicts with sexist religion by setting up a counterworld to it, there is also a more specific and direct opposition developing to the sexism of the churches. This is related to the fact that some of the movement's leading figures as well as an increasing number of its adherents are women who know personally the experience of authoritarian religious conditioning and the experience of breaking through this. Many now recall in amazement their past acceptance of the exclusion of half the human race from priesthood and ministry as if this were "natural." As long as the mask of role segregation was effective, it was possible to believe firmly that no inequality was involved: men and women were just "different." Women were able to accept the fact that any boy was allowed to serve Mass, whereas a woman with a Ph.D. was absolutely excluded from such a function. They could go through marriage ceremonies in which they promised to "obey" their husbands without reciprocal promises from men, and still think that no inequality was involved: they were "subordinate but not inferior." Now that the implications of role segregation in the wider society have received exposure in the media, however, inevitably more women, even the unradicalized, are seeing through the mystifications of religious sexism and our own resistance to consciousness. These women—whatever may be their relationship now to organized religion—are spiritual expatriates, and they bring to the movement intimate and precise knowledge of religion's role in reinforcing sexual caste, focusing criticism precisely upon it. In a particular way, they constitute sisterhood as Antichurch.

The Prevailing Sense of Reality and the Nonbeing of Women

The history of our foremothers has not been recorded. I have already pointed to the fact that women have been wiped out of history. It is important to reinforce our consciousness of this fact, because the prevailing usages of political power are working in every way to blot out such consciousness. Sometimes the existence of this blotting-out mechanism is blatantly admitted. The very fact that men can do this with impunity—as they can with pride assert "I am a male chauvinist" but not "I am a racist"—indicates certitude of male power and female powerlessness.[1] An example of the twofold phenomenon of both reducing women's achievements and publicizing the admission of reducing these can be seen in relation to an undersea study of endurance of aquanauts. It was reported that the observers—all males—had some thoughts about why the women aquanauts outperformed their male counterparts. One excuse given was that screening procedures were more rigorous for the women. In giving this "reason," Dr. William G. Prescott even exposed the built-in bias of the general situation further by adding that this rigor was due to the fact that there were only a few positions available for women. One might ask *why* there were not as many positions open to women as to men. Another excuse that was given for female success on the mission was that there was more publicity about them. "They were really on the spot."[2] Again, this invites the question: Why were they alone on the spot? What does it say about our society that only a small quota of women are allowed to compete in such an experiment, that they are then "on the spot," and that their very success is then attributed to, that is, blamed on, these limitations?

Another example on an entirely different level of this "blotting-out" phenomenon was what was for decades the best kept secret in the history of biology—the fact that initially all mammalian embryos are females. No conscious efforts were made to conceal this finding, yet it has been stubbornly ignored. Since the androcentric theory of women's origin from the male reigns over the popular consciousness, no data really make any difference. The data and their implications are in effect *erased*, so that, as Lester Frank Ward stated, "scarcely any number of facts opposed to such a world view can shake it."

On the level of scholarship, erasing women is the name of the game. I have already referred to the trivialization of the work of proponents of the matriarchal theory. Ludovici comments upon this:

Scholars imprisoned in the patriarchal prejudices of the Zeitgeist *used the oldest trick in the game to repel invasion by the revolutionary theories of both Bachofen and of Morgan. They simply ignored the two protagonists of matriarchy.*[3]

The same treatment was accorded to Robert Briffault's *The Mothers*, a work of a million and a half words published in 1927. To quote Ludovici again:

Scholars resented passionately a theory which would encourage the deracination of our patriarchal culture and the depreciation of its religious values.[4]

What is the most effective response that women, recognizing this process of erasure, can make to the structures that function in such a way? The sociologists of patriarchy have given us a clue, unwittingly. Peter Berger speaks of three processes involved in world-building: *Externalization* is the ongoing outpouring of human being into the world, both in the physical and the mental activity of "men" [sic]. *Objectivation* is the attainment by the products of this activity of a facticity that then confronts the original producers as realities outside themselves. *Internalization* is the reappropriation by "men" [sic] of this same reality, transforming it into structures of the subjective consciousness.[5] Thus spake Peter Berger. The fact is, as one woman acutely pointed out, that under the conditions of patriarchy, it is indeed *men* who do the externalizing, in which case Berger is correct. However, it is women who are conditioned to be the internalizers *par excellence*, a point which the noted sociologist passes over.[6] Realizing this fact, women have a clue to an essential dynamic involved in uprooting the prevailing sense of reality. This is to expel what has been internalized, to recognize that such structures are in some sense less real than our own dreams. Women who have experienced the draining of creativity involved in battling these ghosts *as if they were more real than our own selves* have some sense of how counterproductive such a twisting of energies can be.

The experience itself of battling political power with political non-power—which is all we have in that realm—is revelatory. The techniques of men who have worked themselves into positions of power—whether in civil government, churches, businesses, educational institutions, or in any of the cultural analogues of these—are many-faceted, but by and large they are reducible to the mechanism of "divide and conquer." One of the elements in the "divide and conquer" syndrome is paternalism. Since women have been conditioned to distrust each other and rely upon men with power for support, there is a susceptibility to paternalistic affective tyranny that is omnipresent and subtle. While younger men are also vulnerable in this way, the bonding phenomenon among males promises future deliverance. Recognition of this difference —perhaps not fully conscious—is reflected in behavior on the part of both sexes. In women, one notices "accommodation attitudes," that is, a self-abnegating and flattering manner that is almost "second nature."[7] Conditioning to such accommodation attitudes is intensified by such customs as nonreciprocal first naming, common even when the boss (Mr. Jones, Father Jones, Professor Jones, or Doctor Jones) is thirty years of age and the secretary, who is sixty, is called "Sally." A similar custom is reference by "the boss" to "Sally" as "the girl" in the office. A young male "executive assistant" doing essentially the same work as Sally, for a much higher salary, is of course not referred to as a "boy." Another behavioral difference between men and women, whether the former are in the position of boss or subordinate to each other, is body language. Men assume the initiation of personal touch, the prerogative of undignified postures. Men give nonverbal cues signaling status above women, even when the former still occupy junior or lowly situations on the totem pole. Paternalism toward males—unless they are disadvantaged males by reason of race or some other handicap—is the attitude of a father toward a youngster who will some day grow up. In the case of women, future adulthood is not envisaged.

Another mechanism in the "divide and conquer" battery of weapons is confusion of issues by using women's illusory identification with the categories and ideologies of the male-run culture to keep female bonding from being effective. Among church women, Protestants are persuaded that they do not have the same problems as Catholic women. Among university women, faculty women are separated from faculty wives, from secretaries, students, and female administrators, and within these groups there are further divisions arising from other considerations such as grades and status (female professor as opposed to female instructor, or wife of professor as opposed to wife of instructor, etc.) which are irrelevant to the common condition and problems of women.

Since, then, the experience of battling power structures head-on invites an intensification of this kind of division of women against each other, many are coming to reexamine the problem of where to focus energy. I have just pointed out that there is a species of delusion involved in battling the objectified products of male externalization processes as if these were solid realities—not products, but immutable "nature." A central problem is to get to recognition of our own internalization of such soul-shrinking products and move toward externalizing our own being in objective social reality. This is another way of saying that the creation of new space involves facing nothingness and discovering power of being.

Does this mean that there is no value in struggling on the level of political power? Such a conclusion would be simplistic. I would suggest that the point is *to avoid unrealistic expectations* concerning the outcome. The point is not to negate the value of the tremendous efforts made by women to obtain justice for women within sexist institutions. An outstanding example of such a concerted effort has been the work of the St. Joan's International Alliance, the organization of Catholic feminists that for decades has struggled to obtain justice for women in the wider society as well as within the Church. The courageous efforts of religious activists such as Frances McGillicuddy (President of the American branch of Saint Joan's) and of Dr. Elizabeth Farians (founder of several organizations, including NOW's National Task Force on Women and Religion) have not transformed structures but they have not been wasted. The consciousness of women has been changed immeasurably because of their work.[8]

The process of "fighting," then, has value as an educative and radicalizing activity, but there is a healthy cynicism that comes with recognition that a place in sexist space is not the goal. Women who have repeatedly gone through such processes as struggling to obtain a woman faculty member only to discover that the fruit of endless efforts is the selection of a docile token by male administrators, chosen mainly because of her nonfeminist consciousness and "safe" behavior, have learned something about the need to create being *on the boundary* of patriarchal space. In fighting "within" such space, we should allow it only the minimal degree of power over our expenditure of energies that will serve our own purposes. As a cognitive minority, our war is on a deeper level. It is with the prevailing sense of reality, according to which we must be relegated to nonbeing. Our self-recovery, in part, depends upon our refusal to take *this* "reality" too seriously. To put this in another way, we have to learn to live *now* the future we are fighting for, rather than compromising in vain hope of a future that is always deferred, always unreal. This creative leap implies a kind of recklessness born out of the death of false hope.

Antiworld: Antichurch

To live in this new world is to be creating an Antiworld, by renaming the cosmos. To some it might appear to be a sort of trivialization to call this Antichurch, reducing the phenomenon to contradiction of only one cultural institution. However, this is to forget the power that religion has over the human psyche, linking the unsteady reality of social constructs (objectivations) to ultimate reality through myth. It would be naïve to think that religion in this sense has lost all of its power. The use of religion by both presidential candidates in the 1972 United States election bordered on the grotesque, suggesting that American civil religion has been carried through to the ultimate caricature of the battle between principalities and powers. To affirm that sisterhood is Antichurch is not to speak on the level of denominational quarrels but on the level of a profound struggle within the human psyche trying to free itself from destructive social forces. It is to say we are dealing with powerful symbols that invade our beings from all sides, from the most banal television commercial or textbook, to the doctor's office, to a billboard with a three-dimensional figure of a local political candidate, telling voters to "put your faith in him." All say one thing: that to be human is to be male is to be the Son of God.

What is involved, then, is a religious struggle, and this is so because the conflict is on the level of being versus nonbeing. The affirmation of being by women is a religious affirmation, confronting the archaic heritage of projections that deny our humanity. However, since the conflict is more on the level of creation than of struggle for equal ground in sexist space, the term Antichurch must be understood in a positive way. It is the bringing forth into the world of New Being, which by its very coming annihilates the credibility of myths contrived to support the structures of alienation.

Antichurch and Antichrist

Analyzing medieval Catholicism, Troeltsch wrote:

The Church means the eternal existence of the God-Man: it is the extension of the Incarnation, the objective organization of miraculous power, from which . . . subjective results will appear quite naturally.[9]

Moreover, "in spite of all individual inadequacy the institution remains holy and divine."[10] Just as the incompetencies of the ascendent group count for nothing as evidence that the system is wrong, so too the brilliant "exceptions" within the subordinate group offer no substantial challenge. The system has been closed to new information.

The image of the church as the "bride of Christ" is another way of conveying that it is "the extension of the Incarnation," since a bride or wife in patriarchy is merely an extension of her husband. The potency of this image derives from the notion of the divinity of Jesus, for authority figures can derive credibility from the belief that they are representing the God-Man. The pope, who has been called "the vicar of Christ on earth," and the ecclesiastical hierarchy of Catholicism as distinguished from the laity, participate in this identification.

It has been argued, of course, that unlike the harsh patriarchates of pre-Christian culture, this system was construed as a patriarchalism of love. In regard to the family, for example, Troeltsch claims that "in this respect all that Christianity did was to modify from within this idea of male domination by its teaching about love and good will." It stressed *voluntary* submission. Authority and subordination were to continue as before, he maintains, "although with important and increasing security for the individual personality of women, children, and servants."[11] Such claims are so common that we tend to accept them as "true" without question. However, they leave out of account certain disturbing facts such as the barbarities of "good" Christians toward women, children, and servants that have been sanctioned by the church.[12] Such claims also leave out of account the fact that under Christianity the will to autonomy in women and other "lesser beings" has been stifled in a double way: feelings of fear have been reinforced by feelings of guilt. The alleged "voluntariness" of the imposed submission in Christian patriarchy has turned women against ourselves more deeply than ever, disguising and reinforcing the internalization process. As the Virgin-Mother Mary was alleged to have said: "Let it be done unto me according to *Thy* word."

There is a bond, then, between the significance of the women's revolution as Antichrist and its import as Antichurch. Seen in the positive perspective in which I have presented it, as a spiritual uprising that can bring us beyond sexist myths, the Antichrist has a natural correlative in the coming of the Antichurch, which is a communal uprising against the social extensions of the male Incarnation myth, as this has been objectified in the structures of political power. In order to see the relationship between the Second Coming of female presence not only as Antichrist but also as Antichurch, it will be helpful to consider some aspects of the relationship between myth and ritual.

Reinforcement of Myth Through Cult

Sociologists have perceived well enough the connections between myths and ritual. Durkheim observed:

If the myth were withdrawn from religion, it would be necessary to withdraw the rite also; for the rites are generally addressed to definite personalities . . . and they vary according to the manner in which these personalities are conceived.[13]

Durkheim points out that the cult rendered to a divinity depends upon the character attributed to him [sic], and the myth determines this character. He adds that "very frequently, the rite is nothing more than the myth put into action."[14] If this is the case, then clearly a rejection of Christolatrous symbols in the rising woman-consciousness has an organic consequence in the rejection of sexist rituals. Although one might be tempted to see this as a simple logical consequence, a reduction of the process to "logic" would be utterly naïve. Berger has pointed out that the sacred cosmos provides the "ultimate shield against the terror of anomy."[15] To be in the position of confronting the Christocentric cosmos that shields many from facing "the terror of anomy" is to be exposed to the wrath of those who fear their own latent madness and therefore will inflict madness upon those who threaten their fragile "sanity." To assert this is not to be hyperbolic but rather to make an understatement. Robin Morgan expressed this realization in her poem "Monster":

> Oh, mother I am tired and sick.
> One sister, new to this pain called feminist consciousness
> For want of a scream to name it, asked me last week
> "But how do you stop from going crazy?"
> No way, my sister.
> No way.
> This is a pore war, I thought once, on acid.[16]

Berger, quite unaware that he is describing precisely the spiritual dimension of feminist consciousness as it converges to form Antichurch, writes:

To be in a "right" relationship with the sacred cosmos is to be protected against the nightmare threats of chaos. To fall out of such a "right" relationship is to be abandoned on the edge of the abyss of meaninglessness.[17]

Berger continues to describe powerfully the horrible danger that one may lose all connection with the sacred and be swallowed up by chaos. "All the nomic constructions are designed to keep this terror at bay." Mircea Eliade graphically records human efforts to ward off this terror.[18]

The women's revolution as Antichurch represents this terror of chaos and says it will no longer be kept at bay. It rejects not only the myths of patriarchy but their externalization in ritual. This makes it more threatening than an abstract "intellectual" discussion about "myth and all that." One reason why it is threatening is that religious ritual maintains a continuum between the present and the religious tradition. It is essentially *a memory*. Sexist ritual is a false memory, placing present experience in the context of a history that is in fact a deadly fiction, a pernicious lie. The Antichurch dimension of women's liberation *reveals* that this expression of social memory is a lie. To use Berger again:

Men [sic] forget. They must, therefore, be reminded over and over again. . . . Religious ritual has been a crucial instrument of this process of "reminding."[19]

Nietzsche said more than he realized when he wrote of this process:

Whenever man [sic] has thought it necessary to create a memory for himself [sic] his effort has been attended with torture, blood, sacrifice.[20]

Antichurch means saying "No" to these "reminders."

The import of this "No" to the rituals that externalize the *machismo* myth may be gleaned from facing the fact that males have always marched to war amid blessings and prayers. The presence of military chaplains saying Mass and holding other religious services for "the boys" engaged in the business of killing those on "the other side" speaks for itself.[21] Females and males have been put to death amid rites and incantations. Thus violence is made to appear "sane." It is legitimated and made part of the social reality that is considered part of the normal scheme of things. To persons in whom the effects of socialization so overwhelm critical judgment that their sense of reality is co-extensive with the world legitimated by religious myth and ritual, the "reasonableness" of even the most bizarre and violent events thus legitimated seems unquestionable. Such persons will fearfully resist the "No" of the women's movement as Antichurch to such legitimations. Others, who wield ideological and political power and understand how to manipulate such fears will also resist this "No" by *using* religion and other instruments of social control. Such instruments include the myth and institutions of "mental illness."

In the past, this control was exercised by the execution of heretics. In the present, well, as Robin Morgan puts it in her poem "Monster":

> *I gripped the arms of my seat more than once*
> *to stop my getting up and screaming to the entire planeload*
> *of human beings what was torturing us all—stopped*
> *because I knew they'd take me for a crazy, an incipient*
> *hijacker perhaps, and wrestle me down until Bellevue*
>   *Hospital*
> *could receive me at our landing in New York.*[22]

The worshippers of the Yahweh of patriarchy, as they come to realize the potential of this Antichurch to bring about the transference of consciousness into another world, can be expected to use all the tools of violence at their command. For the social reality that they attempt to link with "Ultimate Reality" is precarious, and the danger of anomy or of "conversion" is a threat that lurks always behind the irrational dogmatism of the High Priests of war. The need for ritual *"reminders"* itself betrays the precariousness of the shields against anomy which these High Priests, both ecclesiastical and civil, wish to keep erect.

Ritual and Repressive Satisfaction

Marcuse wrote:

All liberation depends on the consciousness of servitude, and the emergence of this consciousness is always hampered by the predominance of needs and satisfactions which, to a great extent, have become the individual's own.[23]

Marcuse is here writing of false needs, that is, those "which perpetuate toil, aggressiveness, misery, and injustice."[24] Although his intent and context clearly were not precisely the same as those reflected in this book, there is a coincidence of insights. The rituals of patriarchy *do* create false needs, such as the need to lean on father-figures instead of finding strength in the self, or the need for compulsive "self-sacrifice" because one is brainwashed into thinking that one is sinful and "unworthy."

They then respond to these needs by granting a transitory euphoria of unhappiness. This is repressive satisfaction. To let Marcuse speak again:

The most effective and enduring form of warfare against liberation is the implanting of material and intellectual needs that perpetuate obsolete forms of the struggle for existence. [25]

The women's revolution, just by being ourselves, declares that such needs are not our true needs and such satisfaction is not satisfying. Saying this comes from the depths of feminists' new awareness. Once it is seen and said, we do not need "reminders" because it is the word of our very being that is spoken. We may become confused, lonely, despairing, or mad, but we cannot really "forget." This is because our revolution means life against death. It is not "losing oneself" for a cause, but living for oneself and therefore also living a cause. Because such consciousness is not contrived, its dawning marks a change and the mark is indelible. One of the women who walked out of Harvard Memorial Church in the 1971 Exodus wrote:

What made the Memorial Church Exodus different [from skulking out the side door and feeling guilty for leaving], what made it possible, was the realization that the Church that does belong to me and to my experience is the exodus community of women and men who are prepared to get on with the business of living—living up to our potential, living in relationship, living creatively. [26]

As the same woman remarked over one year later: "It was once and for all. We don't need to walk out of churches over and over again." That is the point. The satisfaction of actively participating in being is real and not repressive. As another woman wrote of the same experience:

As I left, I looked at the different faces in the pews—and kept on smiling. I saw leaving women I knew, old women, middle-aged women, their children, husbands, young women, all kinds and sorts of people. I knew that we were leaving to do whatever we had to do to become persons. [27]

Because this nonrepressive satisfaction is rooted in being, it in itself is not fragile but enduring. Not needing the inane "reminding" by ritual that reinforces false consciousness, it is creative and spontaneous. Women have not walked out of Memorial Church again, but have found other expressions suitable to new situations that arise. Feminist consciousness of being, then, is anti-ritual, because it is so deep.

"Feminist Liturgy": A Square Circle?

A woman who proposed as her project for a course on "The Women's Revolution and Theological Development" an attempt to create a "Women's Liturgy," wrote a twelve-page journal recording her thought process as she tried to work this out. The description of the thought process is in the form of a day by day diary and shows her increasing skepticism of the possibility of a "Women's Liturgy." The problems as they evolved in her consciousness included distrust of anything rigidly structured; unwillingness to do research on "liturgies," which would suggest a mold into which to cast women's experience; dislike of appealing to the old liturgies of patriarchy for legitimation, since these reek of hierarchy; fear of failure in trying to do something completely new, which would be a vehicle rather than a product, so that women would be carried forward.[28]

All of these problems strike deep chords in women who are struggling with the tensions between remembrance of the past and experience of the present which contradicts our old beliefs. Probably the most striking reflection in this woman's journal was that just as antiracist, antiwar services never really seemed to change the racist and warlike beliefs of the participating Christians, so a feminist liturgy would change nothing, for "the *form* was *theirs*." It was the "form" that counted, no matter what the "content." The form was a dead shell, and the growth of the consciousness of women is an attempt to live without such shells. The result of her efforts was the creation of an *event*, a combination of readings and songs expressing anger, change, self-assertion and sisterhood—an event not to be repeated, but the story of which could be told repeatedly. It was called "Something of, by, and for Women."

A "feminist liturgy" is a contradiction in terms, given the legitimating function of liturgy in patriarchy to support sexism and consequently its offshoots: war, racism and all the destructive hierarchies of economic oppression. It is an attempt to put new wine, women's awareness, into the old skins of forms that kill female self-affirmation and turn female consciousness against itself. This is not to say that the impulse behind the desire to have something like a "women's liturgy" is not healthy and alive. There is every reason for women to celebrate our becoming and the discovery of our history, but in ever new ways, not encrusted in stagnant, repetitious ritual. The urge to celebrate is part of a precious new beginning. It springs from an ovarian insight.[29] But the impulse can be twisted against itself if we look for support and legitimation in the forms of patriarchal ritual, whether Jewish, Protestant, Catholic, Moslem, Hindu, or whatever. To know this, one needs only to open one's eyes to the "sacred" symbols and one's ears to the "sacred" words of the "sacred" cosmos that excludes our humanity. To straighten out the thought of Nietzsche: "What are these churches now if they are not the sepulchres of *women*?" In his confusion, Nietzsche wrote "sepulchres of God," but the real problem is that the churches have been the murderers of women. The corpse of "God" they contain is unfulfilled human being.

To put the matter in psychological terms, one might ask the question: "What is a self-actualizing person?" To this question Abraham Maslow has excellent answers in his list of qualities such people exhibit. They tend to have or better exhibit "boldness, courage, freedom, spontaneity, perspicuity, integration, and self-acceptance."[30] These healthy human specimens tend also to have clearer, more efficient perception of reality, more openness to experience, autonomy, detachment, recovery of creativeness, ability to fuse concreteness and abstractness, democratic character structure.[31] Such persons seem to have resolved "the civil war . . . between the forces of the inner depths and the forces of defense and control."[32] We need only to think of such qualities and then to think of what religion in our society has done to wipe them out in women. A "feminist liturgy," despite the healthy impulse behind it, would contribute to the legitimation of this "wiping out" process, because it would be *contained* to some extent in a traditional form (the admission of this is implicit in the word "liturgy"). It would reinforce —though in an ambivalent manner—false memory.

Non-Saint Joan and the Witch Within

Characteristically, the church burned Joan of Arc as a heretic and, when she was safely dead, canonized her as a Christian saint. But what if Joan was *really* a "heretic"—a member of the Dianic cult—as the well-known scholar Margaret Murray maintains? Murray proposes that the questions asked at Joan's trial reveal her accusers' suspicions that she represented an underlying organization which they dreaded—the Old Religion, whose roots go back to a pre-agricultural period. This was an ancient religion of Western Europe which still survives underground. It had "beliefs, ritual, and organization as highly developed as that of any other cult in the world."[33] Murray marshals historical evidence to support her thesis that Joan's accusers were aware of her connection with the ancient religion. She points to the incredible exchange of letters after her execution which reveal that Joan was no ordinary heretic:

After the execution, the judges and counsellors who had sat in judgment on Joan received letters of indemnity from the Great Council; the Chancellor of England sent letters to the Emperor, to the kings and princes of Christendom, to all the nobles and towns of France, explaining that King Henry and his Counsellors had put Joan to death through zeal for the Christian faith; and the University of Paris sent similar letters to the Pope, the Emperor, and the College of Cardinals.[34]

Moreover, Murray's research indicates that there was widespread belief that Joan was God Incarnate. It was a belief of the Old Religion that God could appear as a woman, a man, or an animal. Such a God is found in Italy, Southern France, and the English Midlands, and is commonly called Janus or Dianus. The feminine form of the name, Diana, is found throughout Western Europe. It is the name of the female deity or leader of the so-called Witches. For this reason, the Old Religion is also referred to as the Dianic Cult.[35] The fact that the French never lifted a finger to save Joan—difficult to explain—might be accounted for by their belief that as God Incarnate she was doomed to suffer as the sacrifice for the people.

Joan's trial, then, could be seen as part of the war between Christianity and the Old Religion, or Ritual Witchcraft—an ancient religion of pre-Christian origins, which should *not* be confused with "Black Magic."[36] Christian writers, of course, have wanted to claim Joan as a true Christian. However, Murray's contention is that these have been misled by such phenomena as Joan's "Voices," to whom Joan gave the names of saints, for "the questions showered upon her show that the judges had shrewd suspicions as to the identity of these persons," that is, that the "Voices" were human beings, persons of a different religion than Christianity.[37] I should like to point out another item that might be significant. Joan's questioners were constantly asking whether she marked her letters with the sign "Jesus Maria" and a cross. On March 1, 1431, she gave an interesting answer: "On some letters, Yes; on others, No!" She added: "At times I used the cross to warn those who understood [what it meant] *not* to do what I had written in that letter."[38] Why would a Christian symbol be chosen to bear this negative message?

The issue that Joan's accusers made of her insistence upon wearing male clothing is significant. On this the judges laid most stress. "Though Joan had recanted and been received into the Church, the moment she put on male attire she was doomed on that account only."[39] Murray points out that the simple fact of resuming male garments was a signal for her death without further trial, and suggests that for Joan, as a member of the Dianic cult, the wearing of male attire must have been an outward sign of that faith, and the resuming of it must have meant the relapse.

It may be that future historians, prodded on by the work of scholars like Murray and burning to discover the truth about Joan and about the Old Religion rather than with zeal to entomb her within Christianity, will find more evidence that supports this interpretation of Joan's life and death. Yet even abstracting from this not yet fully explored question, it is clear that there is something deeply significant about the connection between Joan's reassuming of male attire (a "mortal sin") and her execution. Phyllis Chesler points out that Joan begins to step completely outside the realm of patriarchal culture:

For this, she is killed in her own lifetime—and re-experienced by those women who are mad enough to wish to "step outside" but who do not wish to be crucified for doing so.[40]

The essential reason why Joan was killed was that she signaled to some extent an escape from patriarchy.

In some ways it was an ambiguous escape. Joan's fate involved the sacrifice of The Maid. This is a proud title, for traditionally in the Old Religion The Maid was one holding a high position in the Coven

Yet, as Chesler points out, Joan's sacrifice was used for purposes of male renewal.

In the Madonna's case the renewal is achieved through classic patriarchal rape-incest; in Joan's case, first through military victories and then through patriarchal crucifixion, guilt, and expiation.[41]

The final indignity, not stressed by Chesler, was the fact that having killed her, the Church made her a saint. It should be noted that she was killed in the most horrible way—burned alive—whereas her lieutenant, Gilles de Rais, was granted the mercy of strangulation before burning.

As Antichurch, the women's revolution is an affirmation of Joan's escape from patriarchy. It says "No" to whatever there was of cooptation and ambivalence imposed upon her fate. Above all it says "No" to her imposed "sainthood" and "Yes" to her real sainthood—her transparency to the power of be-ing which made her life a sign-event, expressing the witch that burns within our own true selves. Joan's potential stature was reduced by the patriarchal imagination into that of the Virgin-Warrior who aids men to fulfill men's goals. The witch that burns within our being will have to bring out that potential stature, repudiating ambivalence and servitude, refusing the tortures and degrading honors which are their only rewards.

Mothers, Daughters, Comrades

The religions of patriarchy—especially the Judeo-Christian tradition and its hideous blossom, Freudian theory—have stolen daughters from their mothers and mothers from their daughters. Chesler reminds us that Demeter, the goddess of Life, and Persephone, her maiden daughter, were for a long time celebrated in elaborate ceremonies. "But somehow—no one really knows why—such celebrations of mothers and daughters certainly ceased."[42] Christian women go to church and sing of themselves as sons of God. The Virgin Mary was allowed only a son, but no daughter. Mothers in our culture are cajoled into killing off the self-actualization of their daughters, and daughters learn to hate them for it, instead of seeing the real enemy. If they begin to see, the pain drives them to their paternal analysts, who help them to understand that they must hate their mothers for not having destroyed them enough to erase the pain. Still, the destruction has not been complete, and women are beginning to dream again of a time and space in which Mother and Daughter look with pride into each other's faces and know that they both have been victims and now are sisters and comrades.

By the time of Joan of Arc, within the Dianic cult the worship of the male deity seems to have superseded that of the female. Murray holds that only on rare occasions does God appear in a female form and that as a general rule the woman's position, when divine, is that of the "familiar" or substitute for the male God. Yet this ambivalence was probably a late development, and it was still possible to see in the chief woman of the cult the remnants of the Mother-Goddess and her autonomous power.[43] The Old Religion was not "pure," but its women could still be powerful figures not yet reduced to the condition of the bovine Madonnas adored by the artists of Christianity. The New Being of Antichurch is a rising up of Mother and Daughter together, beyond the Madonna's image and beyond the ambivalent Warrior Maiden's image. The togetherness comes from nonimmersion in either role, and it comes from our desperation which has made us remember and look forward to the Golden Age. This remembering/looking-forward already colors our existence in the boundary space and time where some women are beginning really to live.

Antichurch and the Sounds of Silence

Male religion entombs women in sepulchres of silence in order to chant its own eternal and dreary dirge to a past that never was. The silence *imposed* upon women echoes the structures of male hierarchies. It is important to listen to the structures of this imposed silence in order to hear the flow of the new sounds of free silence that are the voice of sisterhood as Antichurch.

Durkheim wrote of the Warramunga tribe in Australia which imposed absolute silence upon women for long mourning periods (as long as two years). As a result, he claimed, the women developed communication through gestures. Some preferred to remain silent even for years after the imposed period of silence.[44] One woman was said to have been silent for twenty-four years. One wonders if the continuation of silence is because the women discover a better means of communication, an underground language of silence that men cannot understand.

The Pauline text screamed (it doesn't matter at all whether this was written by Paul or some pseudo-Paul): "I permit no woman to teach . . . she is to keep silent." The point, it seems, was that women cannot "officially" speak—a claim still shrilly proclaimed by Roman Catholicism and orthodox Judaism and affirmed only a bit more subtly by Reformed Judaism and Protestant Christianity. For the "sacred" words were all written by men and can only be repeated and echoed. In religions that cling to the past, whether by Bibliolatry or by tradition or both, no woman can break out of imposed silence.

In modern times academia and the printed secular word have partially moved in on the territory of the sacred church and its sacred word. Here too women have been entombed in imposed silence, in the gross and obvious way of simply being excluded and in the more subtle way of only being allowed to echo male words. One may not dare to think out loud women's words—at least, not too much. We know the penalties for that.

As a result the new sounds of free silence may be hard for many to understand. They are many-faceted. We speak forth shapes and colors, utter textures, flash forth to each other in a flow of understanding what is too awesome to be understood: our own self-birth in sisterhood. Robin Morgan paints the silence:

> And I will speak less and less to you
> And more and more in crazy gibberish you cannot under-
> stand:
> witches' incantations, poetry, old women's mutter-
> ings. . . .[45]

This multi-faced communication that is being born among women in the modern technological jungle of America is nonspeech in the terms of our culture, just as truly as the gestures of the "primitive" Warramunga women were nonspeech to their men. Multi-leveled communication is of course not unknown to all men, but the rules of patriarchy try to write it out as much as possible. What is new when it happens with women is that it is the interflow of our own being, our affirmation of process that is our own process over and against sepulchral forms that almost but never quite did quench our fire.

Women are starting to know now the defects of language because it is not ours. It reflects the structures blessed by male religion. In order to say that women's speech breaks out of these bounds I have called it silence. It is silence in the sense of going beyond inauthentic speech, but to those who know only inauthentic speech it is meaningless. "Logical positivists" have claimed that one can ask only whatever questions language clearly expresses. To go outside this pre-established box is, supposedly, to use "pseudo-propositions," to say the unthinkable, the meaningless. What the logical positivists did not point out was that the pre-established box is patriarchal, which would mean that our new anti-patriarchal questions are *a priori* pseudo-questions. Other academicians, and non-academicians, though they would not call themselves logical positivists, share this view. To such persons, who crush thought and language into patriarchal space and time past, the new sounds are unhearable. A sexist language-bound world is deaf to these.

Suzanne Langer wrote of the restriction on discourse that sets bounds to the complexity of speakable ideas. She saw this as an inherent defect of language, which is a poor medium for expressing emotions, ever-moving patterns, the ambivalences and intricacies of inner experience, the interplay of feelings and thought, memories and echoes of memories. The fine arts compensate for this built-in defect of language, she maintained.[46] But I would point out that poetry and the fine arts have been *individual* expressions of ontological reason—granting that in the case of great art many people can resonate to such expressions. They have remained by and large within patriarchy, which has neatly labeled them "fine arts," and entombed them in its museums and universities. Contained, they have not made a planetary rebellion. Indeed most art and poetry in our culture expresses patriarchal feelings. (Look at the flabby, unathletic bodies of Renaissance Madonnas; read the diarrheic outpourings of misogynism in Milton, Kipling, Claudel.) By contrast, the new sounds of silence, sparking forth a network of boundary communication, is the dawning of communal New Being. This is neither "public" nor "private," neither "objective" nor "subjective." It is intersubjective silence, the vibrations of which are too high for the patriarchal hearing mechanism. It is, then, ultrasonic.

Beyond the Antichurch

I have already indicated that the merging of feeling and thought, of the personal and the political in the new space being created by the second wave of feminism is a widespread spiritual event. It implies conflict with sexist religion as such, but it also portends transcendence, not only of the sexism, but also of the conflict. This is partially due to the paradoxical fact that there is an *élan* toward transcendence discernible in the women I have called spiritual expatriates, which is at least in part traceable to the influence of religion upon their lives. This influence has been both direct and indirect, that is, by way of direct participation in organized religion and by way of a general cultural climate that has in large measure been shaped by the Judeo-Christian heritage.

A purely negative evaluation of the effects of religion would be inaccurate. It cannot be denied that many people, women and men, have achieved with the help of religion a kind of autonomy, charity, and peace. I have pointed out that these qualities, and particularly this peace, have been attained at too high a price, that is, by leaping over inequities instead of working through these. Certainly, there is something deficient in harmony bought at the expense of insight, in solving problems by not seeing them. Yet it is the human condition always to have only partial insight, and it would be foolish and insensitive to deny all authenticity to the deep experience, the values, and the commitment of those whose religious conditioning rendered them opaque to its own negative aspects. Those who have abandoned institutional religion—or to be more accurate, *been abandoned by institutional religion*—because of these negative elements have often retained a fundamentally spiritual insight, although in many cases they would be reluctant and even hostile to the idea of calling it "religious."[47] At any rate, there is a remarkable radicalization of consciousness among these spiritual exiles, which often manifests itself in refusal to stop short at limited goals and particular issues, however valid and important—such as legalization of abortion, free day care centers, or the equal rights amendment—and constantly seek to understand the deep implications of liberation.

This deeply radicalized consciousness is by no means the unique property of those who at some time have been personally related to the churches, however. It is one of the developing dimensions of sisterhood—a dynamic toward spiritualization of consciousness and communal incarnation of that consciousness. To call this reality Antichurch is good, but we should not stop with this name alone. To say this word and to stop here is to be caught in a mode of expression that leaves us with an "opposition of opposites." "Opposites" are open to seductive advances, to offers of cooptation, as radical women know. This is illustrated by the many incidences of being invited to speak to obviously nonfeminist gatherings, or to be on panels that are carefully "balanced to represent both extreme points of view" (the assumption being that "truth" must lie in between somewhere). "Opposites" are open to seduction not because they are perceived as radical, but because they are perceived as similar to, in the same category with, the "opponent." To recognize this is not to renounce our identity as Antichurch, nor, on the pragmatic level, does it mean that we must always renounce such offers of a forum. It does mean that we have to be wary and that we have to reach toward something *beyond* opposition.

CHAPTER SIX

Sisterhood as Cosmic Covenant

*My friends, do we realize for what purpose we are con-
vened? Do we fully understand that we aim at nothing less
than an entire subversion of the present order of society,
a dissolution of the whole existing social compact?*
—ELIZABETH OAKES SMITH, 1852

*Tyger! Tyger! burning bright
In the forests of the night,
What immortal hand or eye,
Dare frame thy fearful symmetry?*
—WILLIAM BLAKE

It was a temptation to call this chap-
ter "Sisterhood as Cosmic *Church*," in order to express some of
the movement's elements that are in dialectical tension with its mode
of being as Antichurch. However, the negative reactions of feminists
to the term are warning enough. Betty Friedan expressed this gut
feeling by remarking simply that "the church is the enemy." The
word is freighted with an archaic heritage in a specifically Christian
way, and this may never be shaken off. Yet certain functions that
the church claimed to fulfill and never could, essentially because of
its sexism, are being more than fulfilled in the new space of feminism.
Or, to be somewhat more accurate, something *beyond* the claims of
Christianity is coming into being, for the formulation itself of churchly
claims has been anemic, couched in a language reflecting the limits
of the patriarchal imagination and perpetuating those limits. The
church's actualizations of even such shriveled formulations fall far short
of what the advertisements have promised. Still, in order to help our new
words—our sounds of silence—to emerge, it may be useful to look at
some prevalent concepts of "church." The use of these to express analogies can be worthwhile in envisaging sisterhood as *beyond* "church."

A Space Set Apart

The church often has been envisaged as *a space set apart* from the rest of the world, having a special meaning for people and functioning as haven and sanctuary. It is still not uncommon for people to experience the physical interior of a church building in the way described by Eliade as an experience of sacred space.[1] Even the frankly nonreligious person in our culture tends to value certain "holy places" of her or his private universe, places associated with happy memories, usually. Often it is a ritualized and superstitious sense of specialness that attaches to "holy shrines" that has nothing to do with individual or communal insight and growth. A church construed as space set apart, then—whether the term is intended to mean a building, an institution, or an ideological "sacred canopy"—has certain propensities for serving as an escape from facing the abyss. It then becomes a place for spinning webs of counterfeit transcendence.

Yet the image of a space set apart is not worthless. I have already suggested that this revolution provides a space—mainly a province of the mind—where it is possible to be oneself, without the contortions of mind, will, feeling, and imagination demanded of women by sexist society. But it is important to note that this space is found not in the effort to hide from the abyss but in the effort to face it, as patriarchy's prefabricated set of meanings, or *nomos*, crumbles in one's mind. Thus it is not "set apart" from reality, but from the contrived nonreality of alienation. Discovered in the deep confrontation between being and nonbeing, the space of liberation is sacred.

When sacred space is discovered, the possibility of deterioration into escapism or of absolutizing the space into a particular form is there. However, the real danger is that women will succumb to *accusations* of escapism or single-mindedness by those who do not see the transcendent dimensions of feminism. Reduction of women's liberation to escapism because of "personal hang-ups" is still a potent weapon, especially when couched in psychological jargon. Women are vulnerable to accusations of absolutizing the movement and we are accustomed to listen only too well to the voices of alienation. Yet there is something to be attended to here, since the accusation is a typical *reversal* of the real problem, which is the constant temptation *not* to face the universality of sexual caste and the awesome demands of living in the new space.

Since the new space is set apart precisely from the nonreality of sexist alienation and since we are *in* it only insofar as we confront nonreality, it is not static space but constantly moving space. I have said that its center is on the boundaries of patriarchy's spaces, that is, it is not *contained*. R. D. Laing wrote something that is of help in understanding this:

The truth I am trying to grasp is the grasp that is trying to grasp it. . . . The Life I am trying to grasp is the me that is trying to grasp it.[2]

Our space is the life source, not the "container" of contrived covers of life. But whereas Laing was writing of an individual leap or journey through inner space that society would call madness, we are engaged in a journey that is not only utterly individual but also ultimately communal. The kind of communality that it has springs from the fact that there is discovery of "the me that is trying to grasp it." Laing, however, while he does perceive the destructiveness of the social setting, remains to some extent caught in an intrapsychic point of view. The problem remains that even if many persons are "cured," this of itself isn't enough. As Chesler remarks, throughout the book *Sanity, Madness, and the Family* "he remains unaware of the universal and objective oppression of women and of its particular relation to madness in women."[3]

Our space set apart does mean individual freedom, but this becomes possible in recognizing and refuting the structures of objective oppression. I have said that our struggle is not on the enemy's terms. It is self-actualization that is communal, that has as a necessary condition deep rejection of the structures of destruction.

The ever moving center of our space—the opposite of "dead" center—moves because it is ourselves and we are moving, becoming, in a "noospheric net" never dreamed of by Teilhard de Chardin or other prophets of male futurism. This center is the Archimedean point of support, the fulcrum from which, if enough women discover it and do not lose courage, it may be possible to move the world.

Exodus Community

Because of this constantly moving center, the space of the women's revolution can be called an *exodus community*. The church has been characterized by this name, but both the formulations and the social and psychic realizations of the meaning of this image have been limited and limiting to human aspiration. The church as exodus community allegedly has gone forth from bondage toward liberation on the basis of a promise made by Yahweh to the fathers of the people of God. The voyage has not been spectacular, and this is in no small measure due to the fact that there is something contrived about promises handed down from on high. Yet, as in the case of *space set apart*, the image has value when taken out of its paralyzing context and allowed to spark forth our own insight. The moving center which is the energy source of the new sisterhood as exodus community is the promise in ourselves. It is the promise in our foremothers whose history we are beginning to discover, and in our sisters whose voices have been stolen from them. Our journey is the fruit of this promise—a journey into individualization and participation, leaving behind the false self and sexist society. Since one cannot physically leave the planet, however (and extraterrestrial space trips as programmed by the prevailing society will be super-sexist, with the accommodation of space stewardesses, perhaps), our mode of departure has to be appropriate to the situation. We can depart mentally to some extent by refusing to be blinded by society's myths. We can depart physically and socially to a degree also, but simple withdrawal will not change the wider situation. The adequate exodus requires communication, community, and creation. The truly moving space will not be merely unorthodox or reformist, but will be on its way beyond unorthodoxy as well as orthodoxy, discovering and bringing forth the really new.

To those within patriarchal space, and perhaps especially within its religions, it may look as though radical feminists have broken a "promise" by not "living up" to the expectations that have been outgrown. In fact, by living out our own promise, we are breaking the brokenness in human existence that has been effected by means of the constructs of alienation. To put it another way, we are breaking the dam of sex stereotyping that stops the flow of being, that stops women and men from being integrated, androgynous personalities. The admission of the fact of this brokenness into our consciousness brings to light the promise burning within, the potential toward the "fearful symmetry" that the poet glimpsed, and that our culture keeps hidden in the forests of the night. It also puts us in touch with "the flow of the inexhaustible Encompassing" about which the philosopher Jaspers has written, without which there is only "the random swirling of dead husks of words, producing a semblance of external order and meaning in endless, arbitrary variation."[4]

The dawning of this promise within, this rushing of the waters of life that have been dammed and damned by our culture, since it puts us in touch with ourselves and with the "Encompassing," brings us into the deepest possible community. It is the community that is discovered, rather than "formed," when we meet others who are on the same voyage. There is, then, a "covenant" among us, *not* in the sense of an agreement that is *formed* and precisely formulated, but in the sense of profound *agreement that is found.* The word "covenant," then, cannot fully say the reality—it is part of the language that splits, cuts off, divides and tries to paste back together again. If, however, we can get beyond the limits imposed by our inherited nonspeech, we can use the sound to signal something more. The covenant is the deep *agreement* that is present within the self and among selves who are increasingly in harmony with an environment that is beyond, beneath, and all around the nonenvironment of patriarchal splits and barriers. For lack of a better word, this may be called the "cosmos," and the sense of harmony has its source in participation in being, which means being in touch with the deepest forces in the cosmos. Out of this contact comes new speech. "Covenant" has always been bound up with language. Sisterhood as cosmic covenant means beginning to re-name the cosmos.

"Covenant" also has the meaning of a common-law form of action to recover damages for breach of contract. Women's form of action to recover damages begins with a declaration. Those women were not joking when they claimed that all you have to do to become a witch is to say three times to yourself: "I am a witch; I am a witch; I am a witch."[5] This is something like speaking an unspeakable word. It is an exorcism of the internalized demon that divides the self against the self. It is a way of saying, "I am, I am, I am." With this declaration one joins the new coven and discovers the covenant.

The moving center of women's new space is on the boundary of the dead circle of archetypes and repetition. Historians of religion, such as Eliade, have made such claims for Christianity. Eliade maintains:

*Christian thought tended to transcend, once and for all, the old themes
of eternal repetition, just as it had undertaken to transcend all the other
archaic viewpoints by revealing the importance of the religious experience of faith and that of the value of the human personality.*[6]

The only words that save this from being a preposterous statement are
"tended" and "undertaken." Eliade sees the situation through male
lenses. He writes further that Christianity is the religion of "fallen man"
[sic] "and this to the extent to which modern man is irremediably identified with history and progress, and to which history and progress are
a fall. . . ."[7] For Eliade this "fall" means the final abandonment of the
paradise of archetypes and repetition. But has there been real movement out of that "paradise"? The experience of feminists reveals that
women feel very much trapped in this "Eden" of endless circles and
that Christianity is keeping things this way. The poet William Blake
described this paradise very well:

> *In Eden, Females sleep the winter in soft silken veils
>   woven by their own hands to hide them in the darksom grave.
> But Males immortal live renewed by female deaths.*
> (The Four Zoas, *1797)*

Within Christianity, males still live renewed by female deaths, and this
renewal at female expense may well be a delusion of history and
"progress" to those who feel benefited by it. I have already pointed to
the Fall that is on its way, hopefully, and that is the Second Coming
of women. Those who have always lived renewed by female deaths
have every reason to postpone its arrival.

Charismatic Community

The church has been seen by some as essentially a *charismatic community*, in which such gifts as healing and prophecy are experienced.
Unfortunately its apologists have failed to give due attention to the fact
that the healing dispensed within the province of institutional religion
has to a large extent been needed because of the destruction wrought
by such religion. Institutionalized "spiritual" healing traditionally was
supposed to come through such vehicles as the sacrament of confes-

sion, pastoral counseling, and its secular surrogates—psychiatry and psychology. The priestly or quasi-priestly caste using these instruments speaks with prestige and authority, guiding women to see the folly of rebellion against the destiny designed by "God" and/or anatomy. Exceptional members of the religious or clinical priestly caste who actually use their situation to liberate are deviants who do not function according to their role specifications and pay for it.

The healing dispensed institutionally, then, does not go to the cause of sickness. It is not preventive medicine. Rather, an elitism is perpetuated that feeds on illness of soul, mind, and body. It is delayed and partial healing that keeps control in the hands of a few, perpetuating the dichotomy between "agent" and "patient" and reflecting a condition of society in which power is divorced from real love. This dichotomized situation is symbolized in Roman Catholic doctrine by "the power of the keys," applied to the magical power of the priest in the sacrament of confession. It has an analogue in the situation in mental hospitals, in which psychiatrists, staff, and chaplains are basically distinct from patients in that the former have keys whereas the latter are deprived of them.

The guilt that has plagued the apparent beneficiaries of "healing" has in large measure been a creation of religion itself, especially in the case of its female victims. This institutionalized implantation of "guilt" and "healing" is an unending circle of separation and return. Religious charismatic healing has participated in the circle. It has been in demand partly because of psychosomatic illness inflicted by the society that religion justifies. Its curing has been at best a solution for individuals. It has not reached the objective social forms that continue to destroy.

Still, the idea of healing is of value when we use the word to speak something beyond the meaning it customarily bears. Feminists are discovering a healing that is charismatic, not only in the sense that it is noninstitutional, but also in the sense that it is counterinstitutional, recognizing that what the institutions of healing deem "sick" are frequently signs of incipient health. This means setting up a counterforce to the trap designed by society's physicians of the soul. Such counterforce is possible because the center of our new space is not located within the "paradise" of archetypes and repetition but, having been discovered in confrontation with the abyss of nothingness, moves on the tide of ever increasing participation in being. Putting it in more psychological terms, Chesler says that whereas woman's primary identity has been rooted in what pleases a few men, this ego-identity "must somehow shift and be moored upon what is necessary for her own survival as a strong individual." This shift "implies a frank passion for achieving the power necessary to define oneself—a power which is always predicated on the direct control of worldly realities." The transfer of women's primary force of supportiveness to the self and to each other should never be "to the point of self-sacrifice."[8]

Those who have seen the church as a charismatic community have also stressed the role of *prophecy*. It is understood that whereas official priesthoods and hierarchies function to sustain the delusion that whatever is, is right, the prophetic function is to point beyond to what has never been, but can become. Within the Judeo-Christian tradition, however, most recognized prophets have been males and their criticism has not been directed against patriarchy as such. They have been individual voices crying in the wilderness, and their cries have not led us out of the wilderness of sexism. Indeed, the imagery of Old Testament prophets was very sexist. There was a tiresome propensity for comparing Israel to a whore. Isaiah spoke of Zion as a harlot (1:21). Jeremiah told Israel that "she" had lain down like a harlot, abandoning Yahweh for false gods (2:20). Ezekiel not only repeatedly declaims Israel as prostitute and whore (ch. 16), but adds other interesting imagery as well:

The word of Yahweh was addressed to me as follows: Son of man, the members of the House of Israel used to live in their own land, but they defiled it by their conduct and actions; to me their conduct was as unclean as a woman's menstruation. I then discharged my fury at them because of the blood they shed in their land and the idols with which they defiled it.   (Ezekiel 36:16–18)

It did not occur to the prophets to decry Israel as a rapist—which would have been, behaviorally speaking, a more accurate description. As Yahweh's extension, as "his" instrument, Israel did righteously rape the enemies of the "true God." However, having envisaged "her" as Yahweh's bride, the prophets were hardly in a position to evaluate behavior from another perspective. Typically, Yahweh "discharged" *his* "fury" and the sense of uncleanness for violent shedding of blood is projected upon menstruation in women.

Even leaving aside the revealing instances of sexist imagery, the fact stands out that the prophets of the major religions have not challenged sexual oppression in an effective way. As Weber pointed out, the fact that a prophet such as the Buddha was glad to see clever women sitting at his feet and employed them as propagandists, as did Pythagoras, did not necessarily carry over into an evaluation of the entire female sex. "A particular woman might have been regarded as sacred, yet the entire female sex would still be considered vessels of sin."[9] Moreover, even though unconstrained relationships with women were maintained by nearly all prophets, this attitude has not generally carried over among their later followers, beyond the first stage of the religious community's formation. It has been a consistent pattern that "as routinization and regimentation of community relationships set in, a reaction takes place against pneumatic manifestations among women."[10] Patriarchy's prophets have not conveyed a message of liberation that has managed to overcome this process of sclerosis in their followers.

It can be observed that contemporary prophets of so-called revolutionary movements repeat the same syndrome that Weber perceived in the case of the Buddha and of Pythagoras. I have already mentioned in an earlier chapter that within the peace movement in America prophets such as the Berrigans have women among their disciples and propagandists, and yet fail to see sexism as source of the genocidal and warlike propensities of the structures they oppose. There is no clear indication that the new world they would bring into existence if they could would be substantially less sexist and consequently less warlike. So also in the movement for black liberation in the United States, the archetypal prophet, Martin Luther King, was patently unconcerned with women's oppression. His wife, Coretta King, was reported to have said that all through his life her husband had had an ambivalent attitude concerning the role of women. Dr. Pauli Murray, lifelong civil rights advocate and feminist, points out that the Southern Christian Leadership Conference of which Dr. King was the head was almost wholly male dominated. Women were almost invisible in its leadership.[11] When one looks to a newer generation of black radicals, it is again clear that the visible prophets, such as Malcolm X, who came out of the strongly patriarchal Black Muslim tradition, have been unconcerned with sexism and in fact have perpetuated it. Among the sisters of these black leaders there have been women whose voices proclaim links between racism and sexism. These women have varied in background: There is scholar-activist-lawyer-poet Pauli Murray. There is Marxist revolutionary Angela Davis. There is radical feminist Florynce Kennedy. Yet black feminists are voices crying in the desert.

The words "prophecy," "prophet," "prophetic," then, cannot convey the full impact of the communal phenomenon of sisterhood. Yet the words can be useful if we allow them to say more than they have been able to say within the confines of inherited language. First of all, prophets have been persons who do not receive their mission from any human agency, but seize it.[12] The revolution of women has this kind of dynamic, since women have been excluded from the power of politics. However, what we are "seizing" and "usurping" is that which is rightfully and ontologically ours—our own identity that was robbed from us and the power to externalize this in a new naming of reality. This is not a purely individual charismatic gift, but a communal awakening.

Second, prophets have been persons who establish a *breakthrough* to a better cultural order and declare this break to be morally legitimate.[13] This says something applicable to the feminist revolution. But in the prophecies of the major religions, this breakthrough has always been to a cultural order which contained and still "blessed" the structures of destruction, since it was sexually hierarchical. The dynamic of the feminist breakthrough, since it is in total contradiction to this hierarchy, does not contain this self-contradictory destructiveness and therefore cannot itself be contained within the category of prophecy. For Weber, the essential criterion of prophecy is whether or not the message is a call to *break* with an established order. *Yet none* of the major prophets called unambiguously for rejection of the sexist order, and in all cases their followers implemented this system of social arrangements. Because this unambiguous call was always lacking, the "decline and petrifaction of prophecy" which Weber saw as practically unavoidable was indeed inevitable.[14] He does observe that whereas priesthoods have always protected patriarchalism, prophetic religion breaks through patriarchal structures.[15] However, such transcendence has never been radically feminist even in the initial visionary stage. It is hardly surprising, therefore, that it could not be sustained.

A third point of importance for our speaking through and beyond the word "prophet" is the fact that prophets characteristically have invoked "a source of moral authority, an imperative which leads directly into the problem of the conceptions of meaning and order."[16] The language here is inadequate for the prophecy that is feminism. The use of such a term as "authority," for example, suggests legitimation handed down from on high. Also the language about "conceptions of meaning and order" is anemic. It does not express the process of awakening, of emotional and imaginative regeneration that is experienced. Yet it does ineptly say something about the power of conviction that communicates itself in the community of feminism, and that demands not only re-conceptualizing but re-imaging and re-naming of the "world" bequeathed to us.

A fourth useful though inadequate aspect of the language of prophecy—again borrowing from Weber's analysis—is the distinction between the "ethical type" of prophet and the "exemplary type." The concept of the "ethical type" is so totally inapplicable for naming the foretelling power of feminism that it is useful as a blatant illustration of what the cosmic covenant of feminism *is not*. As Talcott Parsons interprets Weber's concept of the ethical prophet, such a person thinks of himself [sic] as an *instrument* of the divine will, having a *mission* to promulgate an order for others which expresses that will. Such a prophet need not become personally sanctified. Parsons continues his explanation by pointing out that such a prophet tends to legitimate his [sic] teachings by reference to a concept of one or more gods who stand *outside* and *above* the world and legislate for it.[17] The language itself here ("instrument," "mission") is phallic, whether intentionally or subintentionally. The whole image is hierarchical. It is a picture of an archetypical male who, as an extension of his archetypically male God, thrusts his will upon others while remaining aloof, not sharing in their experience and concerns. This kind of prophet and divinity has prevailed in Judaism, Islam, and Christianity. The prophet of this type generates hierarchy. He imposes demands, telling others that it is their duty to follow his teachings. His message and image merge with those of the priest, women's ancient and persistent enemy. He (and it must be a "he") cannot foretell outside the circle of separation and return.

By contrast, the "exemplary type" of prophet has the self-image of a vessel, and stands in a relation of personal identification with the divine. The exemplary prophet participates in an immanent, pantheistic principle of divinity and invites others to participate in this.[18] Clearly this image of prophet is more appropriate to describe feminism's foretelling function. Yet it is important to understand its shortcomings, which become evident upon reading Weber's analysis. For a prophet, even of this type, is understood to be a "purely individual bearer of charisma."[19]

The tendencies generated by the ethical prophets (prevalent in Judaism, Christianity, and Islam) have led to a this-worldly and sexist pseudo-transcendence that finds its ambitions realized in sending missiles to the moon or to Mars, so that these "heavenly bodies" may become national colonies. The dynamics of the exemplary prophets (prevalent in India and manifested sometimes in China and the Near East) have been toward escape—whether envisaged as upward or inward—from the babble and unreality of common consciousness. There is validity in this escape insofar as it is escape from *unreality*. But this is not the communal vocational self-awareness that I have called the *creative political ontophany* of women. Exemplary prophets within patriarchy have invited individuals to free themselves from the pain, but this has not brought about a creative transformation of history grounded in confrontation with nonbeing. Women by the millions still die—spiritually and/or physically—of the effects of sexist brutality while the chosen few strive toward Nirvana.

Yet this distinction between ethical and exemplary prophets is useful to remind us of what *our* foretelling is *not*, so that we will not allow linguistic blinders to keep us from seeing the scope of the feminist revolution's potential. It would be easy to stagnate in a shallow activist "translation" of the ethical model or else in a noncreative and unreal "interior freedom" that in no way confronts the problem of objective structures. The cosmic covenant of sisterhood is beyond patriarchal prophecy in the sense of being beyond this split, for its participatory courage is rooted in power of being.

The "gift of tongues" is yet another example of the failure of religious charisma to uproot alienative structures. "Tongues" can be seen as a manifestation of the human psyche's rebellion against the impotence imposed by language. Yet this charism has functioned only as a temporary release for individuals in elite groups. Often these very individuals and groups have been most stubbornly conservative and sexist in their adherence to "real" language, outside the special moments of charismatic occurrences. This phenomenon is characteristic of the Pentecostal movement, in Catholic as well as in Protestant groups. Contemporary Catholic Pentecostals, for example, do not challenge authoritarian Roman Catholicism, but support it. It appears that they do not perceive the release expressed by "tongues" in their small groups as a palliative for the overwhelming oppressiveness of the symbolic and linguistic forms of the institutions they serve. On the contrary, they often come forth from such meetings refreshed to defend the very rigidity from which they have temporarily found release—and not only to defend, but to "convert" others to a sacramental religion that crushes women and corrupts men.[20] The fact of the cooptability of Catholic Pentecostalism is revealed by the ecclesiastical approval it has received.[21]

The truth behind the manifestations of the charism of "tongues" is the need to break out of the iron mask of language forms that are strangling us. Women's new hearing and naming is cosmic upheaval, in contrast to this charism which is a controllable and cooptable ripple of protest. Feminist naming is a deliberate confrontation with language structures of our heritage. It transcends the split between nonrational sounds of "tongues" and the merely rational semantic games of linguistic analysis, for it is a break out of the deafening noise of sexist language that has kept us from hearing our own word.

Healing, prophecy, and other charisms such as "tongues," then, have functioned ambiguously, giving partial and temporary alleviation but not liberation. They serve the male-made structures of oppression. As they become institutionalized and routinized they are used in attempts to coerce even "God Himself" into the service of these alienative structures. If these words are used to describe the event of women's becoming, then, this should be in a context that makes clear the fact that we are only using analogies—that these words fall far below the reality. Or—to borrow and bend an idea of the medieval philosophers —we may say that in thus speaking analogously we are using terms to describe phenomena that are more different from each other than they are similar. These analogies are the gestures of our minds when at times there is nothing better we can do in the effort to say the really new.

Communicating Community

Part of the self-understanding of the Christian church has been that it is a community with a "mission." As Moltmann suggested, the promise (*promissio*) implied a mission (*missio*).[22] There is a consistency of ideas here, though not in the sense that Moltmann intended. A promise handed down from an anthropomorphic deity to the forefathers does imply a mission—an extension of the command. In the history of Christianity the mission has often meant bloody conquest "for Christ." One need think only of the "conversion" of the "barbarians" of Europe or of the Crusades to be reminded of the thrusting and conquering propensities of the Christian conception of mission. Even the peaceful missionaries who have gone to "heathen" lands have felt justified in using questionable tactics to impose "true" beliefs upon others and in so doing have "righteously" allied themselves with economic imperialism. The imagery and the behavior implied in mission, then, is phallic. It is only necessary to think of the word in a very common contemporary military context—"bombing mission"—to perceive the direction implied by the word (outward, thrusting, exploding in many directions from one source). Moreover, the example conveys the burden of violence with which the history of the word is weighted down. Mission, then, is not communication but compulsion, whether this be understood as physcial or psychological compulsion and coercion.

Since the promise which is the source of sisterhood is within women's being and since the cosmic covenant based on that promise is an agreement that is discovered, the mode of communication of this community cannot be expressed adequately by the term "mission." The truth embodied in the term is the "sending" aspect of communication, but this is a relatively superficial aspect of communication, and the word "mission" is essentially wrong because it one-sidedly stresses this aspect. The communication involved is not a thrusting of an objectified "message" to another nor a thrusting of oneself or any model upon the psyche of another. Insofar as there is "sending" at all it is mutual—an interpenetration of insights coming from discovery of participation together in being, in the cosmos. It is, as two women observed, a process of "cosmosis."[23]

The expansion of the new space of women's awareness, then, is not an imperialist expansion that pushes back the territory of others. Rather, insofar as it *is* where being is discovered in confrontation with nothingness, it is an invitation to others to leave the patriarchal space of alienative identity—the sacred circle of eternal return—and enter new space. The Roman church has often "excommunicated" those who disagreed with its dogmas. One woman remarked that the community of sisterhood, which has no hierarchy and no dogmas, involves a process which is the opposite of this. That is, it expands by "incommunication."[24] Those who discover the covenant *find themselves* in the new space. The old territory, then, is not encroached upon: one does not bother to invade nonbeing. Rather, it is left behind by those who follow the promise within, which is the promise of integrated, transformed, androgynous being.

The Cosmic Covenant and Male Liberation

It is evident that the covenant is discovered not only by women but also by men who have been able to hear women's new words and accept these as an invitation to break out of the archetypal circle and face nothingness. Before proceeding to an analysis of authentic response, it is important to be aware of the ways in which men can and do avoid hearing women's new words while appearing to listen.

First, it is clear that men may wish to "dialogue" with women on the subject for various destructive and/or superficial reasons. Such reasons include sadism, curiosity, a desire for emotional, sexual, or intellectual titillation, a desire to "know the enemy" or—on a less gross level—a desire to be "fair" by "hearing the other side of the question." The latter motive is common among liberal intellectuals and often the basic shallowness of the process is revealed in the conditions "set up" for the dialogue. It is not uncommon, for example, for one woman to be invited to address fifteen or twenty male colleagues on the subject without the presence of other women—or perhaps in the presence of one or more "token" and timid women. Under such conditions of "dialogue," she can be sure of being cast into the "you can't win" position. If she shows strength and rationality she will be labeled as "abrasive." If she subtly compromises for the sake of "keeping the door open," thereby selling out herself and her sisters, she may be treated gently but her position, or rather nonposition, will be filed away with other trivialities easily taken care of.

A second point to keep in mind is that merely cerebral comprehension of some aspects of women's oppression will function in the manner that technical reason split off from ontological reason generally does operate. That is, it will use the "information" or "knowledge about" women's liberation in the service of prevailing hierarchies. Sometimes women, new to feminist consciousness, are surprised that they seem to find more understanding among men than among women. It would be important to consider the possible reason for this. Men generally have had more opportunities for seeing through the workings of power structures, having been on the inside to a far greater extent than women. The innocence and naïveté inflicted upon women prevents insight until anger gives the power of release. By contrast men, having learned about political power, can be open to toying with analogies when the idea of women's oppression is first presented to them. However, this is easily exploitable "knowledge about" women's situation. In the case of male administrators, the knowledge can be used to calculate how much women will tolerate, and to what extent the new consciousness can be exploited, whether directly for economic gains (e.g., in universities, in the publishing business, and in the media) or to enhance the image of institutions as "liberal" by extending minor rewards to women, without essentially changing anything. Women who are not totally new to feminist consciousness soon learn to perceive discrepancies between this display of intellectual understanding and the concrete behavior of many liberal males toward the women who serve them and uphold their status, such as wives and secretaries.

A third point to remember is that even male comprehension that extends beyond word games and manipulativeness toward real concern may be limited to particular issues or dimensions which men perceive as directly benefiting themselves as well as women, but which demand no renunciation of privilege. I have pointed out that many men have shown genuine concern about such issues as birth control and abortion, without seeing greater depth to feminism that this. Others have identified feminism with the "sexual revolution" out of motives of self-interest. Some gay men have linked it with the gay revolution and seen in it a useful source of allies, but have not pursued the idea more deeply than this. In all such cases there is partial understanding but not the depth of *agreement* that constitutes the covenant.

Dr. Louis Cutrona, a Boston psychologist who has been a leading activist in men's liberation, has expressed discouragement about the shortsightedness of men in male liberation groups. In his experience with such groups he found that there was a general consensus that sex stereotyping is bad insofar as it oppresses men, by forcing them to suppress emotions, control the urge to cry, always be aggressive and seize the initiative, and be morbidly concerned with performance. However, when it came to the question of relinquishing the *benefits* of sex roles, very few were willing and/or able to see any problem. They perceived themselves as doing their wives a favor by "helping them" with the housework but not as doing this simply because they had equal responsibility.[25]

On the level of ideology, male feminists of modern times, from John Stuart Mill to Theodore Roszak, have frequently comprehended a great deal, but their analysis has never really been ontological. They have not examined the dimensions of the struggle on the level of being and nonbeing. I think that this is the radical reason for the contradictoriness or just falling short of the mark that radical women find irritating even in the most excellent productions. Roszak, for example, in an otherwise excellent historical analysis, disappoints the reader at the end, by misconstruing such activities as learning karate, implying that women want to become "brutes and bastards" like so many men. He suggests concerning the movement that:

Perhaps its historical purpose will be to shatter the sexual stereotypes at the expense of the compassionate virtues, leaving us all, men and women alike, with the nobler task still to achieve: Gandhi's hope: all power renounced but that of love. . . .[26]

Roszak apparently does not perceive the connection between women's learning karate and human overcoming of the dichotomy between power and love. As long as "love" is assigned to one sex and power to the other, the ontological union of love, power, and justice—Gandhi's dream—will be unrealizable. Learning karate is not an act of violence but of prevention of violence, for it is directed to removing potential victims from a rapist world that requires for its perpetuation a caste of people educated to be victims. Male liberation cannot happen without this de-victimization. But perhaps in the long run this is what even male feminists fear, for as Marcuse says of our society in another context, "the real spectre [is] liberation."[27]

Women and men inhabit different worlds. Even though these are profoundly related emotionally, physically, economically, socially, there is a wall that is visible to those who *almost have managed* to achieve genuine interplanetary communication with the opposite sex. The prerequisite of this achievement is communication within the divided self, discovery of the lost self. The adequate meeting of the two worlds, then, cannot be imagined as a simple one-to-one relationship between representatives of humanity's two halves, for half a person really never can meet the objectified other half. The adequate "cosmosis" will require a breakdown of walls within the male psyche as well as within the female. It will require in men as well as in women a desire to become androgynous, that is, to become themselves. Whenever men manage to see this promise in themselves of actually finding themselves, of finally agreeing with themselves, they will have reached the threshold of the new space. They will have begun to discover the covenant. If they do not shrink from the good news because it means loss of undeserved privilege and prestige or because it means setting forth on a long and perilous trip into uncharted territory, they might succeed in becoming human.

After a lecture or discussion men have sometimes asked: "What do I do to join the movement?" They are assured that there is nothing to sign—no card, no contract. Since our covenant is an agreement that is found rather than formed, men who are "graceful" enough to have fallen into the new space and find themselves in agreement are in fact part of the covenant. The only way of falling out again is by standing still. How men will externalize their newly discovered promise will be determined by concrete circumstances. There are no charts or maps for this journey inward, backward, and forward into androgynous being. There are assurances, however: When I am coming alive I know that I am coming alive. The cosmic covenant means coming into living harmony with the self, the universe, and God.

For men in the past—and most are living in the past rather than now—life has meant feeding on the bodies and minds of women, sapping energy at the expense of female deaths. Like Dracula, the he-male has lived on women's blood. Perhaps this is one reason why patriarchal lore has expressed such a horror of female blood. The priests of patriarchy have eaten the body and have drunk the blood of the Sacrificial Victim in their Mass, but they have not wished to know *who* has really been the Victim whose blood supported this parasitic life.

The insatiable lust of males for female blood has resulted in a perpetual blood transfusion throughout the millennia—a one-way outpouring into the veins and arteries of the bloodthirsty monster, the Male Machine that now can continue its obscene life only by genocide. If the Machine dreams, it is of a future filled with megadeaths. The total vampire no longer needs even to speak of blood, which is after all visible, measurable. It drinks instead in quantities calculable only through the highest mathematics. The Vampire Himself has given his life to a Dracula of his own making, the High Computer who drains the life of the planet into the bottomless grey pit of bloodless abstractions.

To understand the opposite of this one-way flow of life in the sapping processes generated by male hierarchy, we may begin with the chemical model of osmosis. This is a diffusion which proceeds through a semipermeable membrane, separating two miscible solutions, and tends to equalize their concentrations. The liberation of males as well as of females requires the breakdown of the obstacle to the flow of life within the divided self, the wall of the opposition of opposites. But it should not be forgotten that our situations are not the same. It is female talent that has been lost to ourselves and the species. It is men who have sapped the life-force of women. The equalizing of the "concentrations," then, will not mean an immediate "give and take," as if those who have been deprived of their own life should "give on a fifty-fifty basis." Since what males *have* to give has in large measure been sapped from women, "the equalizing of concentrations" can hardly be imagined as if from equal but opposite social positions. On the level of social interaction, what has to take place is *creative justice*. It is not a simple transaction that is demanded, but restitution.[28] It is absurd for men to look upon the relinquishing of stolen privilege as benevolence. It is absurd also for men to protest indignantly when women speak of wresting back our own stolen power and being.

The required osmosis within the male as well as within the female psyche, that then has to be externalized in a new society, is a vast harmonic reordering process from an unleashed flow of energy—a "cosmosis." The source of the energy is women's participation in power of being as we hear and speak forth our own new word. It is not yet time for "dialogue" with those who have stolen the power of speech and made all language a system of false words, having made the part stand for the whole. Rather, it is a time for men to learn at last to listen and to hear, knowing that this is how to find their own promise, and to discover at last the way to adequate speech. Perhaps very few men will want to listen, but those who do not will have chosen their own nonbeing. As a well-known prophet once said: "He [sic] who has ears to hear, let him hear."

Earth, Air, Fire, Water: Ecology and the Cosmic Covenant

George Wald has pointed out that we have something to learn from the history of the dinosaurs, who had very small brains for their size. Since the proportion of brains to brawn was very low, they disappeared. Whereas within the individual human being, the proportion of brains to brawn is high, technology has inversed the proportion and we are coming again into the situation of the dinosaurs. Cars, not the people in them (for we realize that the people are not altogether in control), kill more than 50,000 Americans a year. On a more disastrous level, Wald points out that the discovery of a nuclear reaction—the process of turning hydrogen into helium—which could mean that we could shortly make our own sunlight, is turned mainly into a weapon that threatens our lives and the life of the planet. Again, the trips to the moon have been negligible for high level scientific content, but are expected to be useful for future weaponry. Our self-destructive use of brawn need not have been:

It is our western culture at work, our western culture with its beautiful Judeo-Christian ethic. It is our culture alone among the cultures of the earth that sees it that way, that has brought the technology of killing and destruction much further than any culture on the earth ever dreamed of doing before.[29]

There are some points to be added to George Wald's insightful statement: This "beautiful Judeo-Christian ethic" of missions—missions to convert "pagans" over their dead bodies, missions to the moon, missions to drop hydrogen bombs and ultimately to end life on the planet—is the culmination of the masculine-feminine schizophrenia which is causing the race to rape itself to death. The brain which the brawn is overshadowing is essentially not technical reason but ontological reason, that realm where power, justice, and love meet in harmony. The cosmic covenant is the discovery of this harmony.

Farsighted thinkers have pointed out that the moral imperative of respect for life, formerly understood in quantitative terms, must now be understood in terms of the *quality* of life.[30] This has obvious implications, such as the need for population control and for bringing a halt to the waste of resources and pollution of the environment. Such needs are not understood by the *machismo* mind. Marcuse uses the category of obscenity to describe the behavior of the "affluent monster." He points out that "this society is obscene in producing and indecently exposing a stifling abundance of wares while depriving its victims abroad of the necessities of life . . . in its prayers, in its ignorance, and in the wisdom of its kept intellectuals."[31] Meanwhile, of course, the affluent society *pretends* to be *improving* the quality of life, disguising what is actually happening by its usual techniques, which I have called "reversal."

Marcuse observes that the Establishment abuses the term "obscenity" by applying it, not to expressions of its own immorality but to the behavior of another:

Obscene is not the picture of a naked woman who exposes her pubic hair but that of a fully clad general who exposes his medals rewarded in a war of aggression; obscene is not the ritual of the Hippies but the declaration of a high dignitary of the Church that war is necessary for peace.[32]

Marcuse's perception is acute, and he rightly calls for "linguistic therapy" which would free words from almost total distortion of their meanings by "the Establishment." Yet I must point out that the therapy will never be radical enough if the basic obscenity is perceived as capitalism rather than sexism. The very word "obscene" itself, as used by "the Establishment," suggests the locus of the essential perversion and victimization. Marcuse's own insightful juxtaposition of the naked woman and the fully clad general reveals the basic reversal in phallic morality which is still observable in socialist as well as capitalist societies. Such social criticism does not go far enough. It employs revealing instances of the powerful elite's *sexist* behavioral, imaginative, and linguistic distortions while still perceiving these distortions' radical source in capitalism and their cure in socialism.

Another sentence from the same essay of Marcuse is symptomatic of this phenomenon of shortsightedness. He writes:

Thus we are faced with the contradiction that the liberalization of sexuality provided an instinctual basis for the repressive and aggressive power of the affluent society [*emphasis mine*].[33]

It should be stressed—and this is what feminism is doing—that the so-called liberalization of sexuality "provides an instinctual basis for the repressive and aggressive power" *of the sexist society*. For of course it is not a genuine liberation of sexuality that displaces the obscenity of generals and projects it upon naked women, and the essential disease is *not* affluence in itself. The lifting of taboos on genital sexuality does nothing to liberate from sex roles. Marcuse himself says that this relaxation binds "the 'free' individuals libidinally to the institutionalized fathers."[34]

Such expressions of insight into the sexist nature of the oppressive society, strangely coupled with failure to direct the critique *directly* and *essentially* at sexual oppression, is characteristic not only of intellectuals such as Marcuse but also of more "popular" expressions of social criticism. Such films as *The Godfather, The Ruling Class,* and *Deliverance* can be seen as brilliant exposés of the social disease which is patriarchalism. One could almost believe that the writers and directors must be committed feminists. Yet the functioning of these productions, with their amazingly revelatory juxtapositions of sex and violence and their exploitation of phallic symbolism, has not been directed intentionally to the service of feminism. Perhaps one could call such "understanding" of sexual alienation "subintentional." Recognition of the real enemy's identity is so close to the surface of consciousness of the writers and directors of such productions that some feminists tend to find the experience of reading such books and watching such films almost unbearable. "They know not what they say," it would seem. Then it is clear that women will have to speak forth the identity of that which is destroying us all. The subintentional revelations of male critics indicate that some receptivity to this knowledge may be possible—that the capacity to hear is closer to consciousness than we would have expected. The time for us to speak is precisely now.

In writing of the "new sensibility," Marcuse dreams of new people who will have broken identity with the "false fathers" who built Auschwitz and Vietnam, the ghettos and temples of the corporations. He says that "they will have broken the chain which linked the fathers and the sons from generation to generation."[35] But this is precisely the point: What *is* the substance of the chain that has "linked the fathers and the sons," culminating in the Auschwitzes, the Vietnams, the corporations, the ecclesiastical and secular inquisitions, the unspeakable emptiness of the consuming and consumed creatures whose souls are lost in pursuit of built-in obsolescence? This is precisely the chain that derives its total reality from the reduction of women to nonbeing. The strength of the chain is the energy sapped out of the bodies and minds of women—the mothers and daughters whose lifeblood has been sucked away by the patriarchal system. The chain that has drained us will be broken when women draw back our own life force.

The power to regain our own life comes from the discovery of the cosmic covenant, the deep harmony in the community of being in which we participate. The false harmony coerced by the chain of fathers and sons which dominates our constantly deteriorating environment has many manifestations. In economic terms it can be seen as a false concord based upon a false dichotomy of supply and demand. In America, the dominant elite creates the false consciousness of the public, whose alienation is so total that their very being is lost in the commodities they are trained to live for and devour. This is a translation into the realm of economics of the myth of eternal return. It means living out the endless circle of meaningless desires, never fulfilled, pouring human being into the insatiable chasm of nonbeing.

In contrast to this hell-bent "harmony," the concord which is the cosmic covenant is found in the process of rupture with the continuum of rapism, our imposed artificial environment. The power of imagination is unchained and we see, hear, feel, breathe in a new way. Our perception reaches beyond the ugly and the beautiful of the great chain of nonbeing.

In the refusal of our own objectification, those who find the covenant find something like what Buber called I-Thou. This happens first among women, as sisters, and as we have seen, the discovery contains a dynamic that makes us aware of the Verb who is infinitely personal, who is nonreifable, present and future in the depths of our present-future I-Thou. This Verb is the Eternal Thou. The contagion of this refusal of objectification extends outward toward male liberation, opening up the possibility for I-Thou between women and men, and among men. This Great Refusal of rapism clearly means refusal to rape earth, air, fire, water, that is, refusal to objectify and abuse their power.

More than this, it means that the covenant embraces our sister the earth and all of her nonhuman inhabitants and elements. It embraces, too, our sisters the moon, the sun and her planets, and all the farthest stars of the farthest galaxies. For since they *are*, they are our sisters in the community of being. The question arises of how to speak of our relation to these nonhuman sisters who speak their word, but in a non-human way. Paul Santmire has suggested that in order to speak of the relationship to nature we might modify Buber's articulation of the I-Thou, I-It distinction and speak of a "third type" of relation, which can be called an I-Ens (I-Being) relation.[36] The I-Ens, writes Santmire, is intimate, fluid, and present. The Ens is characterized by givenness. It is not perceived as an object to be used, but is beheld in its own splendor, which gives rise to wonder. It therefore does not fit into a utilitarian description of the world. Along with givenness, the Ens exhibits mysterious activity and beauty. The "I" of the relation is characterized by wonder, and can experience both dread and delight. In this relation there is a sense for the presence of the Deity; there is an awareness of the dimension of depth.[37]

But the I-Ens, which Santmire has described with great sensitivity and lucidity, is not the "normal" relation to nature in sexist culture. It is a momentary delusion of poets, madmen, and lovers who must be lured back to "normality," which is utilitarianism. But the cosmic covenant of sisterhood *has* the potential to transform the extraordinary relation of the poet to nature into the ordinary and "normal" relation, changing our environment from a culture of rapism to a culture of reciprocity with the beauty of the earth, the other planets, the stars. Out of women's becoming in the process of confronting nonbeing can come an ever more conscious participation in the community of being. This means that we will look upon the earth and her sister planets as being *with* us, not *for* us. One does not rape a sister.

CHAPTER SEVEN

The Final Cause: The Cause of Causes

The final cause is the cause of causes, because it is the cause of the causality of all the other causes.
                    —SCHOLASTIC AXIOM

If the violation of taboos transcends the sexual sphere and leads to refusal and rebellion, the sense of guilt is not alleviated and repressed but rather transferred: not we, but the fathers, are guilty.
                    —HERBERT MARCUSE

Real liberation is not merely unrestricted genital activity ("the sexual revolution"), but free and defiant thinking, willing, imagining, speaking, creating, acting. It is be-ing.
                    —MYSELF

Rebellion is as the sin of witchcraft.
                    —I SAMUEL 15:23

The time for individual skirmishes has passed. This time we are going all the way.
                    —REDSTOCKINGS MANIFESTO

You are a Witch by saying aloud, "I am a Witch," three times, and thinking about that. *You are a Witch by being female, untamed, angry, joyous, and immortal.*
                    —NEW YORK COVENS

I took a deep breath and listened to
     the old brag of my heart.
I am, I am, I am.
                    —SYLVIA PLATH

A woman at the end of the hall cried,
Comrades, let us remember the women
who died for liberty. And then we intoned
the Funeral March, a slow, melancholy and
yet triumphant air.
                                —MONIQUE WITTIG

May we comprehend that we cannot be stopped.
May I learn how to survive until my part is
   finished.
May I realize that I
              am a
              monster. I am
       a
       monster.
I am a monster.
And I am proud.
                                —ROBIN MORGAN

I n a moment of illumination, a radical feminist exclaimed: "We are the final cause."[1] I believe that she was right. Hence the following philosophical analysis.

The Final Cause and the Future

When Aristotle wrote of the "final cause," he intended "cause" to mean that which brings about an effect. Scholastic philosophers followed the Aristotelian theory of the "four causes" to explain change. According to this theory the material cause is that out of which something is made (as the wood in a table). The formal cause is that which determines its nature (as the shape of the wood which makes it a table and not a chair or something else). The efficient cause is the agent that produces the effect by her/his/its action (as the carpenter who produces the table). The final cause is the purpose which starts the whole process in motion (as the goal of having an object upon which to place books, papers, and other items). The final cause is therefore the first cause, since it moves the agent to act upon the matter, bringing forth a new form.

The example that I have used is obviously very simple. The doctrine of the four causes had many levels of interpretation and meaning for ancient and medieval philosophers. One only has to ask about the "four causes" of the wood itself to glimpse some of the difficulties involved. Yet the theory for centuries provided a framework for thinking about problems of transformation and becoming.[2]

It should be understood that the theory of the four causes was developed in a society encased in a static worldview, lacking any sense of evolution. In Aristotle's philosophy, the role of the efficient cause or agent is to actualize a potential that is already present. For example, the fire as agent brings cold water, which has the potentiality to become hot water, into the condition of actually being hot. Within the context of this mode of thinking, there is literally nothing new under the sun. As medieval philosophers later phrased it: *"Nemo dat quod non habetur."* That is, no one (agent) gives what isn't in some way already possessed. The "new form" is already there. It is actually in the agent (as the heat in the fire) and potentially in the patient (as the capacity in the water to become hot). There is no qualitative leap into the future. All is foreseeable.

Such a static and cyclic understanding of change was plausible in a postfigurative culture, in which one could look to one's grandparents and parents as models, seeing one's own future being acted out in their lives. As Mead has pointed out, we no longer live in such a society.[3] I am proposing that our present situation makes it possible to see "the final cause" in a completely different context. There was an incipient futurism in this idea which was nullified by the conceptual context in which it was expressed and which reflected prevailing societal conditions.

As it was conceived by Aristotle, the final cause or goal inspires the agent to act because it is apprehended as good. It causes by attracting, by drawing unto itself. This idea of the good as attracting, which Aristotle inherited from his teacher, Plato, might seem to be indicative of a futurist vision of a world on the move. However, it did not work out this way. The Greeks identified the concept of "the good" with the Parmenidean conception of "true being," which is changeless and already present. The goal of every action, therefore, already is. The future is essentially closed.

In the medieval philosophical synthesis of Thomas Aquinas, the good and true being were identical—the distinction being only in the mind.[4] Hence his thinking too remained bound within the same nonevolutionary circle. Aquinas did have an important distinction between the way creatures cause and God's causality. He thought that any finite agent can only work upon pre-existing matter, transforming it in a way that its potentiality will allow, which meant that it would "become" essentially the same as something already existing. In contrast to this, God, the First Cause, was said to be cause of being, for God brings creatures into existence out of nothing and sustains them in existence.[5] One could read an incipient futurism in this distinction of Aquinas, since the divine causality is *not* determined by pre-existing matter. But in reality there was not an open future envisaged here, since God was understood as *changeless* Being, from whom all creatures proceed and to whom they return.[6]

Contemporary Christian theology ostensibly has tried to bring the future into the picture. The results have been remarkably unsuccessful. The problem is illustrated in the work of Wolfhart Pannenberg, a prominent exponent of the theology of hope. Pannenberg casts us into a state of real hopelessness by his fixation upon the figure of Jesus. He contrasts the "coming-to-appearance of God in Jesus" with the "epiphanies of gods [sic] in human or animal form," claiming that in the latter cases "any particular form of the appearance, being replaceable, remains external to the essence of the deity." He continues:

In the ministry of Jesus, on the contrary, the God of Israel, the future of his Reign, comes definitively to appearance once. He [sic] manifested himself in this single event conclusively and for all time, and just for this reason only once.[7]

This is indeed a theology of hopelessness. Pannenberg reconfirms this interpretation at the end of the same essay, when he writes:

The arrival of what is future may be thought through to its conclusion only with the idea of repetition (which does not exclude the new), in the sense that in it the future has arrived in a permanent present [emphasis his].[8]

One is compelled to wonder what sort of future this might be. At any rate the symbolic message tells us that the prospects are dismal, and that this perspective is far more paralyzing than that of the Greeks. It is particularly depressing, though consistent, that this theologian finds the epiphanies of the "gods" (small "g") in *human* as well as in animal form to be external to the essence of the deity, apparently because these are *replaceable*. That is, there is no vision here of the universal presence of the Verb who is Be-ing, who has *not* been revealed once for all time, who can be revealed at any moment in a constantly unfolding (not merely repeated) revelation. Genuine *hierophanies* (manifestations of the sacred) are not "replaceable." Rather, they are manifold and unique manifestations of Be-ing. The fact that they are many and new, and not once and for all, is precisely because *they are not external to the essence of the deity*. The manifold and new quality of genuine hierophanies—genuine insofar as they are manifestations of Be-ing—that is, *ontophanies*, is possible because of *participation* in Being which is Be-ing. Be-ing encompasses and engulfs with healing power the false dichotomy between "true being" and becoming, revealing its unreality.

The usual mechanism of reversal seems to have been operative, then, in the recent crescendo of Christian "futurism" which kills the future by Bibliolatry. The gentlemen have protested too much; their speech betrays them.[9] The Greeks, somewhat unfairly blamed for Christianity's decrepitude, did bequeath some useful insights, not least among them the idea of "the final cause." If we can be freed from the Parmenidean delusory dichotomizing of becoming and being, we may be enabled to understand at last the real power of the final cause. Of course this will require lifting the idea out of context.

But how do we overcome the dichotomizing propensities in our culture that give credibility to the split between being and becoming? Clearly, we begin by trying to overcome the dichotomies within ourselves. I have said that this requires ongoing active courage and that androgynous wholeness is the essential healing we seek. But how does this relate specifically to the distinction in our cultural heritage between becoming and "true being"? I propose that we look at this problem with new eyes, seeing the conceptual distinction in the societal context that produced it, for philosophies reflect the vested interests of the cultures that give rise to them. We will have to free our imaginations so that they are not "field dependent" upon habitual (read: patriarchal) modes of perception. It will require "breaking set" and hearing old terms with brand new ears.

We might consider the probability that if the male intellectual elite has been fixated upon a split between becoming and being, this in all likelihood reflects the situation of the elite, who benefit from a static, hierarchical cultural climate and who would be threatened by total openness to the future. "Becoming" then becomes domesticated under the reign of reified "being," which can represent "things as they are" to the consciousness of the privileged who want it that way. It would not serve such interests if "becoming" were to blow off the lid of objectified "being." Marxist criticism of Christian hierarchalism and oppressiveness, while it wasn't deep enough, did manage (along with other influences) to generate a frantic scurry among theologians to leap on the bandwagon of futurism and find a scapegoat for the disease of Christianity. Having managed to blame "the Hellenic influence" for Chrisitan servility to oppressive powers, they now offer us the "future" of incorporation with Yahweh & Son. Women who have finally come to recognize that we are *per definitionem* excluded from management in that "corporation" can recognize here a continued hardening of the arteries that should link "being" and "becoming." The institutional fathers are still running the show In the Name of the "Future," which is another word for past.

Bachofen pointed out that the patriarchal principle is one of restrictions and that after the crushing of the original matriarchy, which was characterized by openness to others, the principle of hierarchy took over. I am adding that as long as this system prevails, human becoming is held down by objectified "being," which is the demonic distortion of Be-ing. Women have the power to open the channel so that being and becoming find their essential unity. We can do this by be-ing. But time is short. The senior and junior executives of the secular corporations that are the natural offspring and allies of Yahweh & Son are already programming us out of any significant role in the future. The gynocidal-and-therefore-genocidal mania of the patriarchs has already been transferred to The Holy Father Computer, who is heir to the papal throne of a secular Christendom that wills to devour the world. The Corporation of God the Father has formed a merger with the Earthly Town Fathers on the sly (soon to be subject to an antitrust suit). Together they have sent nocturnal emissions beyond the earth's atmosphere, bringing forth signs and wonders in the heavens, converting nearby outer space into a celestial junk yard. The Kingdom of Heaven, then, is at hand. Before it is too late, let it be said that Heaven is not a Kingdom. Let it be spoken by the word of our lives.

"The Final Cause" in Modern and Contemporary Philosophy

In the history of modern philosophy, prior to our own century, the final cause had a rather bad reputation. I shall give a brief sketch of some of the highlights of its unfortunate history as background for an analysis of what was wrong and of what is right.

Francis Bacon saw the final cause as a "sterile virgin" in philosophy, "barren" of results in physical investigations, and having no proper use except in the realm of human actions. In this way, Bacon tried to dodge the deadly device of using this concept as an explanatory principle. However, he was willing to allow it to stay around unchallenged in the realm of sacred theology in the form of a divine plan revealed in Scripture. This freed philosophy from its tyranny within philosophy's own territory, but it did not adequately challenge the mind-set of Christians.

Descartes thought that God has set an end for the universe and hence exercises final causality, but he insisted that the infinite depths of the divine purpose are inscrutable to us and banished this consideration from physical investigations. Again, this did not really challenge the claims of those who believed they had "divine revelation" in the Bible. It bestowed a kind of autonomy upon philosophy, helping it to get out from under the control of sacred theology. It helped to free philosophy but not to free people still mesmerized by Christian doctrine.

Spinoza removed the final cause not only from the philosophy of nature, but from *all* philosophical investigation. This was a logical consequence of his pantheism and of his conception of the final cause as a perfection to be acquired. Since the modal world (finite things) cannot "acquire" God, it would be contradictory to speak of causality in this sense. Spinoza was in this sense more radical than Descartes. The "final cause" which he removed from philosophical investigation deserved to go. But banished also from consideration were Insights about human becoming that are made available by more adequate envisionings of the final cause.

Leibniz tried unsuccessfully to rehabilitate the final cause in order to supplement his mechanistic view of nature. For him, souls and minds act according to the laws of final cause. There are conscious desires and chosen ends. There is, he thought, a pre-established harmony between the realms of mechanism and teleology. Within the context of the world of "nature" and efficient causes, a social communion—a teleological order—comes to birth. This constitutes the "City of God." However, as Bergson later pointed out, Leibniz's finalism was expressed in spatial terms. This spatial model was nonevolutionary. For Leibniz, God has chosen the best possible plan for the universe. Since "He" is all-perfect, "He" could hardly have chosen otherwise. Within this philosophical framework, there was hardly room for real freedom or a real future.

Kant used teleology to make sense out of sense impressions, but he did not think that there can be philosophical evidence for genuine purpose at work in nature. For him, the mind proceeds upon the *assumption* of purposiveness, but metaphysical certainty of this is impossible. In Kant's moral philosophy, clearly, purposiveness is assumed in responsible human behavior. However, this is not understood in ontological terms.

Schelling's system had room for purposiveness, not only as a regulative concept in minds, but also as a constitutive principle operating in nature itself. However, the presence of finality in nature is not known by induction. It is a deductive consequence of Schelling's doctrine on the absolute. Nature is the field not only for our moral strivings, but also for the strivings of the absolute spirit. This is interesting speculation, but its starting point is hardly communal consciousness of oppression and it is not therefore promising as a vision of an open future.

The positivist philosopher, August Comte, rejected metaphysical arguments for a final cause in the sense of transcendent being. Yet he considered "humanity" as final cause. John Stuart Mill favored a kind of teleology or final causality, but this was on the level of psychological description transferred into the realm of norms. His discourse was not ontological.

I suggest that the rejection of *ontological* final causality—a rejection that has manifested itself in various ways—has often really been a kind of metaphysical rebellion, even on the part of those philosophers who have been most disdainful of metaphysics. It has been an effort to overthrow the tyranny of the allegedly "supernatural end" that seemed to block the dynamics of thought and action. But this "block" was often a shallow and reified conception of the final cause. When those doing the rejecting have had no deep awareness of the dynamism in being, that is, of the ontological force of final causality, the reified Block has not wholly disappeared. It has tended to reappear in various ways. In the cases of some professed Christians, it was excluded from philosophy but was allowed to stay around in the realm of "faith" as what might be called the "Divine Block," alias the divine plan as revealed in Scripture. With the nonreligious it stayed around in the name of humanity, or universal happiness, or some dogmatic social theory or language theory. I suggest that both refusal to recognize the ontological power of final causality and blind adherence to a Final Block (divine or man-made) spring essentially from the same source: failure to confront the nonbeing of the structures of alienation and to affirm being In a creative and participatory way.

In some twentieth-century philosophical arenas, the Final Block has lost ground. Bergson's philosophy, for example, tried to break through it. He saw the surge of evolution as moving toward bringing life into reflective possession of itself, so that human intuitive consciousness becomes the "end" of the evolutionary process. He made it clear that he rejected the finalism of Leibniz which is based upon a spatial model of reality.[10] Yet, as Whitehead pointed out, it is regrettable that Bergson went so far as to see the tendency to spatialize as a vice necessary for intellectual apprehension of nature.[11] As a result of this belief, Bergson opted for a kind of anti-intellectualism, viewing theoretical concepts as incapable of expressing or unfolding intuition. Opposing this view, Whitehead saw the inadequacies of conceptual language as diminishable, though not eliminable. Although the history of Western philosophy would seem to support Bergson's conclusion that the distortion of "spatializing the universe" is unavoidable in philosophy, I would point out that this philosophy has been created by a male intellectual elite who have reflected the conservative and dichotomizing propensities of our culture. Bergson indicated that he himself was not free of these propensities when he opted against the use of theoretical concepts to analyze process, choosing instead poetic imagery. I do not think that radical women trying to express our intuition of being can settle for this route. We will have to reject this "either/or," and conceptualize as well as image our process in a manner that breaks out of stale male spatial patterns.

The process philosophy of Whitehead and some of his intellectual progeny comes closer to anticipating the dawn of the rising woman-consciousness. It is not my intention here to sketch the salient features of Whitehead's philosophy (a job already done many times over by his critics and admirers), or to initiate a feminist "dialogue" with this. I should merely like to indicate a few aspects of his thought which are hopeful indications that androgynous creative theorizing is in some way happening here, even though the specific relevance of such intellection to sexist oppression hardly leaps forth from every page or from any page. I would point out that Whitehead has presented his basic ideas in a manner intended to overcome all of the classical dualisms, as these are usually understood, while affirming them in another sense.[12] In his view, the future is open. Consistently with this, Whitehead's God is not a Creator God, that is, not merely *before* all creation but *with* creation.[13] Furthermore, for him "the purpose of philosophy is to rationalize mysticism."[14] That is, he neither opts for shallow objective consciousness nor gives up on intellectuality, but seeks a unity which I would still prefer to call a union of technical and ontological reason. I might add that Whitehead's refusal to dichotomize purposeful human beings from what has sometimes been considered nonpurposive nature is encouraging. The fact that the aesthetic plays an important role in his teleology is a hopeful sign. We may hope that this kind of thinking reflects and encourages a trend toward a more sensitive and less exploitative attitude toward "nature," an at-oneness with it.

Process philosophy's inclination to define being through becoming is an especially encouraging indication. Charles Hartshorne writes that "to be is to be available for all future actualities."[15] In his thought, process is a creative synthesis. With this kind of perspective, there is minimal danger of falling into dead-end notions of final causality. As Hartshorne put it, "an absolute and inexorable purpose, supposing this meant anything, would deny individuality, self-activity, hence reality, to the lesser individuals, the creatures."[16]

Yet one may question the relevance of this kind of intellection to social reality, especially to the objectified structures of alienation. I have stressed already that the essential task of feminism is *not* to go looking around for a ready-made theory and then try to make it relevant to our (little?) "issue" or "problem." This is self-depreciating in the extreme, a fact that is obvious if one realizes that feminism is cosmic in its dimensions. There is a seductiveness about philosophies (even more than in the case of theologies) which use language that is not totally distorting, but which do not explicitly move out of patriarchal space. The fact that philosophers of the future do not speak directly to the problem of sexism is a warning. "Whiteheadians" can be oblivious to the "process" of the female half of the species in our struggle to become. The essential thing is to hear our *own* words, always giving prior attention to our *own* experience, never letting prefabricated theory have *authority* over us. Then we can be free to listen to the old philosophical language (and all philosophy that does not explicitly repudiate sexism is old, no matter how novel it may seem). If some of this language, when heard in the context of female becoming, is still worth hearing, we need not close our ears. But if we choose to speak the same sounds they will be formally and existentially new words, for the new context constitutes them as such. Our process is *our* process.

The Cause of Causes

As Aristotle and the medieval philosophers understood it, the final cause is the goal perceived as good and attracting the agent to act. In "nonrational" nature the goal is also present in an anticipatory fashion as "entelechy." That is, there is an indwelling of the goal as yet unattained, but unfolding itself. I have pointed out that the implicit futurism is braked and broken within a thought-context that denies real newness: Plants, animals, and human beings unfold to become essentially the same as their parents; there is no qualitative leap envisaged. To paraphrase an ancient axiom: Whatever is, *was*.

But if we perceive the good, the final cause, as *not* identical with the static, timeless being of Parmenides, and *not* identical with the intentions of the institutional fathers and their Heavenly Father, but rather with Be-ing in which we participate actively by the qualitative leap of courage in the face of patriarchy, the magic collar that was choking us is shattered.

The circle of eternal return that neutralized the implicit futurism in Greek thought and that constitutes the alleged futurism of Christian symbols can be broken if women break the chain of nonbeing by be-ing.

In this sense, our cause can function as "the final cause," that is, by incarnating the desire to break out of the circle and communicating that desire, awakening women and consequently men to become ourselves. The final cause is the beginning, not the end, of becoming. It is the first cause, giving the motivation to act. The feminist movement is potentially the source of real movement in the other revolutionary movements (such as Black Liberation and the Peace Movement), for it is the catalyst that enables women and men to break out of the prison of self-destructive dichotomies perpetuated by the institutional fathers. Radical feminism can accomplish this breakthrough precisely because it gives rise to an intuition of androgynous existence. Only radical feminism can act as "the final cause," because of all revolutionary causes it alone opens up human consciousness adequately to the desire for non-hierarchical, nonoppressive society, revealing sexism as the basic model and source of oppression. Without the power of this vision to attract women and men so that we can will to transcend the whole array of false dualisms, there will be no real change. The liberation "movements" that leave sexism unchallenged can, of themselves, only spin delusions of progress, bringing about endless, arbitrary variation within the same senescent system.

It requires a kick in the imagination, a wrenching of tired words, to realize that feminism is the final and therefore the first cause, and that *this* movement *is* movement. Realization of this is already the beginning of a qualitative leap in be-ing. For the philosophers of senescence "the final cause" is in technical reason; it is the Father's plan, an endless flow of Xerox copies of the past. But the final cause that *is movement* is in our imaginative-cerebral-emotional-active-creative be-ing.

Diverging from the Omega Point: Versus Teilhard de Chardin

In his essay "The Grand Option," Teilhard de Chardin sets up several dichotomized alternatives which supposedly are our options in determining the "future of man" [sic].[17] I hasten to point out that when Teilhard says "man" he does mean "man." An ardent devotee of "the eternal feminine," he has bequeathed to us abundant examples in his writings of the nonactualized, nonreal condition which he admired in the female half of the species. Let it be admitted and mourned that he probably found no female in his circle of women disciples who had the mental vigor necessary to turn his quintessentially stereotypic thinking around. The level of feminist consciousness among Frenchwomen several decades ago was not astronomic, and it is certain that Simone de Beauvoir did not belong to the circle. Feminists perceive that Teilhard's conception of the generic and specific meanings of "man" (l'homme) coalesced. So also apparently do some of his male admirers who have written laudatory books on the subject of "women according to Teilhard."[18] Briefly, Teilhard favored "a certain emancipation" but was fearful lest this "masculinize" women.

The first pair of alternatives that Teilhard saw facing us is being and nothingness. Obviously, he would have us choose being. Although on the verbal level this is not a false dichotomy or the "wrong" choice, it remains in the realm of sterile abstractions since the becoming of women, which alone can direct the evolution of our species toward psychically androgynous being, is excluded from serious consideration.

The second dichotomy is involvement in the world versus withdrawal. It is clear that the prescribed option is "involvement." However, this is essentially a superficial split, for as I have attempted to show, "withdrawal" into boundary space and time constitutes the most radical involvement/participation in the cosmic community.

The third option envisaged is between unity and plurality, that is, between "convergence" and "divergence." This is a revealing dichotomy. Opting for convergence, Teilhard attempts to establish that the Universe is narrowing to a center. He unabashedly sees totalitarian regimes as essentially on the right track in this respect.[19] He asserts that a convergent world, "whatever sacrifice of freedom it may seem to demand of us, is the only one which can preserve the dignity and the aspirations of the living being."[20] The choice for convergence, which he sees as destined to become the common choice of "the mass of Mankind" is the "Grand Option."

Teilhard's dichotomy between convergence and divergence is hardly satisfactory. The imagery behind the terms is explicitly spatial. Convergence is narrowing to a center, while divergence is "spreading out like a fan." It is a way of expressing the dualism between monism and pluralism, the various ambiguous meanings of which are left unclarified. I suggest that if one wishes to speak adequately of "convergence," then this has to have as a basic element in its meaning a coming together and harmonizing of traits *within individual human psyches* that have been split apart and objectified by sex role socialization. *This* fundamental convergence, or unity, or individuation will mean increasing human potential for participation in society as unique, diverse individuals. It will mean "divergence."

Teilhard sees both Marxism and Christianity as offering options toward convergence. But as opposed to the "senescence" of the utopian classless society, Christianity supposedly offers the possibility of a "paroxysm," a breaking of the bonds of space-time to reach the irreversible loving center of all evolution, the Omega Point, the "Cosmic Christ." Teilhard's language is revealing. Insisting that Christ is identical with the Omega, he writes:

In order to demonstrate *the* truth *of this* fundamental proposition, *I need only refer to the long series of Johannine—and still more Pauline—texts in which the* physical supremacy *of Christ* over *the universe is so magnificently expressed* [emphasis all mine].[21]

To the nondogmatic mind it appears odd that Teilhard thought it was possible to "demonstrate" the truth of anything merely by the fact that it is proclaimed in biblical texts. This is hardly recognizable as the product of an evolutionary scientist-philosopher's mind and imagination. The language about Christ is consistent with the dogmatic, authoritarian tone of the whole "proposition" of this renowned Jesuit philosopher.

Teilhard tends to split off and reify being:

The world travails not to bring forth from within itself some supreme reality but to find its consummation through a union with a pre-existing Being [emphasis mine].[22]

His Omega Point is a static, spatial image, and in using it he spatializes time. He *visualizes* the Omega as an *apex* of conic time, as a *point*, as the *closing bulb* on the tree of life, as the *North Pole*.

In brief, Teilhard's Omega Point inspires claustrophobia. It is the repulsive metaphor of the Mystical Body of Christ revisited. It is "true being" clamping its iron jaws upon "becoming." His Christolatry cuts down his dream of "cosmogenesis" and closes the door to the future. "All that rises must converge"? Perhaps. But if this is convergence, who would want erection? Teilhard constantly uses the imagery of "rising," but as we float upward with him we notice that we are destined to bump into a reified Something. Describing the Seer, he writes:

Gazing upward, towards the space held in readiness for new creation, he dedicates himself . . . to a Progress which will bear with it or else sweep away all those who will not hear. His whole being seized with religious fervour he looks towards a Christ already risen but still unimaginably great.[23]

Enlivened by a dynamic intuition of being, women now coming alive hardly need or want a paroxysm toward a deadly Omega Point. Participation in Be-ing is the final cause, and because this is "the end," we can look forward to endless divergence. It makes us citizens of the future, where we are already finding it possible to know a new past. In organic Space-Time our movement is not linear. If, as Nietzsche said, God is dead, "Is there any up or down left?" Correction: To the degree that God the Father is dead, swept under by the Living Final Cause, our movement is in all directions: backward, inward, sideward, forward, as is the case with life itself.

Conclusion: The End of the Looking Glass War

An unwitting description of the cause of the peace movement's built-in obsolescence was made by biblically based Dan Berrigan during an interview reported in December 1972:

This seminary [Union Theological in New York] is like a playpen. I see signs in the elevators and in the halls, signs about raking leaves, sherry parties, women's liberation [emphasis mine] and so forth, but never anything about the war. It's forgotten. There is, practically speaking, no church resistance to the war anymore. But I can't forget about the war.[24]

Berrigan's commitment and courage are unquestionable. But . . . "raking leaves, sherry parties, women's liberation. . . ." When will they understand? It is rapism that has spawned racism. It is gynocide that gives rise to genocide.

In November 1972, the American people elected Richard Nixon to a landslide victory. December 1972 witnessed the heaviest bombing raids on Hanoi since the beginning of the Vietnam war. When will they understand? Can it be that we are beginning to witness "the fullness of the Gospel"? The Elected One points us toward the Omega Point. It is a time of warfare between principalities and powers.

On December 20, 1972, the news was telecast that Phil Berrigan was released from prison. Mass was celebrated among a gathering of family and friends. During the Mass, Pete Seeger's song "Turn, Turn" was sung. The words that came over national television were: "To everything, turn, turn. . . .A time to kill, a time to heal. . . ." The song, of course, has its origin in the Bible, in Ecclesiastes 3, 1–8. The chapter begins: "There is a season for everything, a time for every occupation under heaven." Among the approved dichotomies listed in this wisdom literature:

> *A time for killing,*
> *A time for healing;*
> *A time for knocking down,*
> *A time for building. . . .*
> *A time for loving,*
> *A time for hating,*
> *A time for war,*
> *A time for peace.*

And so the eternal circle turns. When will they understand? George Wald has written:

One has to begin to ask, are there such highly superior technological civilizations elsewhere in the universe, or is there not only a time when such a creature arrives, but a somewhat later time, perhaps not very much later, in which he [sic] departs? That problem now very much concerns us.[25]

One answer is: If they are humanoid creatures, split against themselves by an alienative opposition of opposites in the very depth of their psyches, and if they do not resolve *that* problem, then surely they do depart.

Our planet is inhabited by half-crazed creatures, but there is a consistency in the madness. Virginia Woolf, who died of being both brilliant and female, wrote that women are condemned by society to function as mirrors, reflecting men at twice their actual size. When this basic principle is understood, we can understand something about the dynamics of the Looking Glass society. Let us examine once again the creatures' speech.

That language for millennia has affirmed the fact that Eve was born from Adam, the first among history's unmarried pregnant males who courageously chose childbirth under sedation rather than abortion, consequently obtaining a child-bride. Careful study of the documents recording such achievements of Adam and his sons prepared the way for the arrival of the highest of the higher religions, whose priests took Adam as teacher and model. They devised a sacramental system which functioned magnificently within the sacred House of Mirrors. Graciously, they lifted from women the onerous power of childbirth, christening it "baptism." Thus they brought the lowly material function of birth, incompetently and even grudgingly performed by females, to a higher and more spiritual level. Recognizing the ineptitude of females in performing even the humble "feminine" tasks assigned to them by the Divine Plan, the Looking Glass priests raised these functions to the supernatural level in which they alone had competence. Feeding was elevated to become Holy Communion. Washing achieved dignity in Baptism and Penance. Strengthening became known as Confirmation, and the function of consolation, which the unstable nature of females caused them to perform so inadequately, was raised to a spiritual level and called Extreme Unction. In order to stress the obvious fact that all females are innately disqualified from joining the Sacred Men's Club, the Looking Glass priests made it a rule that their members should wear skirts. To make the point clearer, they reserved special occasions when additional Men's Club attire should be worn. These necessary accoutrements included delicate white lace tops and millinery of prescribed shapes and colors. The leaders were required to wear silk hose, pointed hats, crimson dresses and ermine capes, thereby stressing detachment from lowly material things and dedication to the exercise of spiritual talent. They thus became revered models of spiritual transsexualism.

These annointed Male Mothers, who naturally are called Fathers, felt maternal concern for the women entrusted to their pastoral care. Although females obviously are by nature incompetent and prone to mental and emotional confusion, they are required by the Divine Plan as vessels to contain the seeds of men so that men can be born and then supernaturally (correctly) reborn as citizens of the Heavenly Kingdom. Therefore in charity the priests encouraged women to throw themselves gratefully into their unique role as containers for the sons of the sons of the Son of God. Sincerely moved by the fervor of their own words, the priests educated women to accept this privilege with awestruck humility.

Since the Protestant Reformation, spiritual Looking Glass education has been modernized in some rooms of the House of Mirrors. Reformed Male Mothers gradually came to feel that Maleness was overstressed by wearing dresses all the time and even decided to include a suitable proportion of females (up to one half of one percent) among their membership, thereby stressing that the time for Male Snobbism was over and the time for Democracy had come. They also came to realize that they could be just as supernatural without being hemmed in by a stiff sacramental system. They could give birth spiritually, heal and console, and give maternal advice. They therefore continued the Looking Glass tradition of Mother Adam while at the same time making a smooth transition to The Modern Age.

Thus, Western culture was gracefully prepared by its Supernatural Mothers called Fathers to see all things supernaturally, that is, to perceive the world backward clearly. In fact, so excellent had been our education that this kind of thinking has become like second nature for almost everybody. No longer in need of spiritual guidance, our culture has come of age. This fact is evident to anyone who will listen to it when it talks. Its statesmen clear-headedly affirm the fact that this is "the Free World." Its newscasters accurately report that there has been fighting in the demilitarized zone, that several people were killed in a nonviolent demonstration, that "our nation" is fighting to bring peace to Southeast Asia. Its psychiatrists proclaim that the entire society is in fact a mental institution and applaud this fact as a promising omen of increasing health for their profession.

In the Looking Glass society females, that is, Magnifying Mirrors, play a crucial role. But males have realized that it would serve no good purpose if this were to become known by females, who then might stop looking into the toy mirrors they have been taught to use incessantly. They might then begin looking inside or outside or backward or forward. Instead of settling for the vanity of parakeets they might fall into the sin of pride and refuse to be Magnifying Mirrors any longer.

The females, in the terrifying, exhilarating experience of becoming rather than reflecting, would discover that they too have been infected by the dynamics of the Mirror World. Having learned only to mirror, they would find in themselves reflections of the sickness in their masters. They would find themselves doing the same things, fighting the same way. Looking inside for something there, they would be confused by what at first would appear to be an endless Hall of Mirrors. What to copy? What model to imitate? Where to look? What is a mere mirror to do? But wait—How could a mere mirror even frame such a question? The question itself is the beginning of an answer that keeps unfolding itself. The question-answer is a verb, and when one begins to move in the current of the verb, of the Verb, she knows that she is not a mirror. Once she knows this she knows it so deeply that she cannot completely forget. She knows it so deeply that she has to say it to her sisters. What if more and more of her sisters should begin to hear and to see and to speak?

This would be a disaster. It would throw the whole society backward into the future. Without Magnifying Mirrors all around, men would have to look inside and outside. They would start to look inside, wondering what was wrong with them. They would have to look outside because without the mirrors they would begin to receive impressions from real Things out there. They would even have to look at women, instead of reflections. This would be confusing and they would be forced to look inside again, only to have the harrowing experience of finding *there* the Eternal Woman, the Perfect Parakeet. Desperately looking outside again, they would find that the Parakeet is no longer *out there*. Dashing back inside, males would find other horrors: All of the other Others—the whole crowd—would be in there: the lazy niggers, the dirty Chicanos, the greedy Jews, faggots and dykes, plus the entire crowd of Communists and the backward population of the Third World. Looking outward again, mirrorless males would be forced to see—people. Where to go? Paroxysm toward the Omega Point? But without the Magnifying Mirror even that last refuge is gone. What to do for relief? Send more bombing missions? But no. It is pointless to be killing The Enemy after you find out The Enemy is yourself.

But the Looking Glass Society is still there, bent on killing itself off. It is still ruled by God the Father who, gazing at his magnified reflections, believes in his superior size. I say "believes," because the reflection now occasionally seems to be diminished and so he has to make a renewed act of faith in Himself.

We have been locked in this Eden of his far too long. If we stay much longer, life *will* depart from this planet. The freedom to fall out of Eden will cost a mirror-shattering experience. The freedom-becoming-survival of our species will require a continual, communal striving in be-ing. This means forging the great chain of be-ing in sisterhood that can surround nonbeing, forcing it to shrink back into itself. The cost of failure is Nothing.

Is this the war to end wars? The power of sisterhood is not war-power. There have been and will be conflicts, but the Final Cause causes not by conflict but by attraction. Not by the attraction of a Magnet that is All There, but by the creative drawing power of the Good Who is self-communicating Be-ing, Who is the Verb from whom, in whom, and with whom all true movements move.

Notes

Preface

1. Conversation with Jean MacRae, Boston, October 1972.

Introduction

1. See Mary Daly, *The Church and the Second Sex* (New York: Harper and Row, 1968). Among my articles, see: "After the Death of God the Father," *Commonweal*, XCIV (March 12, 1971), pp. 7–11; "The Courage to See," *The Christian Century*, LXXXVIII (September 22, 1971), pp. 1108–11; "Abortion and Sexual Caste," *Commonweal*, XCV (February 4, 1972), pp. 415–19; "The Spiritual Revolution: Women's Liberation as Theological Re-education," *Andover Newton Quarterly*, XII (March 1972), pp. 163–76; "The Women's Movement: An Exodus Community," *Religious Education*, LXVII (September-October 1972), pp. 327–35; "A Call for the Castration of Sexist Religion," *The Unitarian Universalist Christian*, XXVII (Autumn/Winter 1972), pp. 23–37.
2. Gerald D. Berreman, "Caste in India and the United States," *American Journal of Sociology*, LXVI (1960–61), pp. 120–27. In the same volume see Berreman's "Rejoinder," pp. 511–12. See also Helen Mayer Hacker, "Women as a Minority Group," *Social Forces*, XXX (1951–1952), pp. 60–69.
3. See Gordon Zahn, Letter to the Editor, *Commonweal*, XCV (February 18, 1972), pp. 470–71. Professor Zahn strongly objects to the use of the term "caste" as inaccurate for describing the male-female situation, and yet in the same paragraph refers to legalized abortion as the "oppression" of "a human being."
4. Jo Freeman, "The Legal Basis of the Sexual Caste System," *Valparaiso University Law Review*, V (Symposium Issue, 1971), pp. 203–36.
5. See Daly, *The Church and the Second Sex*. An earlier scholarly work of considerable merit is D. S. Bailey, *Sexual Relation in Christian Thought* (New York: Harper and Row, 1959). Rich also in historical material is Elizabeth Gould Davis, *The First Sex* (New York: G. P. Putnam's Sons, 1971). See Rosemary Radford Ruether, ed., *Images of Women in the Jewish and Christian Traditions* (New York: Simon and Shuster, 1973). Dr. Ruether has written a number of articles on sexism and religion, including "Male Chauvinist Theology," *Cross Currents*, XXI (Spring 1971), pp. 173–85, and "Women's Liberation in Historical and Theological Perspective," in *Women's Liberation and the Church*, edited by Sarah Bent-

ley Doeley (New York: Association Press, 1970, pp. 26–36. See also Sister Albertus Magnus McGrath, O.P., *What a Modern Catholic Believes about Women* (Chicago: Thomas More Press, 1972). See Emily C. Hewitt and Suzanne R. Hiatt, *Women Priests: Yes or No?* (New York: Seabury, 1973).

6. Reported in the Boston *Globe*, December 10, 1972, p. 14.

7. See Robin Scroggs, "Paul and the Eschatological Woman," *Journal of the American Academy of Religion*, XL (September 1972), pp. 283–303. A shorter and more popularized version of the article is "Paul: Chauvinist or Liberationist?" in *The Christian Century*, LXXXIX (March 15, 1972), pp. 307–09. Although Professor Scroggs' articles are sensitive attempts to distinguish Paul's own views from the pseudo-epigraphical works attributed to him, I do not think that they confront the issues raised by the women's movement.

8. Karl Barth is of course well known for this approach to theology, which implicitly holds as sacred the presuppositions of patriarchy.

9. Male authors who are now claiming that they can write accurately "about women" give away the level of their comprehension by the use of this expression. The new consciousness of women is not mere "knowledge about," but an emotional-intellectual-volitional rebirth. An example of inauthentic male claims is Donald McDonald, "The Liberation of Women," *The Center Magazine*, V (May-June 1972), pp. 25–42.

10. Paul Tillich's method is one of correlation. Although I find it less inadequate than the methods of other systematic theologians of this century, it clearly does not offer the radical critique of patriarchal religion that can only come from women, the primordial outsiders.

11. See Josiah Royce, *The World and the Individual*, 2 vols. (New York: Macmillan, 1900–1901).

12. See Paulo Freire, *Pedagogy of the Oppressed* (New York: Herder and Herder, 1970). Freire wrote acutely of the namelessness of the oppressed without even acknowledging in this book the prototypic namelessness of women.

13. Nelle Morton gives a profound and moving analysis of this in her article "The Rising Woman Consciousness in a Male Language Structure," *Andover Newton Quarterly*, XII (March 1972), pp. 177–90.

14. This is the sense in which "exodus" was applied to the walkout from Harvard Memorial Church called for in my sermon of November 14, 1971. See my article, "The Women's Movement: An Exodus Community," which contains the sermon and some letters from women who participated in the event, reflecting upon its meaning for them.

15. The Harvard Exodus and its continuing aftermath exemplifies the process. So also did the takeover by women students of a Harvard Divinity School course which supposedly dealt with liberation but failed to take into account women's liberation. See *Newsweek*, December 6, 1971, p. 58. The slick article, called "Pronoun Envy," distorts and trivializes, of course.

16. Women who were present at the seven days of exploring theology at Grailville, Loveland, Ohio (June 18–25) describe the experience somewhat in

these terms. A packet of stimulating articles, "Women Exploring Theology at Grailville," is available from Church Women United, 475 Riverside Drive, New York, N.Y. 10027.
17. Suzanne Langer, *Philosophy in a New Key*, a Mentor Book (New York: New American Library, 1951), p. 19.

CHAPTER ONE

After the Death of God the Father

1. Alice Rossi, "Sex Equality: The Beginning of Ideology," *Masculine/Feminine*, edited by Betty Roszak and Theodore Roszak (New York: Harper and Row, 1969), pp. 173–86. Rossi points out some inadequacies of assimilation into male models.
2. See Jean Piaget, *Structuralism* (New York: Basic Books, Inc., 1970).
3. Arnold Toynbee, *Christianity among the Religions of the World* (New York: Charles Scribner's Sons, 1957), p. 19.
4. See Robert N. Bellah, "Civil Religion in America," *Daedalus*, XCVI (Winter 1967), pp. 1–21. Bellah points out that the inauguration of a president is an important ceremonial event in American civil religion. It involves religious legitimation of the highest political authority. At Nixon's inauguration in 1973, Cardinal Cooke of New York was reported to have used the expression "heavenly Father" approximately seven times (conversation with Janice Raymond, who counted, January 20, 1973).
5. Rabbi Louis Finkelstein, in *White House Sermons*, edited by Ben Hibbs (New York: Harper and Row, 1972), p. 68. This sermon was delivered June 29, 1969. Similar sentiments have been expressed by the Rev. John McLaughlin, S.J., "the Catholic Billy Graham." See *National Catholic Reporter*, October 6, 1972, p. 9.
6. Charles Henderson, *The Nixon Theology* (New York: Harper and Row, 1972). See also Henderson's article "The [Social] Gospel according to 1) Richard Nixon 2) George McGovern," *Commonweal*, XCVI (September 29, 1972), pp. 518–25.
7. Dr. Paul S. Smith, in *White House Sermons*, pp. 82–83.
8. Cited in Henderson, *The Nixon Theology*, p. 175.
9. *Ibid.*, p. 176.
10. This is exemplified in a statement of John L. McKenzie, S.J., in *The Two Edged Sword* (New York: Bruce, 1956), pp. 93–94: "God is of course masculine, but not in the sense of sexual distinction. . . ."
11. See Mary Baker Eddy, *Science and Health* (Boston: Published by the Trustees under the Will of Mary Baker G. Eddy, 1934). Eddy wrote what she believed to be the "spiritual sense" of "The Lord's Prayer." It begins: "Our Father-Mother God, all-harmonious . . ." (p. 16). In the same work she uses the image of God's motherhood a number of times. Ann Lee's ideas have been studied by sociologist Henri Desroches. See, for example, *The American Shakers: From Neo-Christianity to Presocialism*, translated

and edited by John K. Savocool (Amherst: University of Massachusetts Press, 1971).

12. See Karl Barth, *Church Dogmatics*, edited by G. W. Bromiley and T. F. Torrance (Edinburgh: T. & C. Clark, 1956–1962), III/4, pp. 116–240. Barth goes on and on about woman's subordination to man, ordained by God. Although he goes through a quasi-infinite number of qualifications, using such jargon as "mutual subordination," he warns that we must not overlook the "concrete subordination of woman to man" (p. 175). He writes: "Properly speaking, the business of woman, her task and function, is to actualize the fellowship in which man can only precede her, stimulating, leading, and inspiring. ... . To wish to replace him in this, or to do it with him, would be to wish not to be a woman." In case the point is not clear, he adds the rhetorical question: "What other choice has she [than to be second] seeing she can be nothing at all apart from this sequence and her place within it?" (p. 171). This is justified as being the divine order, according to Barth. See also Dietrich Bonhoeffer, *Letters and Papers from Prison*, edited by Eberhard Bethge, translated by Reginald H. Fuller (New York: Macmillan Paperback, 1966), p. 47: "You may order your home as you like, save in one particular: the woman must be subject to her husband, and the husband must love his wife." See also Reinhold Niebuhr, *The Nature and Destiny of Man: A Christian Interpretation*, Vol. 1 (New York: Charles Scribner's Sons, 1941), p. 282. Niebuhr writes: "A rationalistic feminism is undoubtedly inclined to transgress inexorable bounds set by nature. On the other hand, any premature fixation of certain historical standards in regard to the family will inevitably tend to reinforce male arrogance and to retard *justified efforts* [italics mine] on the part of the female to achieve such freedom as is not incompatibie with the *primary function of motherhood* [italics mine]." As for Teilhard de Chardin, his writings are replete with spiritualized androcentrism. For examples, see Henri de Lubac, S.J., *The Eternal Feminine: A Study on the Text of Teilhard de Chardin*, translated by René Hague (New York: Harper and Row, 1971). The sexism is of course unrecognized by de Lubac. See also André A. Devaux, *Teilhard et la vocation de la femme* (Paris: Editions universitaires, 1963).

13. Gregory Baum, *Man Becoming* (New York: Herder and Herder, 1970), p. 195.

14. I would agree with Gordon Kaufman that Tillich himself does not completely escape hypostatization in his God language. The "Unconditioned" and the "Ground" are almost reified. See Gordon D. Kaufman, "On the Meaning of 'God,' " in *Transcendence*, edited by Herbert W. Richardson and Donald R. Cutler (Boston: Beacon Press, 1969), pp. 114–42.

15. Paul Tillich, *The Courage to Be* (New Haven: Yale University Press, 1952), pp. 32–63. See also Michael Novak, *The Experience of Nothingness* (New York: Harper and Row, 1970).

16. See Richardson's essay "Three Myths of Transcendence," in *Transcen-*

dence, edited by Richardson and Cutler, pp. 98–113. Richardson is more explicit on the problem of sex roles in his recent book *Nun, Witch, Playmate* (New York: Harper and Row, 1971).

17. See James Cone, *A Black Theology of Liberation* (Philadelphia: Lippincott, 1970).

18. Enlightening on this point of positive ontological experience is the work of Abraham H. Maslow, *Toward a Psychology of Being* (Princeton, New Jersey: Van Nostrand, 1962).

19. This was illustrated a few years ago in Michael Novak's book, *The Experience of Nothingness*. In various ways it has been expressed in writings and music of the counterculture.

20. This problem is acute in the work of Wolfhart Pannenberg. See, for example, his *Theology and the Kingdom of God* (Philadelphia: The Westminster Press, 1969). It is evident also in Jurgen Moltmann, *Theology of Hope*, translated by James W. Leitch (New York: Harper and Row, 1967). These theologians, of course, handle philosophical questions in a sophisticated and knowledgeable fashion, but the perspective is so biblical that it alienates "nonbelievers."

21. Unfortunately, in the Christian theological tradition this "image" was recognized as existing unambiguously only in the male. While Augustine saw the male as being to the image of God, he conceded that woman is restored to the image only where there is no sex, that is, in the spirit (*De Trinitate*, XII, 7). Aquinas was a little more generous, granting that the image of God is in both man and woman, but adding that in a special sense it is only in the male, who is "the beginning and end of woman, as God is the beginning and end of every creature" (*Summa theologiae* I, 93, 4 ad 1).

22. Dietrich Bonhoeffer, *Letters and Papers from Prison*, p. 190.

23. Peter Berger, *The Sacred Canopy: Elements of a Sociological Theory of Religion* (New York: Doubleday, 1967), pp. 53–80. Berger, however, does not recognize implications of this from the standpoint of radical feminism.

24. Peter Berger, *A Rumor of Angels: Modern Society and the Rediscovery of the Supernatural* (New York: Doubleday–Anchor Books, 1970), p. 12. Unfortunately, however, Berger goes rather far in "liquidating" the work of theologians whose views are less orthodox than his own.

25. Max Weber, *The Sociology of Religion*, translated by Ephraim Fischoff (Boston: Beacon Press, 1963), p. 198.

26. *Ibid.*, pp. 198–99.

27. Johannes Metz, "Creative Hope," *New Theology No. 5*, edited by Martin E. Marty and Dean G. Peerman (New York: Macmillan, 1968), pp. 130–41. See also Metz, *Theology of the World*, translated by William Glen-Doepel (New York: Herder and Herder, 1969).

28. Jacques Maritain, *Existence and the Existent*, translated by Lewis Galantiere and Gerald B. Phelan (New York: Doubleday–Image Books, 1956). Although he was hardly a feminist or social revolutionary, Maritain had an

exceedingly fine sensitivity to the power of this intuition, which, if it were carried through to social consciousness, would challenge the world. See also *Distinguish to Unite: The Degrees of Knowledge*, translated from the fourth French edition under the supervision of G. B. Phelan (New York: Charles Scribner's Sons, 1959).

29. Paul Tillich, *Systematic Theology* I (Chicago: University of Chicago Press, 1951), p. 74: "Whenever technical reason dominates, religion is superstition and is either foolishly supported by reason or rightly removed by it."

30. Maritain, in *Existence and the Existent*, p. 76, remarks: "When a man [sic] is awake to the intuition of being he is awake at the same time to the intuition of subjectivity. . . . The force of such a perception may be so great as to sweep him [sic] along to that heroic ascetism of the void and of annihilation in which he will achieve ecstasy in the substantial existence of the *self* and the 'presence of immensity' of the divine Self at one and the same time. . . ."

31. Max Weber, in *The Sociology of Religion*, p. 25, points out that "a power conceived by analogy to living persons may be coerced into the service of man." This means that whoever has the requisite charisma "is stronger even than the god." He also indicates that such a god can conveniently be blamed when things go wrong (p. 32).

32. Conversation with Linda Barufaldi, Boston, August 1972. Buckminster Fuller has referred to God as a verb.

33. It is clear that from such an experiential context there is not likely to come much rapport with language about God as "ultimate Limit" or Limiter.

34. Some of Sartre's thinking consequent to this rejection is in Jean Paul Sartre, *Being and Nothingness: An Essay on Phenomenological Ontology*, translated by Hazel E. Barnes (New York: Philosophical Library, 1956).

35. Karl Jaspers and Rudolf Bultmann, *Myth and Christianity* (New York: Noonday Press, 1958), p. 14.

36. Johannes Metz, *Theology of the World*, p. 104.

37. See Mircea Eliade, *Patterns in Comparative Religion*, translated by Rosemary Sheed (New York: Sheed and Ward, 1958). See Jay J. Kim, "Hierophany and History," *Journal of the American Academy of Religion*, September 1972, pp. 334–48.

38. Paul Tillich, *Systematic Theology* III (Chicago: University of Chicago Press, 1963), p. 310.

39. *Ibid.*, pp. 309–10.

40. *Ibid.*, pp. 308–9.

41. The *National Organization for Women*, the *Women's Equity Action League*, and the *Saint Joan's International Alliance* (Catholic feminists) are organizations with dues-paying members. While these have important functions, the movement as I use the term is not reducible to membership in these organizations. It is far more widespread, complex, and immeasurable than the concept of organizational membership can encompass.

42. Janice Raymond, "Beyond Male Morality," a paper delivered at the International Congress of Learned Societies in the Field of Religion, Los Angeles, September 1–5, 1972. Published by the American Academy of Religion

(University of Montana) in *Proceedings of the Working Group on Women and Religion, 1972*, edited by Judith Plaskow Goldenberg, pp. 83–93.

43. Leslie Dewart made the point that relative atheism is probably more indicative of an open consciousness than absolute theism. See *The Future of Belief* (New York: Herder and Herder, 1966), pp. 52–76.

44. Roger Garoudy, *From Anathema to Dialogue*, translated by L. O'Neill (New York: Herder and Herder, 1966), p. 94.

45. See William James, *The Will to Believe* (New York: Dover Publications reprint, 1956). See also *A Pluralistic Universe* (New York: Longmans Green, 1909).

46. See Alfred North Whitehead, *Process and Reality* (New York: Macmillan, 1929).

47. Well-known sources for these are treatises attributed to Denis the Areopagite, including *On the Divine Names* (*De divinis nominibus*) and a short treatise *On Mystical Theology* (*De mystica theologia*). Thomas Aquinas used the "three ways" for deriving the divine attributes in his *Summa theologiae*.

48. See Huston Smith, "The Reach and the Grasp: Transcendence Today," in *Transcendence*, edited by Richardson and Cutler, pp. 1–17.

49. See for example Thomas Aquinas, *Summa theologiae*, I, q. 6.

50. For a brief discussion of this see Etienne Gilson, *History of Christian Philosophy in the Middle Ages* (New York: Random House, 1955), pp. 368–72. See also Jacques Maritain, *Distinguish to Unite: The Degrees of Knowledge*.

51. Thomas Aquinas, *Summa theologiae*, I, 13, 2.

52. Martin Buber, *I and Thou*, translated by Ronald Gregor Smith (New York: Charles Scribner's Sons, 1958), p. 6.

53. Paul Tillich, *Systematic Theology* I, especially pp. 71–81.

54. Conversation with Emily Culpepper, Boston, November 1972.

55. *Ibid.*

CHAPTER TWO

Exorcising Evil from Eve: The Fall into Freedom

1. Nicolas Berdyaev, *The Beginning and the End*, translated by R. M. French (Gloucester, Mass.: YMCA Press, 1952), p. 246.

2. For striking examples of this punitive attitude as implied in abortion legislation, see Lawrence Lader, *Abortion II: Making the Revolution* (Boston; Beacon Press, 1973).

3. Dr. A. Hesnard, *Morale sans péché* (Paris: Presses universitaires de France, 1954).

4. Elizabeth Cady Stanton, Letter to the Editor, *The Critic* (1896), cited in *Up from the Pedestal*, edited by Aileen S. Kraditor (Chicago: Quadrangle Books, 1968), p. 119.

5. H. R. Hays, *The Dangerous Sex: The Myth of Feminine Evil* (New York: G. P. Putnam's Sons, 1964), p. 88. Unfortunately, not all women scholars

share Hays' willingness to acknowledge the implications of the myth of feminine evil. Phyllis Trible, a biblical scholar, asserts that the myth of the Fall does not legitimate the oppression of women. Dr. Trible's method is an attempt to "reinterpret" the Bible and to prove that "the Hebrew Scriptures and Women's Liberation do meet and that their encounter need not be hostile." See her article, "Depatriarchalizing in Biblical Tradition," *Journal of the American Academy of Religion* XLI (March 1973), pp. 30–48. It might be interesting to speculate upon the probable length of a "depatriarchalized Bible." Perhaps there would be enough salvageable material to comprise an interesting pamphlet.

6. Freire, *Pedagogy of the Oppressed*, p. 32.
7. *Ibid.*, p. 37.
8. Berger, *Rumor of Angels*, p. 7.
9. See Vivian Gornick, "Why Women Fear Success," *Ms. Magazine* I (Spring 1972), pp. 50–53. Gornick here records an interview with Dr. Matina Horner, a prominent psychologist who has done extensive research demonstrating a pervasive fear of success in women. According to Dr. Horner, this is not a simple will to fail. It is an active, anxious desire to avoid success.
10. Statement of Mrs. Norma Folda, President of the National Council of Catholic Women, May 13, 1970, Washington, D.C. The statement was made before the Subcommittee on Constitutional Amendments of the Committee on the Judiciary: U.S. Senate. Part of the statement: "Again we strongly reiterate our opposition to the proposed 'Equal Rights' Amendment to the U.S. Constitution as a threat to the nature of woman, which individuates her from man in God's plan for His creation."
11. See Barbara Burris, "The Fourth World Manifesto," *Notes from the Third Year: Women's Liberation* (New York, 1971), pp. 102–19. Reprinted in *Radical Feminism*, edited by A. Koedt, E. Levine, and A. Rapone (New York: Quadrangle Books, 1973), pp. 322–57. See Frantz Fanon, *A Dying Colonialism*, translated by Haakon Chevalier, Evergreen Edition (New York: Grove Press, 1967), pp. 35–67. In the chapter entitled "Algeria Unveiled," Fanon justified the fact that the Algerian woman was restricted to the home: "The Algerian woman, in imposing such a restriction on herself, in choosing a form of existence limited in scope, was deepening her consciousness of struggle and preparing for combat" (p. 66). Fanon apparently chose to see no problem with calling this a *choice* by women, although he resented bitterly this kind of hypocritical rhetoric when it was used by the French regarding the condition of Algerians (males).
12. See Eleanor E. Maccoby, "Woman's Intellect," *The Potential of Woman*, edited by Seymour M. Farber and Roger H. L. Wilson (New York: McGraw Hill Book Company, 1963), especially pp. 33, 37. See also *The Development of Sex Differences*, edited by Eleanor E. Maccoby (Stanford, California: Stanford University Press, 1966).
13. An obvious example of such an organization was the group of Swiss women who joined together specifically to oppose the right of women to vote in the Swiss national elections.

14. See Joel Kovel, *White Racism: A Psychohistory*, Vintage Books (New York: Random House, 1971). See also David H. Krichbaum, "Masculinity and Racism: Breaking out of the Illusion," *The Christian Century* XC (January 10, 1973), pp. 43–46.

15. See Angela Davis, "Reflections on the Black Woman's Role in the Community of Slaves," *The Black Scholar* III, No. 4 (1971), pp. 2–15. See also "Angela Davis on Black Women," *Ms. Magazine* I (August 1972), pp. 55, 57, 59, 116.

16. Pauli Murray, "The Liberation of Black Women," *Voices of the New Feminism*, edited by Mary Lou Thompson (Boston: Beacon Press, 1970), pp. 87–102.

17. For example, see "A Letter from the Berrigans," in *American Report*, December 31, 1971, p. 5.

18. See Lionel Tiger, *Men in Groups* (New York: Random House, 1969). In this and subsequent writings, Tiger not only gives abundant evidence of male bonding but also proposes the thesis that this tendency is innate and inevitable—a thesis for which he fails to give adequate supporting evidence.

19. See Janice G. Raymond, "Nuns and Women's Liberation," *Andover Newton Quarterly*, XII (March 1972), pp. 201–12. The author demonstrates that the traditional inauthentic roles assigned to women have been especially operative in religious communities of women. Even the role of sex object is incorporated into the ideal of the nun. "Though virginity is certainly opposite to sacred prostitution in a behavioral sense, it is yet identical to it in a psychological and cultic sense. For the nun in her own mind becomes the 'bride of Christ' supposedly on her profession day and henceforth is initiated into the divine 'harem' chosen to have sacred 'intercourse' with the divine" (p. 206). The same author has done an extensive study of the situation of Catholic religious sisterhoods within the historical-cultural context of patriarchy in general and of Roman Catholicism in particular. See Raymond, "Nuns and Women's Liberation: A Study of the Effects of Patriarchy upon Roman Catholic Religious Communities of Women and an Alternative." Unpublished M. A. thesis, Andover Newton Theological School, Newton Centre, Massachusetts, 1971.

20. See writings of women who have "graduated" from submergence in the Radical Left, for example: Ellen Willis, "Women and the Left," *Notes from the Second Year: Major Writings of the Radical Feminists* (New York, 1970), pp. 55–56. This publication is obtainable from P.O. Box AA, Old Chelsea Station, New York, N.Y. 10011.

21. See Thomas S. Szasz, *The Manufacture of Madness* (New York: Harper and Row, 1970). See also Erich Neumann, *Depth Psychology and a New Ethic*, translated by Eugene Rolfe (New York: G. P. Putnam's Sons, 1969).

22. Augustine, *De ordine*, Liber secundus, caput iv, 12: "Quid sordidius, quid inanius, dedecoris, et turpitudinis plenius meretricibus lenonibus ceterisque hoc genus pestibus dici potest? Aufer meretrices de rebus humanis, turbaueris omnia libidinibus; constitue matronarum loco, labe ac dedecore dehonestaueris."

23. Thomas Aquinas, *Opuscula* xvi, 14.
24. See Leo Kanowitz, *Women and the Law: The Unfinished Revolution* (Albuquerque: University of New Mexico Press, 1969), pp. 15–18.
25. *Ibid.*, p. 16.
26. *The "Malleus Maleficarum" of Heinrich Kramer and James Sprenger*, translated with introductions, bibliography, and notes by the Rev. Montague Summers (New York: Dover Publications, Inc., 1971), p. 47 [Originally published in 1928].
27. *Ibid.*
28. *Ibid.*, p. 41. See also Barbara Ehrenreich and Deirdre English, *Witches, Midwives, and Nurses: A History of Women Healers* (Glass Mountain Pamphlets, P.O. Box 238, Oyster Bay, N.Y. 11771).
29. Jules Michelet, *Satanism and Witchcraft: A Study in Medieval Superstition*, translated by A. R. Allinson (London: Arco Publications, 1958), especially the Introduction and pp. 77–88.
30. See Margaret A. Murray, *The Witch-Cult in Western Europe*, Oxford Paperbacks (New York: Oxford University Press, 1971) [Originally published in 1921]. See also Murray, *The God of the Witches*, Oxford Paperbacks (New York: Oxford University Press, 1970) [Originally published in 1931]. Witchcraft as used here refers to the Old Religion. Murray makes a sharp distinction between Ritual Witchcraft (the Old Religion) and Operative Witchcraft. The latter is taken to include all charms and spells, "whether used by a professed witch or by a professed Christian, whether intended for good or for evil" (*The Witch-Cult*, p. 11). Sybil Leek, a contemporary witch, writes: "The trouble comes from the confusion between witchcraft (the Old Religion) and Black Magic, which is certainly *not* a religion but a debased art." *Diary of a Witch* (New York: New American Library, 1968), p. 11.
31. Henry Charles Lea, *A History of the Inquisition of the Middle Ages* (3 vols.; New York: Harper and Brothers, 1888), III, p. 514.
32. Szasz, *The Manufacture of Madness*. See especially Part I: "The Inquisition and Institutional Psychiatry." On Elizabeth Packard, see Phyllis Chesler, *Women and Madness* (New York: Doubleday, 1972), *passim*.
33. Barbara Roberts, M.D., "Psychosurgery: The 'Final Solution' to the 'Woman Problem'?" *The Second Wave* II, No. 1 (1972), p. 13. Roberts writes: "The widest target group, according to all the large-scale studies, is women. Dr. Lindstrom, a prominent California neurosurgeon writing in 1964, said that 72 percent of psychotics and 80 percent of neurotics operated on are women. . . . And Dr. R. F. Heatherton, at the Kingston Psychiatric Hospital in Ontario, admitted at a 1970 medical conference that the hospital administration refused to allow lobotomies on men because of the unfavorable publicity given to lobotomy in Canada; that publicity did not, however, deter the hospital from performing lobotomies on seventeen women" (p. 14).
34. Albert Camus, *The Rebel*, translated by Anthony Bower (New York: Alfred Knopf, 1957), p. 4.
35. Mircea Eliade, *The Sacred and the Profane: The Nature of Religion*, trans-

lated by Willard R. Trask, Harper Torchbooks (New York: Harper and Row, 1961), p. 213.

36. Felix Morrow, Foreword, in Montague Summers, *The History of Witchcraft and Demonology* (Secaucus, New Jersey: Citadel Press, 1971 [c1956, University Books]), p. xiii. Summers, a Catholic priest, was totally convinced that the church was justified in its means of persecuting witches. It is fascinating to read the dedication of his book, indicating an extraordinary devotion to the Blessed Virgin Mary. Summers in his studies of witches, of the tortures to which those accused of practicing witchcraft were subjected, apparently found nothing disconcerting about the church's inhumanity to concrete, existing women.

CHAPTER THREE

Beyond Christolatry: A World Without Models

1. Paul Tillich, *Dynamics of Faith* (New York: Harper and Row, 1957), p. 98.
2. Henry Nicholson, *Jesus Is Dead* (New York: Vantage Press, 1971), p. xi.
3. See Thomas J. J. Altizer, *The Gospel of Christian Atheism* (Philadelphia: Westminster Press, 1966).
4. I expressed this idea in a 1971 article: "After the Death of God the Father." The idea was also used in an original way by Dr. Elizabeth Farians in her article "The Coming of Woman: The Christa," in *Seminarians for Ministerial Renewal*, April 1971. Since then, I have concluded that the idea of the Second Coming of women can be more accurately understood in a wider context than that of Christian symbolism.
5. Leonard Swidler, "Jesus was a Feminist," *The Catholic World*, January 1971, pp. 177–83.
6. Margaret Mead, *Culture and Commitment: A Study of the Generation Gap* (New York: Doubleday, 1970), p. 75.
7. Paul M. Van Buren, *The Secular Meaning of the Gospel* (New York: Macmillan paperback, 1966), p. 134.
8. Thomas Szasz, *The Manufacture of Madness*, p. 261.
9. Nicholson, *Jesus Is Dead,* p. 127.
10. Thomas Szasz, *The Manufacture of Madness*, p. 262.
11. *Ibid.*
12. Neumann, *Depth Psychology and a New Ethic*, p. 53.
13. *Ibid.*, p. 55.
14. On the influence of sanctions, see Ralf Dahrendorf, *Essays in the Theory of Society* (Stanford: Stanford University Press, 1968).
15. Berger, *A Rumor of Angels*, p. 92.
16. Tillich, *Systematic Theology* I, p. 128.
17. Some of the recent ecumenical discussion is presented by Titus Cranny, S.A., in *Is Mary Relevant?* (New York: Exposition Press, 1970). The author's

thought is totally within the framework of orthodox Catholicism, but the book has some useful materials.

18. Conversation with Emily Culpepper, October 1972, who heard this idea repeatedly from Sunday school teachers and ministers in the South.
19. Gordon D. Kaufman, *Systematic Theology: A Historicist Perspective* (New York: Charles Scribner's Sons, 1968), p. 413.
20. John Macquarrie, *Principles of Christian Theology* (New York: Charles Scribner's Sons, 1966), p. 258.
21. *Ibid.*, p. 259.
22. Karl Barth, *Church Dogmatics*, I/2, p. 177.
23. This idea was developed in a paper by Penelope Washbourn, "Differentiation and Difference: Reflections on Ethical Problems Raised by Women's Liberation," *Women and Religion, 1972*, pp. 95–105.
24. See Janice Raymond, "Nuns and Women's Liberation," Unpublished M.A. thesis.
25. Thomas Aquinas, *Summa theologiae* III, 27, 2c.
26. *Ibid.*, II, 27, 2 ad 2.
27. Pope Pius IX, Bull *Ineffabilis Deus*, in Denzinger, *Enchiridion Symbolorum*, n. 1641.
28. In Denzinger, n. 2333.
29. *Dogmatic Constitution on the Church* (*Lumen Gentium*) n. 59, in *The Documents of Vatican II*, edited by Walter M. Abbott, S.J. (New York: America Press, 1966).
30. C. G. Jung, *Psychology and Religion* (New Haven: Yale University Press, 1938), p. 77.
31. *Ibid.*, p. 92.
32. C. G. Jung, *Memories, Dreams, Reflections*, recorded and edited by Aniela Jaffé, translated by Richard and Clara Winston (New York: Random House, 1961), p. 332.
33. *Ibid.*, p. 202.
34. The idea of women rising is not peculiar to Christian symbolism. One woman noted the analogy in the stories about witches flying through the air. Conversation with Emily Culpepper, Boston, December 1972.
35. Conversation with Jean MacRae, Boston, December 1972.
36. Tillich, *Systematic Theology* I, p. 128.
37. Nicolas Berdyaev, *The Beginning and the End*, p. 246.
38. Henry Adams, *The Education of Henry Adams: An Autobiography* (Boston and New York: Houghton Mifflin Co., 1918), pp. 388–89.
39. Elizabeth Gould Davis, *The First Sex*, pp. 243–44.
40. See the book of E. O. James, *The Cult of the Mother Goddess: An Archaeological and Documentary Study* (New York: Praeger, 1959).
41. Davis, *The First Sex*, p. 246.
42. Karen Horney, *Feminine Psychology*, translated by Harold Kelman (New York: Norton, 1967), p. 136.
43. For some examples, see Simone de Beauvoir, *The Second Sex*, translated by H. M. Parshley (New York: Alfred A. Knopf, Inc., 1953); Kate Millett, *Sexual Politics* (New York: Doubleday, 1970); Eva Figes, *Patriarchal At-*

titudes (New York: Stein and Day, 1970). A brief and excoriating collection is to be found in the essay: "Know Your Enemy: A Sampling of Sexist Quotes," *Sisterhood is Powerful*, edited by Robin Morgan (New York: Random House, 1970), pp. 31–36.

44. Erich Fromm, *The Forgotten Language* (New York: Holt Rinehart, 1951), p. 210.

45. Davis, *The First Sex*, p. 75.

46. *Ibid.*, p. 77. Among the sources that Davis uses to support her conclusion are studies by James Mellaart, U. Bahadir Alkim, and Frederic-Marie Bergounioux. These studies (all done since 1965) tend to support ideas proposed earlier in E. O. James, *The Cult of the Mother Goddess*.

47. See de Beauvoir, *The Second Sex*; Davis, *The First Sex;* Daly, *The Church and the Second Sex.*

48. Michelet, *Satanism and Witchcraft*, p. x.

CHAPTER FOUR

Transvaluation of Values: The End of Phallic Morality

1. Herbert Marcuse, "Marxism and the New Humanity: An Unfinished Revolution," *Marxism and Radical Religion*, edited by John C. Raines and Thomas Dean (Philadelphia: Temple University Press, 1970), pp. 7–9.

2. Norman Brown, *Love's Body* (New York: Random House, 1966), pp. 132–33.

3. Theodore Roszak, *The Making of a Counter Culture* (New York: Doubleday, 1969), p. 86.

4. Alice Rossi, "Sex Equality: The Beginning of Ideology," *Masculine/Feminine*, edited by Betty Roszak and Theodore Roszak, Harper Colophon Books (New York: Harper and Row, 1969), pp. 173–86.

5. See Valerie Saiving Goldstein, "The Human Situation: A Feminine Viewpoint," *Journal of Religion* XL (April 1960), pp. 100–12.

6. Thomas Aquinas, *Summa theologiae* I, q. 92, a. 1, ad 2. For Aquinas, this inferiority was so inherent in female nature that women even would have been in a state of subjection before the Fall, which he understood as a historical event in the past.

7. *Ibid.*, II–II, q. 47, a.2. See Aristotle, *Nichomachean Ethics* vi, 5.

8. See, for example, Thomas Aquinas, *Summa Theologiae*, II–II, q. 50, a. 2c and ad 1. For Aquinas, the prudence of those in a state of subjection falls short of what is called regnative prudence. Persons in a state of subjection "direct themselves in obeying their superiors."

9. See Tillich, *Systematic Theology* I, pp. 72–73.

10. Joseph Fletcher, *Situation Ethics* (Philadelphia: Westminster Press, 1966), p. 59. Fletcher goes even further: "It is a Christological ethic, not simply a theological ethic. . . . Take away the doctrine of the incarnation and the Christian ethic is nothing special whatsoever" (p. 157).

11. *Ibid.*, p. 156.

12. *Ibid.*, p. 104. Fletcher elaborates upon this point: "Just as neighbor-concern can find a place for friendship but need not, so it has a place for the self's good as well as the neighbor's, but always only if the self takes second place" (p. 110).
13. I have already indicated that one of the most insightful criticisms of sacrificial love morality is that of Henry Nicholson, in his book *Jesus Is Dead*.
14. Janice Raymond, "Beyond Male Morality," *Women and Religion,* 1972, pp. 83–93.
15. Linda Thurston, "On Male and Female Principle," *The Second Wave* I (Summer 1971), p. 39.
16. George Huntston Williams, "The Sacred Condominium," *The Morality of Abortion: Legal and Historical Perspectives*, edited by John T. Noonan, Jr. (Cambridge: Harvard University Press, 1970), p. 164. All of the essays in this book are by male authors.
17. See Debbie Margolin and Ann Sheldon, "Rape," *Women: A Journal of Liberation* III, No. 1 (p. 18–23).
18. Bernard Häring, "A Theological Evaluation," in *The Morality of Abortion*, edited by Noonan, p. 141.
19. Ralph Potter, "The Abortion Debate," *The Religious Situation: 1968*, edited by Donald R. Cutler (Boston: Beacon Press, 1968), p. 157.
20. Jean MacRae, "A Feminist View of Abortion," *Women and Religion, 1972*, pp. 107–117.
21. John Noonan, "An Almost Absolute Value in History," in *The Morality of Abortion*, edited by Noonan, pp. 1–59.
22. See Daniel Callahan, *Abortion: Law, Choice, and Morality* (New York: Macmillan, 1970), pp. 67–75. Callahan's study is a most useful source. The author makes every attempt to be objective. His "objectivity" about women's liberation, however, at times manifests itself as noncomprehension. The deficiencies as well as the advantages of this sort of "objectivity" are evident in a more recent article: Callahan, "Abortion: Thinking and Experiencing," in *Christianity and Crisis* XXXII (January 8, 1973), pp. 295–98. Here the author uses the familiar method of "balancing" supposed extremes, a method which leads him to make some insensitive remarks. Sample: "No evidence has ever been offered that women freed by abortion from unwanted pregnancies are profoundly more liberated than those who haven't been" (p. 295). Perhaps persons freed by medicine from crippling diseases are not "profoundly" more liberated than those who haven't been, but the relevance of such a remark is hard to discover. Callahan is troubled by a "reconstruction of history . . . creating a highly charged mythology of male repression, or religious persecution, or puritanical fanaticism" (p. 297). The loaded words "reconstruction" and "mythology" reveal something of the author's noncomprehension of feminism.
23. See Lawrence Lader, *Abortion* (Indianapolis: Bobbs-Merrill Co., 1966; Boston: Beacon Press, 1967 [paperback]), p. 23.
24. This confusion is sometimes evident in· Lawrence Lader's writings, even though they are very helpful in other ways. In *Abortion II: Making the*

Revolution (Boston: Beacon Press, 1973), Lader conveys the impression that he actually thinks the legalization of abortion is the final step in women's liberation.

25. *Ibid*. There are scattered references throughout the book.
26. Statement released in conjunction with a presidential order reversing liberalized abortion policies at military hospitals, April 3, 1971. Cited in *Ms.* I (November 1972), p. 109.
27. Dr. Joseph Stanton, M.D., Letter to the Editor, the Boston *Globe*, March 9, 1972.
28. Regina Barshak, Letter to the Editor, the Boston *Globe*, March 18, 1972.
29. See Joyce Goldman, "The Women of Bangladesh," *Ms.* I (August 1972), p. 84.
30. *Ibid*., p. 88.
31. *Ibid*.
32. Quoted in *The Providence Sunday Journal*, January 16, 1972, p. E-1.
33. E. Ionesco, in *Nouvelle Revue Française,* July 1956, as quoted in Herbert Marcuse, *One-Dimensional Man* (Boston: Beacon Press, 1964), p. 80.
34. Paul Mayer, "Jeremiah and Jesus," *American Report*, October 23, 1972, p. 2.
35. Guenther Lewy, *The Catholic Church and Nazi Germany* (New York: McGraw-Hill, 1964), p. 341.
36. *Ibid*., p. 107.
37. As reported and quoted in *National Catholic Reporter,* October 6, 1972, p. 1.
38. Gordon Zahn, "A Religious Pacifist Looks at Abortion," *Commonweal* XCIV (May 28, 1971), pp. 279–82.
39. Some information on the cooptation of German Protestants by Hitler and on Bonhoeffer's struggle with this can be gleaned from *I Knew Dietrich Bonhoeffer*, edited by W. Zimmerman and R. G. Smith, translated by K. G. Smith (New York: Harper and Row, 1966).
40. Theodore Roszak, "The Hard and the Soft," in *Masculine/Feminine*, edited by Betty Roszak and Theodore Roszak, pp. 91–92.
41. *Ibid*., p. 92.
42. Paul Ramsey, *The Just War* (New York: Charles Scribner's Sons, 1968), p. 215.
43. *Ibid*., p. 213.
44. *Ibid*., p. vii.
45. Paul Ramsey, "Points in Deciding about Abortion," *The Morality of Abortion*, edited by Noonan, p. 63.
46. James M. Gustafson. "A Protestant Ethical Approach," *The Morality of Abortion*, edited by Noonan, p. 122.
47. Quoted in *American Report*, November 6, 1972, p. 4.
48. Edmond Cahn, *The Moral Decision: Right and Wrong in the Light of American Law*, Midland Book (Bloomington, Indiana: Indiana University Press, 1966), p. 104.
49. Paul Mayer, "Jeremiah and Jesus," *American Report*, October 23, 1972, p. 2.

50. The unwholeness of the Christian Trinitarian symbol is evident in the one-sidedness of the images of the Father and the Son. The Holy Spirit has been called the spirit—the fire—of love and unity. In a sexist culture this is socially unrealizable. Language about the Holy Spirit is used in a privatized and often hypocritical way and is not generally perceived as the spirit of love that *confronts* loveless institutions. The qualities attributed to the Holy Spirit in traditional theology are stereotypically "feminine," but "he" is referred to by the masculine pronoun. Moreover, "he" was said to have impregnated the Virgin Mary (Matthew 1:18). Limited in this way, the potentially liberating symbol of the Holy Spirit is perverted into the Unholy Spirit who can be invoked to guide the "righteous" in their mission to kill and destroy. Emily Culpepper referred to this spirit of consuming "love" as "theological napalm" during a conversation in Boston, 1972.

51. Anselma Dell'Ollio, "The Sexual Revolution Wasn't Our War," *Ms.* I (Spring 1972), p. 109.

52. Dana Densmore, "Independence from the Sexual Revolution," *Notes from the Third Year: Women's Liberation*, p. 58; also in *Radical Feminism*, p. 111.

53. *Ibid.*

54. Herbert Marcuse, *One-Dimensional Man*, p. 79.

55. Anne Koedt, "Lesbianism and Feminism," *Notes from the Third Year: Women's Liberation,* p. 85; also in *Radical Feminism*, p. 248.

56. *Ibid.*, pp. 248–49.

57. *Ibid.*, p. 253.

58. Phyllis Chesler, *Women and Madness*, p. 185.

59. Radicalesbians, "The Woman Identified Woman," *Notes from the Third Year: Women's Liberation*, p. 82; also in *Radical Feminism*, pp. 242–43.

60. See Janice Raymond, "Beyond Male Morality," *Women and Religion, 1972*.

61. Janice Raymond has done a study of transsexualism, seeing the core of the problem in sex role socialization, in a paper delivered at the New England Regional Meeting of the American Academy of Religion, May 1972.

62. Paul Tillich, *Love, Power, and Justice: Ontological Analyses and Ethical Applications*, Galaxy Book (New York: Oxford University Press, 1960), p. 18.

63. R. D. Laing, *The Politics of Experience* (New York: Ballantine Books, 1968), p. 168.

64. Tillich, *Love, Power, and Justice*, p. 65.

65. Aristotle, *Nichomachean Ethics*, Book V, ch. 10.

66. Helmut Thielicke, *The Ethics of Sex*, translated by John W. Doberstein (New York: Harper and Row, 1964), p. 81.

67. *Ibid.*, p. 84.

68. Gunnar Myrdal, Appendix 5, "A Parallel to the Negro Problem," *An American Dilemma* (New York: Harper and Row, 1944, 1962), p. 1073.

69. Jerome Frank, *Courts on Trial: Myth and Reality in American Justice* (New York: Atheneum, 1971), pp. 384–85.

70. Henry Adams, *Mont Saint-Michel and Chartres* (New York: Collier Books, 1963), p. 260.

71. For a clear, accurate treatment of feminism and justice see Elizabeth Farians, "Justice: The Hard Line," *Andover Newton Quarterly* XII (March 1972), pp. 191–200. Dr. Farians has written and compiled a packet of useful articles under the general title *The Double Cross: Writings on Women and Religion*. She has also compiled a *Selected Bibliography on Women and Religion, 1965–72*. These are available from the Ecumenical Task Force on Women and Religion, of the National Organization for Women. They have also been reprinted by KNOW, Inc.

CHAPTER FIVE

The Bonds of Freedom: Sisterhood as Antichurch

1. Kate Millett, "On Angela Davis," *Ms.* I (August 1972), p. 105. Millett describes her encounter with chief defense attorney Howard Moore, who "jokingly" described himself as a sexist as he shook her hand. It would be impossible to describe oneself as a racist with such cock-sure urbanity. The author points out that sexism is pleased with itself.
2. Reported in *MGH News* (Boston: Massachusetts General Hospital, November 1972), pp. 1–2.
3. L. J. Ludovici, *The Final Inequality*, A Tower Book (New York: Tower Publications, Inc., 1971), pp. 151–52. Ludovici points out that matriarchal society was in stark contrast to Christianity, "the religion whose implacable hostility to women stands out as its most notable and distasteful feature" (p. 151).
4. *Ibid.*, p. 152.
5. Peter Berger, *The Sacred Canopy*, p. 4.
6. Conversation with Jean MacRae, Boston, May 1972.
7. Cf. Freeman, "The Legal Basis of the Sexual Caste System," *Valparaiso University Law Review* (Symposium Issue, 1971), pp. 203–36.
8. For many years Elizabeth Farians and Frances McGillicuddy have been untiring activists in the cause of women's rights, especially within the Catholic Church. Bernice McNeela has worked together with Dr. Farians as co-chairperson of the Joint Committee of Organizations Concerned with the Status of Women in the Church.
9. Ernst Troeltsch, *The Social Teaching of the Christian Churches*, translated by Olive Wyon, Harper Torchbooks (2 vols.; New York: Harper and Row, 1960), I, p. 338.
10. *Ibid.*
11. *Ibid.*, p. 287.
12. See the works of Simone de Beauvoir, Kate Millett, and Elizabeth Gould Davis, already cited.
13. Emile Durkheim, *The Elementary Forms of Religious Life*, translated by Joseph Ward Swain (New York: The Free Press, 1965), p. 101.
14. *Ibid.*
15. Berger, *The Sacred Canopy*, p. 27.

16. Robin Morgan, *Monster* (New York: Vintage Books, a division of Random House, 1972), p. 85.
17. Berger, *The Sacred Canopy*, p. 27.
18. Mircea Eliade, *Cosmos and History: The Myth of the Eternal Return*, translated by Willard R. Trask, Harper Torchbooks (New York: Harper and Row, 1959), especially pp. 141–62. See also Eliade, *The Sacred and the Profane*.
19. Berger, *The Sacred Canopy*, p. 40.
20. Friedrich Nietzsche, *The Birth of Tragedy and the Genealogy of Morals*, translated by Francis Golffing (New York: Doubleday, 1956), pp. 192–93.
21. See Gordon Zahn, *Chaplains in the R.A.F.: A Study in Role Tension* (Manchester, England: Manchester University Press, 1969).
22. Morgan, *Monster*, p. 84.
23. Marcuse, *One-Dimensional Man*, p. 7.
24. *Ibid.*, p. 5.
25. *Ibid.*, p. 4.
26. Linda L. Barufaldi, Letter in *Religious Education* LXVII (September-October 1972), p. 334.
27. Mary Rodda, Letter in *Religious Education* LXVII (September-October 1972), p. 335.
28. Emily Culpepper, "Something of, by, and for Women" (unpublished paper delivered at Boston College, February 9, 1972).
29. Suzanne Langer wrote of "generative ideas," *Philosophy in a New Key*, p. 19.
30. Abraham H. Maslow, *Toward a Psychology of Being* (Princeton, New Jersey: D. Van Nostrand Co., Inc., 1962), p. 136.
31. *Ibid.*, p. 148.
32. *Ibid.*, p. 132.
33. Murray, *The Witch-Cult in Western Europe*, p. 12.
34. *Ibid.*, pp. 271–72.
35. *Ibid.*, p. 12.
36. *Ibid.*, p. 11.
37. *Ibid.*, pp. 272–73. See also Murray, *The God of the Witches*, p. 176 ff.
38. These words are recorded in *The First Biography of Joan of Arc*, translated and annotated by Daniel Rankin and Claire Quintal (Pittsburgh: University of Pittsburgh Press, 1964), p. 81. It is interesting that the authors of this book, who certainly would not agree with the Murray interpretation, commented upon Joan's answer as follows: "Then she revealed a secret agreement." Whatever these authors consciously had in mind, the comment still invites speculation: Agreement with whom?
39. Murray, *The Witch-Cult in Western Europe*, p. 273.
40. Chesler, *Women and Madness*, p. 27.
41. *Ibid.*, p. 26.
42. *Ibid.*, p. xviii.
43. Murray, *The Witch-Cult in Western Europe*, pp. 13–14.
44. Emile Durkheim, *The Elementary Forms of Religious Life*, p. 437.
45. Morgan, *Monster*, p. 85.

46. Langer, *Philosophy in a New Key*.
47. This reluctance or refusal is related to the phenomenon which Marcuse describes as "the transfer of moral standards (and of their validation) from the Establishment to the revolt against it." See Herbert Marcuse, *An Essay on Liberation* (Boston: Beacon Press, 1969), p. 8.

CHAPTER SIX

Sisterhood as Cosmic Covenant

1. See Mircea Eliade, *The Sacred and the Profane*, pp. 20–65.
2. Laing, *The Politics of Experience*, p. 190.
3. Chesler, *Women and Madness*, pp. 92–93.
4. Jaspers and Bultmann, *Myth and Christianity*, p. 13.
5. From a statement of the New York Covens, quoted in *Sisterhood is Powerful*, edited by Robin Morgan (New York: Random House, 1970), p. 540.
6. Eliade, *Cosmos and History*, p. 137.
7. *Ibid*., p. 162.
8. Chesler, *Women and Madness*, pp. 299–301.
9. Max Weber, *The Sociology of Religion*, p. 239.
10. *Ibid*., p. 104.
11. Conversation with Pauli Murray, November 1972.
12. See Max Weber, *The Sociology of Religion,* p. 51.
13. See Talcott Parsons' Introduction to Max Weber's *Sociology of Religion*, p. xxxiii.
14. Weber, *The Sociology of Religion*, p. 78.
15. *Ibid*., p. 217.
16. See Parsons' Introduction, p. xxxiv.
17. *Ibid.*, pp. xxxv–xxxvi.
18. *Ibid*.
19. Weber, *The Sociology of Religion*, p. 46.
20. Those who speak for the Catholic Pentecostal movement reveal their uncritical loyalty to institutional Catholicism. For example, Kevin and Dorothy Ranaghan wrote: "They [Catholic Pentecostals] have shared the desire to be good Catholics and to grow in the life and love of Christ." See Ranaghan, *Catholic Pentecostals* (New York: Paulist Press, 1971), pp. 142–43. Both women and men within the Catholic Pentecostal movement subscribe to the Pauline "headship-subordination" jargon and glorify the sexist syndrome. Some women in the Rhode Island Catholic Pentecostal group reportedly said that they would give up leadership roles as soon as men were "ready" to assume them.
21. The following statements are excerpted from the Report of the Committee on Doctrine of the National Conference of Catholic Bishops submitted to the bishops in their meeting in Washington, D.C., November 14, 1969. The report was presented by Bishop Alexander Zaleski of Lansing, Michigan, chairman of the committee: "They [Catholic Pentecostals] seem to grow

in their attachment to certain established devotional patterns such as devotion to the Real Presence and the Rosary. It is the conclusion of the Committee on Doctrine that the movement should at this point not be inhibited but allowed to develop. Certain cautions, however, must be expressed. . . . We must be on guard that they avoid the mistakes of classic Pentecostalism. It must be recognized that in culture there is a tendency to substitute religious experience for religious doctrine. In practice we recommend that Bishops involve prudent priests to be associated with this movement. Such involvement and guidance would be welcomed by the Catholic Pentecostals."

22. Moltmann, *Theology of Hope*, p. 203.
23. Linda Barufaldi and Emily Culpepper, "Pandora's Box," in *Women and Religion, 1972*, p. 51.
24. Conversation with Janice Raymond, November 1972.
25. See Louis Cutrona, Jr., "What Goes on Inside a Men's Liberation Rap Group," *Glamour*, August 1971, pp. 206ff.
26. Theodore Roszak, "The Hard and the Soft," *Masculine/Feminine*, pp. 103–04.
27. This idea is developed in Herbert Marcuse, *Eros and Civilization: A Philosophical Inquiry into Freud* (New York: Vintage Books, 1965), especially ch. 4. Recognizing the shortcomings of most attempts at "men's liberation," Kenneth Pitchford and other Revolutionary Effeminists have taken a more radicalized stand and are developing a far-reaching critique of sexism, including sexism in the gay liberation movement. See "The Effeminist Manifesto," in *Double-F: A Magazine of Effeminism* (Winter/Spring 1973).
28. On the concept of creative justice, see Tillich, *Love, Power, and Justice*, pp. 64–66.
29. George Wald, "The Human Enterprise," in *Population, Environment, and People,* edited by Noël Hinrichs (New York: McGraw Hill, 1971), p. 222.
30. See Elizabeth Farians, "Population, Environment, and Women," in *Population, Environment, and People,* pp. 97–103.
31. Marcuse, *An Essay on Liberation*, pp. 7–8.
32. *Ibid.*, p. 8.
33. *Ibid.*, p. 9.
34. *Ibid.*
35. *Ibid.*, p. 25.
36. H. Paul Santmire, "I-Thou, I-It, I-Ens," *The Journal of Religion* XLVIII (July 1968), p. 266.
37. *Ibid.*, p. 272.

CHAPTER SEVEN

The Final Cause: The Cause of Causes

1. Conversation with Linda Barufaldi, Boston, December 1972.
2. See Aristotle, *Physics* II, 7; *Metaphysics* I. For a medieval exposition and commentary on these texts, see Thomas Aquinas, *In Octo Libros*

Physicorum Aristotelis Expositio (Rome: Marietti, 1954), and *In Duodecem Libros Metaphysicorum Aristotelis Expositio* (Rome: Marietti, 1950).

3. See Margaret Mead, *Culture and Commitment*, esp. pp. 51–76.
4. This identification is clear in the medieval synthesis of Aquinas. See his *Summa theologiae*, I, q. 5, a. 1: "Hence it is clear that goodness and being are the same really. But goodness presents the aspect of desirableness, which being does not present."
5. *Ibid.*, I, q. 45, a. 1 and 2.
6. *Ibid.*, I, q. 9, a. 1; q. 44, a. 4. For Aquinas, God is an agent who is in no way a patient. That is, God does not act to acquire anything but to communicate the divine goodness, which is the final cause of all things.
7. Wolfhart Pannenberg, *Theology and the Kingdom of God*, pp. 134–35.
8. *Ibid.*, p. 142.
9. The problem, of course, is not restricted to the writings of Pannenberg. Moltmann writes that "knowledge of the future has its stimulus nowhere else than in the riddle of Jesus of Nazareth. It will thus be knowledge of Christ in the urge to know who he is and what is hidden and prepared in him" (*Theology of Hope*, p. 203).
10. Henri Bergson, *Creative Evolution*, translated by Arthur Mitchell (New York: Henry Holt and Co., 1911), especially pp. 39–40.
11. Alfred North Whitehead, *Science and the Modern World* (Cambridge: University Press, 1953), p. 64.
12. See Voctor Lowe, *Understanding Whitehead* (Baltimore: Johns Hopkins Press, 1962). Whitehead thought that "throughout the universe there reigns the union of opposites which is the ground of dualism"—from "Objects and Subjects," *The Philosophical Review* XLI (March 1932), p. 146.
13. See Alfred North Whitehead, *Process and Reality: An Essay in Cosmology* (New York: Macmillan, 1929), especially pp. 519–33.
14. Alfred North Whitehead, *Modes of Thought* (New York: Macmillan, 1938), p. 237.
15. Charles Hartshorne, "Introduction: The Development of Process Philosophy," in *Philosophers of Process*, edited by Douglas Browning (New York: Random House, 1965), p. xix.
16. *Charles Hartshorne, The Logic of Perfection and Other Essays in Neoclassical Metaphysics* (Lasalle, Illinois: Open Court Publishing Co., 1962), p. 206.
17. Teilhard de Chardin, "The Grand Option," *The Future of Man* (New York: Harper and Row, 1964), pp. 37–60.
18. I have already referred to the work of André Devaux, *Teilhard et la vocation de la femme* and of Henri de Lubac, *The Eternal Feminine: A Study on the Text of Teilhard de Chardin.*
19. Teilhard de Chardin, "The Grand Option," p. 46.
20. *Ibid.*, p. 52.
21. Teilhard de Chardin, "My Universe," in *Science and Christ*, translated by René Hague (New York: Harper and Row, 1968), p. 54.
22. Teilhard de Chardin, "The Mass on the World," in *The Hymn of the*

Universe, translated by Simon Bartholomew (New York: Harper and Row, 1965), p. 31.

23. Teilhard de Chardin, "A Note on Progress," *The Future of Man*, p. 24.
24. Interview reported by Charles Fager in *National Catholic Reporter*, December 22, 1972, p. 15.
25. George Wald, "The Human Enterprise," in *Population, Environment, and People*, p. 220.

Index